بسم الله الرحمن الرحيم

DEDICATION

To the Memory of my Parents:

May Allah grant them His Mercy
for the loving wisdom with which they
nourished me.

Also to my brother Jamīl:

With deep appreciation for his love and
encouragement.

And to my Muslim Colleagues, al Shuhadā' Dr. Tīgānī abūJidīrī and Dr. Ismā'īl R. al Fārūqī; may Allah grant them His Mercy; and to the ones who are still working for the Supreme Cause of Islam and Khilāfah, Islamization of contemporary knowledge, reform of Muslim thought, the revival of the 'Ummah and the peace, progress and sense of fulfilment and happiness of all human beings. May Allah grant us strength, success and the reward promised to the sincere and efficient workers in this life and in eternity.

CONTENTS

The Islamic Theory of INTERNATIONAL RELATIONS: NEW DIRECTIONS FOR ISLAMIC METHODOLOGY AND THOUGHT

Dr. ʻAbdulḤamīd ʼA. ʼAbūSulaymān

555 Grove St., Herndon, Va. 22070

Library of Congress Catalog Card Number: 87-081432

ISBN No. 0912463-09-0

Printed by International Graphics Printing Service
4411 41st Street
Brentwood, Maryland 20722 USA

ILLUSTRATIONS

PREFACE

This book serves two major purposes. The first is to present the Islamic point of view, develop familiarity with the basic resources of Islamic thought, and try to introduce to the non-Muslim and Muslim, secular and non-secular intellectuals, the Islamic theory of International Relations in a specialized academic style. The second purpose is to study and examine the reasons why Islamic thought apparently has failed to play an active and constructive role in the contemporary world of thought and ideas, as well as to offer new insights and alternatives in order to make up for the failure of Western thought in the field of International Relations to successfully address the growing need for peace, security, cooperation and participation.

The origin of this book goes back to my experience in preparing an earlier book in Arabic, entitled "*The Theory of Islam in Economics: Philosophy and Contemporary Means*" (Cairo, 1960). For a good summary of that book see *Contemporary Aspects of Economic Thinking in Islam: The Proceedings of The Third East Coast Conference of The Muslim Students' Association of the United States and Canada, April, 1968*, published by American Trust Publication, Plainfield, Indiana, 1976.

That experience showed me that stagnation and narrow application of classic Muslim methodology was behind the rigidity and remoteness of Islamic thought. This specialized study in the field of International Relations provides an opportunity to test and spell out the approach, fresh thoughts, ideas, and style of that book on the Islamic philosophy of economics. The methodology applied in that book started with comprehensive assembly of all Islamic textual materials (*nuṣūṣ*) in the Qur'an and *Sunnah* related to the field of economics. The next step was to identify, construct explicitly, and explain the internal line of logic in these materials. This required linguistic study, analysis of the historical circumstances, means, capabilities, and environment, and systematic use of my technical knowledge as a graduate in the field of political science and economics. Applying the line of thought and logic in the texts of the Qur'ān and *Sunnah* concerning Islamic objectives and goals in the field of economics helped me to develop a coherent and systematic approach and method.

This method enabled me to see the relevance and significance of the different actions, policies, and stages of development in this historical experience of early Islam and thereby avoid any temptation to ignore, twist, abrogate, or jump to conclusions of holy purpose beyond human understanding or comprehension (aḥ Kām tawqīfiyyah). The distinction between the goals and principles of the *Sharī'a* and the policy considerations of the specific time and place where they were articulated by scholars was very useful in opening the door for policy reconsiderations needed in order to suggest new alternatives to fit contemporary needs and means.

This book tries to offer fresh insights in the Islamic understanding and approach to the pursuit of peace, security, cooperation, and participation in relations among peoples and nations. Also it serves as a vehicle to study and analyze the classic Islamic methodology and the traditional way of applying it in the field of Islamic thought.

Specifically, this book takes a new look at many problematic issues in contemporary Islamic thought, such as *Riddah* (Apostasy), freedom of belief, *Jizyah* (Poll tax). It also thoroughly examines *Uṣūl* (Islamic methodology), its role, and the role of *al-'Ulamā'* (Sharī'a scholars), as distinct from the secular scholars and intellectuals, in the persistent stagnation of Muslim thought and of the *Ummah*.

This book contends that the Islamic theory and philosophy of relations among nations is the only adequate philosophy of peace in the contemporary world. It is the only philosophy, concept, and approach that emphasizes the common origin, the common interest, and the common destiny of man as the only firm base for understanding man's nature, interpersonal relations, and group interactions. Man's nature, interests, and relations in Islam look like overlapping circles. Other world ideologies and philosophies focus on conflict management and consequently on war. The Western philosophies of nationalism and class conflict emphasize the negative factor of conflicting perceptions, interests, and destinies. This attitude of conflict always leads to war and destruction.

History shows that lasting peace can come only from an attitude of mutual understanding and appreciation based on a firm belief in our common nature, common interests, and common destiny.

The long road the world community has already travelled along the road of global functionalism and world organizations is a great achievement and should be maintained, but it can be further developed only in the frame and shade of the constructive philosophy and attitude of harmony and peace offered by Islam and the *holy* commitment of Muslim people to it.

This book, by revealing and explaining objectively the Islamic philosophy and understanding of relations among human communities, nations, and states is offering a fresh hope for human civilization.

Muslim intellectuals, scholars, and leaders, it is hoped, can better appreciate from this book what Islam means to them and how they can best work to secure the future of human civilization and existence. Muslim scholars may benefit also from this analytical study of the Islamic methodoogy of thought so that they can introduce in their studies a systematic and scientific approach to human nature, human relations, and the human environment in line with Islamic goals, principles, values, and directions. This should produce not merely insights, but whole new disciplines of Islamic social, human, natural, and technical science. (The Khilāfah Sciences).

In this book, it may seem that I unduly emphasize the shortcomings of the Muslim Umma and of its past life and thought. This emphasis on the practice of Muslims is needed in order to probe deeply into the roots or causes of the Umma's decline, cultural, economic, political, technological, and military.

As a Muslim and social scientist, I am well aware and appreciative of the Islamic goals and ideology, as well as of the Muslims' historical achievements. And it is precisely because of this appreciation that I try to apply an open and critical mind without inhibition to the task of restoring the health and proper role of the Muslim 'Ummah in the contemporary world.

I also clearly see the need of the contemporary world for Islamic values and concepts and for Islam as a faith. Thus I have attempted to identify in this book these basic values and concepts which can provide an essential framework for relations among nations in the contemporary world.

Non-Muslim intellectuals are urged to look in this comprehensive study for a more thorough understanding of the reasons behind the conditions of the contemporary Muslims, including the Muslims' distortion of their own religion, so they can appreciate the Islamic point of view in the contemporary world, set aside their historical hatred and prejudices against Islam and Muslims, and cooperate as partners in building a common destiny in accordance with these principles and values.

It is important for Muslims and non-Muslims to appreciate the responsibility of Muslims, according to their ideology and religion, in establishing, guarding, and maintaining a world order of peace and cooperation. The Islamic world order is a world where all individuals and peoples are free to live according to their deepest beliefs and to maintain their freedom to cooperate on the basis of understanding and respect.

This kind of outlook, attitude, and philosophy can bring humans together and develop common human parameters of purpose, value, interest, and understanding, broad enough to establish workable political structures and the rule of law among human communities at all levels from the neighborhood to the single community of all mankind. This is the only valid and practical way that can lead to a workable world order of peace, security, cooperation, and partnership.

Muslims must start with themselves to restore their vision; their psychological, and civilizational health and strength; and restore their brotherhood and solidarity. They should restore the best of their thought and methodology and the institutions based thereon. They must be true and useful to themselves before they can be respected and taken seriously by others and thereby contribute usefully in building a better and more peaceful world.

This work, originally written more than fourteen years ago to offer a new healthy and dynamic vision for the new Muslim generations, is meant to open the discussion on how to revive Islamic thought and methodology. The work concerns not so much what is correct but what went wrong and how to correct it. The condition of the *'Ummah* is so troubled that we can lose little and gain much if we open our minds and start thinking, analyzing, and discussing what is wrong with our life, our thought, and our way of doing and approaching life.

What is offered here are not *fatāwā* or decrees but analysis and opinions offered to others for their own analysis and discussion in order to correct any false ideas and produce more new dynamic ideas and approaches. This process of interaction makes the goals of a healthy *'Ummah* and healthy Islamic thought more possible and plausible.

It is a great honor for this book to carry as an introduction the last words in writing of Prof. Isma'īl al Fārūqī. In these pages we read a typical example of his beautiful sincerity and love for Islam, the

'Ummah, and humanity. The ideas in this introduction and of his many Islamic works and writings will be, Insha-Allah, *raḥmah* and a blessing for his soul in the hereafter and will give lasting benefits for Muslims and for all sincere people in this world.

Finally as author of this work I would like to emphasize and make clear that I welcome all analysis and criticism that can contribute to the common goal of reviving Islamic values, principles, and objectives in Muslim life, methodology, thought and culture.

I ask Allah to give me the two rewards in the now and the hereafter by guiding me to say what is right and true. I ask Allah to guide more Muslim brothers to join me in the search for what is right and true and to help us all promote the reign of truth and make it possible for man to understand, follow, and benefit from the message of Islam.

Ramadan, 1407
May, 1987
Washington, D.C.

'AbdulḤamīd 'A. 'AbūSulaymān, Ph.D.

INTRODUCTION

by al-Shahīd Dr. Isma'īl R. al-Fārūqī

This book, which the International Institute of Islamic Thought is presenting to the reader, was originally submitted to the University of Pennsylvania as a doctoral dissertation in international relations. Its academic merit is certainly great, but its value far transcends that merit; for its subject matter is Islamic international relations. From these as they developed in early Muslim history the author endeavored to cull the general principles which governed the practices of the early Islamic world. In fact, this dissertation has rendered a service far greater than winning a doctorate for its author. It has exposed truths of Islam which are relevant to one of the most important fields of study in this century—namely, world order.

Nothing could be more urgently needed nowadays than the enlightenment of mankind concerning the threat of annihilation that the present world order poses for it. The hegemony of the West over the world in the last two centuries is certainly responsible for the terror under which humankind lives today. The world's present predicament is the result of the tortuous history of the ideal of the universal community in the West. To understand and solve this predicament, we must know the history of that ideal.

I. THE UNIVERSAL COMMUNITY IDEAL UNTIL THE END OF THE NINETEENTH CENTURY

In contrast to Judaic Christianity, which regarded itself as a reform movement within Judaism and as meant for "the lost tribes of Israel," Western Christianity proclaimed the universal community ideal as a substitute for the Imperium Romanum. For centuries thereafter the Church continued to proclaim this ideal. Its success was extremely limited; and no sooner had it succeeded in establishing a state with potential to become universal than the state divided into two or more states. The challenge to the worldly dominion of the Church was constant, arising both from within and outside the Christian state.

Without having to recount the long list of grievances the Christians of Europe suffered at the hands of the Church, there can be no doubt that the Reformation was right in dismantling the Church's worldly authority. Her political and economic dominion, however, was not to go down alone. Along with it, the Reformation destroyed the Church's magisterium, liberating the mind to plumb the depths of nature and unravel the secrets of the stars. Equally significant was Europe's repudiation of the Christian faith as the basis of identity and the elevation of reason as the definer of selfhood, criterion of judgment, and foundation for citizenship.

This trend grew rapidly following the Reformation and brought forth the Enlightenment which raised again the ideal of the universal community, this time on the grounds of reason rather than faith. The European Enlightenment, however, did not have the courage of its own convictions. On the one hand, its advocates compromised their rationalism in order to accommodate faith, thus providing a cracked foundation on which no universal superstructure could be secured. On the other, the advocates of the Enlightenment gave the lie to their own profession when they naively spoke of humanity and the universe but actually meant only Europe and its peoples. Indeed, the Enlightenment met with devastating opposition: Christianity regarded it as a threat on account of its claimed rationalism; and the princes of Europe resisted it because it threatened the gains they had made as substitutes for Church authority. The former favored romanticism; the latter, nationalism.

Thus, the universal community ideal of the Enlightenment was doomed from the beginning. The "reformed" churches of Europe joined hands with the European dynasties to combat rationalism and its consequent universalism. They promoted romanticism, a movement which secured Christianity by basing truth and value upon feeling rather than reason. And they secured the princes' seats of power by founding group loyalty on nationalism or ethnocentrism which defined the public good in terms of the group's egotistic self-interest and of loyalty to prince or "nation." Schleiermacher was responsible for the former; Fustel de Coulanges for the latter; and both wrote the best defenses and expositions of two aspects of one and the same disease, namely, romanticism, a variety of particularism blown up into a metaphysic and an axiology.

Under their hammering pens, the universal community ideal was shattered.

The debacle of the Enlightenment produced two more results. Reason, as the prime faculty of science, became the sole and absolute master of nature and keeper of her truths. Its major prompting came from competition of the nations to unlock more of nature's secrets and place her processes entirely under national control, at the service of national interest and, above all, defense. The realms of value, of ethics and aesthetics became lost as provinces in which the truth may be discovered and in which reason had anything to say. As domains of feeling and personal experience, those realms were "free and open fields" for anyone to ride through as he pleases. This relativism and subjectivism to which Christianity recoursed in order to save itself from the onslaught of Enlightenment-rationalism soon showed their effect upon Christianity itself.

II. THE UNIVERSAL COMMUNITY IDEAL UNTIL MID-TWENTIETH CENTURY

Repudiation of Christianity's main tenets as well as of the universal community ideal was in the making. On the collective level, Europe gave religion itself its bad name in the world, and enabled Friedrich Engels and Karl Marx to call it "the opium of the people." And on the personal level Friedrich Nietzsche and Sigmund Freud analyzed the religious ethic and psychology to death, predicting "the end of" religion as "illusion" and bringing about the "transvaluation of its values."

All this happened in Europe where the only dominant religion was Christianity. Like their Enlightenment predecessors, these European critics spoke of religion when they meant Christianity. Communism combined these forces raging in the soul of Europe and added to them the opposition to the absurd order of competition and war among the nations of Europe. It condemned romanticism as the base of an unholy alliance between religion and nationalism, both resting, as they did, on feeling, personal experience and cultural relativism.

Communism raised again the ideal of the universal community. But this time, instead of feeling and personal experience, matter and the material interpretation of history were to be the foundation. Until World War II, Communism combated both Christianity and nationalism;

and promoted the universal community ideal as the goal of a world dominated by matter and the proletariat. During and following World War II, the ideal was abandoned in favor of "Mother Russia;" and thereafter, in favor of the consumer society. Picked up for an instant by the Chinese Revolution at the conclusion of World War II, the ideal collapsed, even before the death of its author, Mao Tse Tung, in reaction to its violation by the U.S.S.R. Had the U.S.S.R. remained true to the universalist ideal, and had it helped China to overcome its ethnocentrism, the ideal of the universal community might have had a chance to survive. Unfortunately, in the West as well as in the Communist world, that ideal lies today as dead as a doornail.

Between the two world wars, Great Britain and France, the powers in control of the League of Nations, tried in vain to maintain a semblance of world order through the League. But their manipulation of it was crassly offensive since they used it to cover up their colonial policies in Asia-Africa and their competition with one another. Influenced by Enlightenment idealism, and in response to American isolationist opposition to ratification, President Woodrow Wilson pulled the United States out from the League in disgust at Europe's manipulation of its decision-making process. The U.S.S.R. was excluded beforehand by virtue of both its opposition and its deliberate isolationism.

After World War II, the ideal of the universal community was raised again, for the fourth time, through the United Nations Organization which it was hoped would out perform its predecessor. But the same weaknesses affected both world organizations. The constitutive principle of membership in the United Nations was again declared to be the nation-state as sovereign and able to pursue its own self-interest. In consequence, implementation of resolutions by the member states had to be voluntary and no nation was to be forced to comply. Of course, the big powers always found a way to twist the arms of the smaller nations and obtain compliance. But among themselves, consent was absolutely necessary. In the League of Nations, conflicts were referred to the International High Court of Justice for solution. After World War II, the International Court of Justice continued to exist, but only as a showpiece and propaganda platform. As to the United Nations, its authority and jurisdiction was divided between the General Assembly and the Security Council. The latter, consisting of five super powers as permanent members possessing the right of veto, and a number of General Assembly members chosen on rotation, controls the executive machinery and can render the decisions of the General Assembly pointless. Furthermore, the Security Council hardly acts as an integrated body, since each of its five permanent members can and does take recourse to its veto power against the other four whenever decisions run counter to its national self-interest.

Obviously, both world organizations were built on a self-contradictory foundation. The qualification for membership is nationhood; that is, national sovereignty over territory and people, and nationalism, the principle that the national interest is the ultimate good, the ultimate criterion and justification. For the nationalist state to serve the universal community is impossible, since its very constitution dictates that it sacrifice everything in pursuit of its own self-interest.

Nationalism precludes surrender of national sovereignty, the first prerequisite of an effective universal community that seeks to actualize justice among the member states. National interest as the ultimate criterion compels the nation-state to pursue that interest at all costs and at the expense of morality and justice. Hence, to protect their own self-interest against one another and the world, the superpowers vested themselves with the right to veto any resolution in the Security Council. To frustrate any resolution of the General Assembly, the superpowers made its execution dependent upon the executive machinery which they controlled through the Council. The United Nations created other organs either for special projects or problems or for dealing with a permanent need of the world's nations. Some of these, the superpowers control directly; others indirectly through their contributions to the budget. In either case, only what the superpowers wish gets done. Where resolutions run against their wishes, they withdraw or threaten to do so, bringing the executive machinery to a halt. Where they do not agree with one another, they use the veto to stop the passing of any resolution. On countless occasions, Israel defied the will of the General Assembly representing the overwhelming majority of humankind. Not only devoid of will, the United Nations is also devoid of a standing army with which to stop aggression among the nations. Often, because the superpowers themselves or their satellites are the perpetrators of aggression, the United Nations stand impotently on the sidelines, allowing its general assembly to vote against the aggressor while the latter proceeds with its aggression unabashed.

By definition, the United Nations is not a world government. It was designed to play only the negative role of stopping aggression among the members. But even for this minor role, it proved itself incapable. It continues to exist, like its predecesor, as a theater for the world's orators. Where the national interests of the superpowers are involved, the United Nations has been either a rubber stamp or an impotent observer. For a brief time following World War II, the superpowers spread the idea and hope that there would henceforth be no war, and that the United Nations would bring about a federal union of the world's nations for peace and justice. Today only the naive simpleton entertains this hope.

Competition among the European powers to control the political, economic, military and educational machineries of their liberated colonies continues just as fiercely as before, though with different forms and techniques. The struggle between the former colonies and their old colonizers has been further exacerbated since World War II by the entrance of the two superpowers, the United States and the U.S.S.R. These sought to replace the colonial empires of Europe with their own, and to extend their dominions to cover the globe.

III. THE IDEAL OF THE UNIVERSAL COMMUNITY AND AMERICA

Born as a satellite of the European Enlightenment, as it were, revolutionary America presented the universal ideal as an alternative to Europe's predicament. Since its independence in 1776, it was sufficiently isolated from Europe and the world to be able to play the role of the world's haven from religious and nationalist particularism, and to acclaim under the aegis of a "new world" all those who emigrated to her shores. This lent credence to the claim that it is America's "manifest destiny" to supplant the old world with its own new universal community. The enthusiasm this idealism has generated lasted but a few decades; and universalist language began to give way to nationalism *a l'Europeenne*. Competition with Britain and Spain had aroused America to assert its nationalist will through the Monroe doctrine of "America for the Americans." Her victory in the Spanish American War enabled her to press nationalism yet further, this time by redefining herself in Anglo-Saxon terms over and against the Latin American states and their cultural progenitor, Spain. After a brief period self-isolation following World War I, and the upset of European colonialism after World War II, America emerged as the full heir of Europe's ethnocentrist self-esteem and colonialist view of the rest of the world.

IV. THE FAILURE OF THE WEST

This, in brief, is the story of the failure of the West, including Eastern Europe, to provide a world order of peace and justice for the world's population. The failure is due to the fact that neither of them knows a principle which makes the ideal of the universal community operative. The mind and culture of the West have never risen beyond "the nation" as a form of social organization. Surely, Christianity cherished that ideal and taught it through the ages; but it contradicted it with its separation of Church and state and its eschatological hope for a kingdom that is other than this world. The religiously oriented advocated the universal community ideal, if at all, out of contempt for the world and history, which they held to be forever fallen, hopeless, and the domain of Satan. As a substitute, they sought the universal community in the Church as the Mystical Body of Christ. Naturally, they could not entertain the ideal as an organization with law, law-courts and an army. On the other hand, the secular-oriented in east or west gave only lip service to the ideal, and used it, as the political history of this century amply shows, to further the "national interests" of their own peoples.

Far greater in implication for world history and far more dangerous for the peace and security of mankind is what the superpowers have done in this century. The undisputed hegemony of Western culture in the last two hundred years led to the division of the world between two giants capable of destroying each other and the whole world many times over. It is told that the firepower at their command equals more than 500 pounds of high explosives for every man, woman and child on earth. Their differences are infinite and irreconcilable. Each wants to subdue the other, dominate the world, and exploit the resources of the earth and the energies of its people. If any peace or accommodation is possible, it is always for their own aggrandizement at the cost of the rest of the world which is the victim. By definition therefore such arrangement is temporary until one or the other giant gets ready to devour another chunk of the world. Though called "the cold war," the last 40 years of peace were due to the "balance of terror" the superpowers themselves had established between themselves; i.e., their nearly equal capability to destroy each other totally, not to any will for peace or justice. Humanity trembles whenever one of them complains or threatens, never sure whether the moment has come for either giant to start the tragic end of mankind. In the last three decades, the world may have stood on the brink of extinction several times because of their disagreement on Berlin, Palestine, Hungary, Cyprus, Viet Nam, Cuba and Korea. The two giants press their preparations for war constantly, making no point on earth secure.

The two giants, and to a lesser extent their European allies, spend an inordinate proportion of their national incomes on research, development, manufacture, and deployment of the tools of war. Is it to subsidize this expenditure, and partly to test the efficacy of their weapons against one another, that the two blocks promote hostility among the peoples of the Third World? These peoples were organized by the colonial powers into nation-states with boundaries designed to create perpetual conflict with neighbors. Both power blocks continuously encourage hostilities among the Third World nations, fan the old conflicts, or create new ones and prod the nations of the Third World to open hostility against one another. They subsidize all sorts of subversive movements within each nation-state, precisely in order to instill in the ruling classes of the Third World fear of their own people and of their neighbors, all to the purpose of making them more dependent for their security upon the superpowers. Is it unreasonable to see in this a Western drive to compel these poor nations to buy Western weapons, to use and have to replace them, to destroy their development projects through stalemated wars so they can build them again—all with materials, equipment and expertise supplied by either of the two blocks? If the victimized nation is strong, this Machiavellian policy aims at draining it of its resources and diverting such resources from being used for a really constructive purpose, thus perpetuating its dependent status. If, on the other hand, the nation is poor, they lend it money in order that it will buy their weapons and consumers' products and thus be forced to mortgage its future.

An impoverished Third World, rent with internecine conflicts and armed hostilities, producing raw materials which the two power blocks buy at prices dictated by them, using products of European and American industry and agriculture, and dependent for their staple foods and other essentials (even their daily bread) upon the bounty of either block—that is the order the superpowers and their allies have designed for the Third World. The principles of secularism dominate, and their policies are utterly devoid of moral consideration. The separation of the realms of Caesar and Christ, as Reinhold Niebuhr had affirmed, liberates national policy from the ethic of Christ and permits the nation-state to flout every moral precept.

This is why it makes perfect sense for the West to pay its citizens from the national treasury in order to produce below their capacities so as not to cause prices to fall. Their moral logic permits them to buy, stockpile and, when the warehouses are filled to capacity, to destroy the foodstuffs they had bought so as to maintain their price and trade patterns. The core of immorality and inhumanity in this Western practice is that all this prevention of production and stockpiling and destruction of foodstuffs takes place while the majority of mankind goes undernourished, while hundreds of millions suffer from hunger, and scores of millions of humans perish from hunger and famine every year.

For humanity to live under the shadows of terror and annihilation, and for the two power blocks to prosper on the production, destruction, and re-supply of the tools of war constitutes a terrible sin against humanity. It is truly satanic to be unconcerned about the fact that the war industry (with sales topping one trillion dollars in the current year) is the most crucial economic activity, and to give reign to a vested interest in developing interhuman hatred and hostility in order to maintain one's power or egotistical advantage. But that is precisely the result of the West's hegemony over the world during the last two centuries. The world is neither safe, nor peaceful nor contented. It is a time bomb whose hour to explode can strike at any moment. A very few millions in the two power blocks sit at the summit of power and affluence while the majority of their compatriots are poor, devoid of spirit or idealism, some of them pining for a lottery miracle to bring them some of the power or affluence of the fortunate few. The rest of humanity is undernourished, hungry or dying. That is not only a capital failure; it is indeed a tragic disaster.

V. POVERTY OF THOUGHT IN THE FIELD OF WORLD ORDER

The Western tradition of thought in the field of international law or world order is extremely poor. With the little inspiration that tradition has provided, it is no wonder that the West's record in world-order affairs is little more than convention and force. Was this poverty of ideas the cause or the mirror of the practice? In the realm of practice, the West has never known or applied international law except on the basis of convention. Differences between one state and another were solved by negotiation, or with reference to previous agreement. In most cases, the appeal was to some treaty or convention between the parties from which the conflict in question was regarded as a departure. In the total absence of such agreement, treaty or convention, the conflict was deemed soluble only by force, or *ad baculum*.

The doctrine of natural law, known and discussed in the Middle Ages, especially after the rise of scholasticism—remained an academic/theological matter and was never applied to the field of international relations. It was not until the 17th century that any Western thinker first sought to link international relations to law. The religious wars and the scramble for colonies in the New World, Asia and Africa, with all the conflicts it brought in its trail among the states of Europe, inspired Grotius to appeal to the law of nature as a ground for inter-European agreement and harmony. The Enlightenment repeated the appeal for a while; but its voice was soon silenced by the advent of romanticism. The actual processes of international activity remained far removed from theory and were never affected. As to relations with non-Europeans, there was neither treaty nor convention to invoke. Furthermore, the Asians and Africans were infidels already condemned by God. Only the argument of force would hence apply to them. Nothing therefore could stop the Europeans from recourse to the harshest measures of force and brutality in defeating and subjugating them individually and collectively.

We have seen the circumstances under which the League of Nations and the United Nations were formed. We have noted their failure. Surprisingly, that failure did not stimulate the Western mind, either after the First World War or after the Second, to think of alternatives. That mind, whether American, Western or East European, has remained unmoved and incapable of thinking through the failure or of reaching a solution to the predicament.

VI. THE PRESENT NEED FOR A NEW WORLD ORDER

There is a great need of the world today for an international order which would establish a just and permanent peace without tyranny, one which recognizes the differences and distinctions—religious, cultural, social and economic—of the peoples of the world as legitimate, and founds its law upon their common need to order their lives as they wish in justice and freedom. Such world order would establish a federal or confederal world government with the executive and police machinery necessary for implementation. It would be backed by an international law and a system of courts that would place international justice within reach of all—governments, institutions, communities and individuals. Without such an order, the world will not find peace. Justice and reassurance will never come if the nation-state does not give up its "national sovereignty" in favor of the government of a federated world.

World government—whatever its form—has become in this age an absolute and inevitable necessity. With atomic weapons proliferating, the world population exploding, the superpowers' greed for the world's wealth growing as rapidly as their atomic arsenals, and—most importantly—the majority of humanity seething with hatred and discontent and growing ever more radical and restive, this world order of ours, brought about by the West and propped up by it for the last two centuries, cannot last. Either it will come down in a holocaust, or it has to change peacefully and rationally in fulfillment of the aspirations of humanity.

Either the inhabitants of the planet earth act as sheep and jump over the cliff to their death for no reason but to follow their leader, to use Arnold Toynbee's expression, or as rational beings they give up their nationalist madness and establish the new world order. To design and articulate the new world order, to elaborate its implementation—that is humanity's first duty. But humanity has no legacy of thought concerning world order except that of Islam.

Only very recently, the United Nations tried to institute such a law to govern the relations of its members. Its efforts resulted in the Universal Bill of Human Rights, a document which contains much good—genuinely universal and truly basic human rights—but which falls far short of the ideal. Some of the values it has incorporated were purely Western values, and they were accepted by puppet nation-states which did not represent the peoples or their moralities. The Charter of Human Rights was defeated by its own enthusiastic promulgators, who used it as a means of propaganda war against their competitors or enemies. It never produced a court system under which the individual sufferers could voice their grievances and obtain justice against the violators of those rights. Thus the charter remains, to this day, mere ink on paper whenever the violation of human rights agrees with the national interest of a superpower or of one of its satellites. The charter appears to be merely a tool of propaganda.

VII. THE WORLD ORDER OF ISLAM

The fact remains that in the field of international ethics, as well as law and jurisprudence, the world is dependent on the Islamic heritage. All the more justification therefore for publishing this book and presenting it for public debate. Our hope is to stimulate humans everywhere—Muslim and non-Muslim—to ponder over the principles of the international order presented and to begin to lay the foundation in the mind and will for its implementation.

Rather than summarize or evaluate the contribution of Islam as presented in this work—such being the conclusion of the expected debate—it is the intention to present in this introduction, in addition to the foregoing and by way of introduction to the subject, a skeleton outline of the Islamic thesis as a whole.

A. *ISLAM'S COMMITMENT*

Islam and its adherents regard themselves as committed to the task of bringing about a new world order. They regard this commitment as the only viable response to the present predicament; first, because this is how we can render obedience to God, who has commanded all humans to enter the realm of peace and to organize their affairs and order their lives in justice and responsible brotherhood; and second, because this is the only way to save humanity from endless competition and meaningless suffering in the present and from imminent destruction in the future. Thus Muslim commitment to a world order of peace, justice and brotherhood is both religious and utilitarian. Islam holds that desiring this world order, working for it, and sacrificing to bring it about are constituents of heroism and virtue, of piety and saintliness. To lay down one's life in the process of its actualization is *shahadah* – martyrdom—earning for its subject eternal Paradise. No nobler or stronger motivation is possible.

B. *PAX ISLAMICA*

The world order that Islam seeks is one from which war is banished once and for all. Islam's commitment to peace is absolute, universal and comprehensive. For any people to enter the new order, it is necesary for them to disband their army, destroy their weapons, or surrender them to the world government, except those necessary for maintenance of public order or for the enforcement of the verdicts of the courts of law. The covenant of peace under which no dispute or claim may be settled except through adjudication, arbitration or negotiation, must be offered to all peoples. Every people is entitled to it, as well as obliged, to join it. To reject adjudication under international law, or the invitation to enter the covenant of peace, is indeed to opt for war or isolationism, neither of which is rationally or morally tenable. Islam demands that all nations and all peoples enter the realm of peace, and it commands its adherents to do so with enthusiasm. It justifies coercive action by the whole (i.e., by those who have entered the order of peace) against the recalcitrant nation. If a nation repudiates the peace accepted by everyone else on the same universal terms, Islam understands this to be a declaration of war.

C. *BASES FOR MEMBERSHIP*

Islam's international law regards the *Millah*, or religious society, as the basic identity framework; and the Islamic world order has been composed of the Muslim, Christian, Jewish, Zoroastrian, Sabaean, Hindu and Buddhist religious communities. The reasoning of Islam is founded on the repudiation of tribalism and nationalism; for it regards ethnocentrism, whether based on racial, real estate, linguistic or cultural particularism, as evil and unbecoming of humans whom God created equally and whom He endowed with His spirit. Ethnic characterization is demeaning of man; every man would rather be identified by his thoughts and ideals, by his voluntary deeds and accomplishments, rather than by circumstances of birth and biological or social formation, which are never of the person's own choosing. The Jews were the first non-Muslim group recognized by the Islamic constitution of Madinah in 1 A.H./622 A.C.; and they were followed by the Christians, Sabaeans, Hindus and Buddhists who opted for self-identification by religious affiliation. Islamic jurisprudence equally recognizes those peoples who opt for non-religious identification provided they have a legacy of laws (even if secular) by which they wish to order their lives. The only group which may be barred from membership is that whose law is anti-world order and anti-peace. Whatever the religious, ethical and socio-political content of their dominant ideology, their title to join the world order rests on their humanity and will to peace alone. Islamic jurisprudence thus enables one to affirm today that any group claiming itself to be a *millah* on whatever grounds is entitled to membership.

D. *LIBERTY*

Islam holds, and the world order envisaged by it affirms, that unless born in captivity to captive parents, humans are all born free, and remain so as long as they live. Capture of fighters in the field of battle is the only recognized source of captivity. Such captives, however, are legally susceptible to ransom by anyone concerned for them, and are capable by themselves to contract for their own liberation or manumission by their captors for a reasonable consideration. In the eyes of Islamic law, it is illegitimate for the captor to reject the captives' offer to ransom themselves by their own productive work.

Equally, by virtue of their humanity, humans may not be seized, detained or incarcerated without due legal process. And no law is regarded by Islam as legitimate which empowers any government to seize, detain or incarcerate any human without legal charge before a court of law. All humans enjoy the full liberty to educate their children as they please and to order their lives according to the dictates of their conscience as formulated, institutionalized and interpreted by the tradition of the *millah* with which they are affiliated. Nobody may be coerced into membership of any *millah*, including the Muslim; and anyone may move from one *millah* to another if he so chooses. As long as his movement is his own free and solemn decision, it must be honored by all concerned.

E. *OPENNESS*

The world order Islam seeks to build regards the planet earth as a manor of God in which His human creatures are free to seek His bounty. This means that humans may not be restricted in their movements. They should be free to settle wherever they choose. As long as they are willing to abide by the laws governing the territory and its people, they must be free to enter, to reside, as well as to leave. Movement of persons and their goods must remain unhampered by entry and exit permits, residence or work permits, protectionist custom clearances and the like. All these measures, which are hardly older than a century, as well as the government institutions which administer them, must be abolished. The choice of man's profession or work is an inviolable right in God's cosmic order. And so is one's title to one's earthly possessions, one's freedom to move such possessions wherever one desires. A person's liberty may not be hampered except in cases where its exercise constitutes a trespass or aggression upon another person's property. In a truly Islamic world order, the economy and administration of any country would be in tune with the situation of the globe as a whole.

F. *EGALITARIANISM*

All humans are born equal, and remain so in the eye of the law. They are entitled to equal opportuniy in education and employment, in work and compensation. Distinction must be purely by intelligence and knowledge, work and productivity, by excellence, virtue or righteousness. Certainly, a person's wealth may pass to the heirs through death, gift or will; and this may significantly increase their opportunities in life over and above those of the others. That is no threat to egalitarianism, though it may result in the stratification of society. But no social stratum or class may be a closed club. An Islamic world order would know of no group, class, or association which is not open to anyone who qualifies and wishes to join it; and no qualification requisite would be legitimate that is not realizable by voluntary decision and/or personal effort. Islam regards any kind of apartheid built on race and biology, language or culture, geography or age, as an offense against humanity as well as its Creator, and treats it as punishable crime.

G. *UNIVERSALISM*

In the world order of Islam all humans would be members of one brotherhood. Ethnic particularity, whether biological, social or cultural, would provide no basis for distinction or discrimination. On the contrary, it has fuelled war and hostility among the tribes, nations and states of the world for millennia. The laws of citizenship, immigration and naturalization enacted by the nation-states to safeguard and perpetuate their ethnocentric identity or their advantaged socio-economic and political position would be abolished. Nothing would prevent the communities of the world from intermixing with one another, and they would indeed be encouraged to do so.

No doubt, true universalism would cause great social changes in the fabric of humanity; and under it, many communities might be submerged along with their ethnocentrisms. But this is necessary if the human community is to be purged of its particularism and humans are to be regarded as truly human and judged on the basis of their personal excellence as humans. The emerging universal community or human brotherhood is a far nobler and stronger social ideal; and it would constitute a significant advance for its members over their previous status in the ethnic or national community. It would enable them to remain in local or intermediate communities open to all and at the same time to rise to the universal humanistic ideal.

H. *JUSTICE*

No minority in the world would remain a minority compelled to live under the laws of the surrounding majority, and thus to suffer its own character to be eroded or changed, even though gradually. The world order of Islam would recognize the minority as a *millah*, constitutionally empowered to order the lives of its members by its own laws. If another human group were of the same *millah*, both would be free to merge by emigration and thus constitute a larger whole. The Islamic law of nations is pluralistic, providing legitimacy and protection to the laws of all human groups. Under it, no minority would be a "minority" since it enjoys as much legitimacy in the eye of the world-law as any larger or majority community. If, this legitimacy notwithstanding, the minority group loses a member to the majority, it would be by the voluntary and free choice of that member, a decision which the world order must respect and honor.

If a *millah* should encroach upon another, the victim could bring its complaint to court. The law being public, any court of law would be empowered to consider the litigation and give a verdict. The law courts would also be empowered to look into any complaint brought about by any individual against his *millah* or against the world order itself. Justice being free, its process unencumbered, and its verdict swift of execution, every citizen of the world order of Islam would stand reassured that his rights are sacrosanct.

Above all, every citizen would be reassured that justice is possible, that it is indeed reachable. This ready availability of justice is not expected to increase litigation nor make it unmanageable. For in Islamic law, contempt of court, perjury, and false witness would receive the severe punishment of loss of legal status, in addition to retributory or compensatory fines; and where the latter are not possible due to poverty or bankruptcy, they would be translated into corporal punishment. Finally, the public implementation of corporal punishment would act as didactic and preventive pedagogy for the people. To the victim of injustice, however, there is nothing greater than the reassurance that, despite his weakness, justice is his for the asking.

I. *THE FREEDOM TO CONVINCE AND BE CONVINCED*

Finally, the world order of Islam would confer upon every man by virtue of birth and humanity, the ultimate right and honor, namely, the capacity to think and make up his mind as to which *millah* he wishes to belong and hence, by which law he desires to order his life and that of his dependents. It regards the human person as endowed by God at birth with the capacity to judge between alternatives presented to the mind, and as responsible in the exercise of his faculties and choice. Islam countenances no tutelage whatever in this matter. On the contrary, it regards censorship and spiritual guardianship in matters of religion and law as an affront to the person and to humanity and a compromise of the divine design for creation. Islamic international law would tear down all "curtains" erected by the nation-states to "shield" their citizens against counter-claims to the truth, confident that the truth will ultimately prevail. For the truth theoretically is God's knowledge, and the truth practically and axiologically is His will.

Philadelphia, Pa. February, 1986

Chapter 1

Background

The Muslim world, which is internally weak, relatively backward, frustrated, suffering from internal tensions, full of conflicts, and often controlled and abused by foreign powers, is in a state of crisis. Its modern history is a tragedy. At an earlier time during the sweeping revolution of Islam, Muslims became guardians of human civilization and both the center and master of the civilized world. At present the Muslim polity is neither a master nor even a partner, and both Muslims and Islam are often regarded as a problem in world politics.[1]

How did such a state of affairs come about, and in what ways can the Muslim peoples alter this condition?

In Muslim countries, it is usual to blame external powers and old imperialism for all ills. Although this habit may point up many of the grievances and obstacles Muslims face, it cannot explain the internal causes of the ills. These ills put in motion a process of decay that dissipated the internal power of the Muslim world. The resultant weakness brought external powers into the picture, complicating the difficulties. The problem of the external factors along with the complications they caused for the Muslim world cannot be dealt with before the internal factors are fully understood.

I. PRELIMINARY AND BASIC DEFINITIONS:

The elucidation of this subject requires a discussion of the basic historical background and some definitions.

Islam as a religion and complete way of life made its appearance in the early seventh Century A.C. Muhammad, the last Prophet of Islam (PBUH) (570–632 A.C.), belonged to the well-known Arab tribe of Quraysh. Quraysh, descendant of Ishmael son of Abraham were the custodians of the holy city of Makkah in the western part of the Arabian Peninsula. At the mature age of forty, Muhammad (PBUH) received *wahy* (revelation) from Allah that he had been appointed Prophet and Messenger of Allah. Basically this *wahy*, recorded in the Qur'an constitutes the first source of the *Sharī'ah* (the revealed Will of Allah through the Prophet (PBUH) regarding the conduct of all human life on earth).[2] The *Sunnah* (way) of the Prophet, that is, the collection of reported sayings, actions, and approvals or disapprovals, is regarded as the second source of the *Sharī'ah*.

Muslim jurisprudence (*fiqh*), for the systematic deduction of law, developed a methodology of its own to interpret and make deductions in line with the *Sharī'ah*, for example, *qiyās* (analogy), *'ijmā'* (consensus). The source material coupled with the methodology is called *'uṣūl* (source and methods of Muslim jurisprudence). Some of the *'usul* are basic and some are supplementary. The basic *'uṣūl* are four: Qur'an *Sunnah, 'ijmā'* and *qiyās*. The various schools of Muslim jurisprudence differ on the number of *'uṣūl* to be used or emphasized, although all of them include the Qur'an and the *Sunnah*. In Chapter 3 we will deal with *'uṣūl* in detail when the methodology of Muslim thought is discussed.

By the end of the tenth century A.C., Muslims had reduced the recognized schools of jurisprudence to four. These are called the four Sunni schools of jurisprudence. Since then Muslim thought, with few exceptions, has been rigidified, and imitation (*taqlīd*) has been the dominant approach.[3] In the nineteenth century, modernists introduced the concept of "piecing together" (*talfīq*) to Muslim jurisprudence and legislation as the dominant force of the so-called modern *'ijtihād*.[4] As N.J. Coulson put it:

> The so-called modern 'Ijtihad' amounts to little more than forcing from the divine texts that particular interpretation which agrees with preconceived standards subjectively determined.... In sum, it appears that modern (Muslim) jurisprudence has not yet evolved any systematic approach.... Lacking any consistency of principle of methodology, it has tackled the process of reform as a whole in a spirit of juristic opportunism. Furthermore, many of the substantive reforms must appear, on long term view, as temporary expedients and piecemeal accommodations.

The "medieval" juristic thought pertaining to the area of international relations constitutes what will be referred to here as the classical theory or thought.[5]

II. TRADITIONALISM AND WESTERNIZATION

While Muslim thought, technology, and social system became stagnant with *taqlīd* as the established way of life, Europe began to develop new ideas and methods. By the seventeenth century, Europe had surpassed the Muslim world in warfare and political organization. Muslims were forced into a defensive posture.

As a result of closer and more frequent contacts with Europe, Muslim authorities became aware of the need to learn and adapt European technology, especially in the military and related professions. Muslim political authorities established military and professional schools, hired European instructors, and sent students to European schools to acquire the new skills and technical knowledge. This step created a serious problem in the Muslim social structure, pitting the religious sector of society against the secular, a concept fundamentally alien to Islam. This situation developed because the *'ulamā',* the Muslim theologians and learned men were for centuries deeply involved in *taqlīd* and arid legalism, providing little leadership. Their education lacked the concept of systematic empirical observation and left them alienated from the newly evolving social sciences with their emphasis on application and methods. They were unaware of the repercussions of the new knowledge and methods on the composition, interaction, and organization of society, nor were they able to see the potential of this new knowledge harnessed to the values, goals, and overall paradigm of Islam.

The rising power of the newly emerging Muslim professionals and bureaucrats, who lacked the specialized Islamic knowledge, commitment, and ideological awareness of the *'ulamā',* and of the non-Muslim minorities with their leading professional role, as well as the increasing influence of European powers, led to the polarization of education and knowledge into religious and secular areas and drove the *'ulamā'* into virtual isolation.

Religious education became the symbol and protector of a rigid set of historical religious traditions, built originally on the Islamic ideology. Alien to Muslim thought, secular education increasingly absorbed European ideas and attitudes. This process did not contribute to a revitalization of Muslim thought and education. Systematic empirical observation did not become a tool of Muslim religious education, which remained moribund.

This dichotomy had a crippling effect on motivation and determination in either direction, Islamic or secular, resulting in the isolation of the *'ulamā'* from public life, the separation of the bureaucracy and government from the people, the polarization of the traditionalists, who drew blindly on the past, and of the secularists, who relied totally on Western sources for inspiration and ideas. *Taqlīd* and *talfiq* as practiced by either segment of contemporary Muslim intellectuals have done more harm than good to the cause of creating a new Muslim psychology and outlook based on a revival of Islam. Unification of "sacred" and "secular" in Islam makes it necessary for the devout Muslim's conscience in the modern world to arrive at an agreement between Islamic outlook and the material aspect of life. Thus, it behooves Muslims to clear up the place-time issue pertaining to their understanding and application of Islam. The resolution of this dilemma would bring about the badly needed original dynamic and realistic policies. To make this task possible, we must explain and elaborate on the mechanisms developed and used in the classical Muslim social system, especially in the area of external relations, where political as well as legal factors were clearly present and where both war and peace with non-Muslim parties were involved.

III. SIYAR: A SOURCE OF LAW

Some writers, when analyzing and discussing Islamic works in the field of relations among nations, wrongly emphasizse the idea that *fiqh* is law in itself and not a secondary source of Islamic law. It is very important, in the modern context, to recognize this aspect of *fiqh*. Moreover, it is essential to concentrate on the study of Muslim governmental systems in the Middle Ages if efforts by Muslims to reorganize and systematize the modern Muslim process of law making are to bear fruit.[6]

The difference in meaning among *fiqh*, *'uṣūl al fiqh*, and the *Shar¯ i'ah* must be clarified. The Islamic *Sharī'ah* is the divine will revealed to the Prophet pertaining to the conduct of human life in this world. *'Usul al-fiqh* is the science of deducing and extrapolating rules and injunctions from their sources in the data of revelation. *Fiqh* is the body of rules and injunctions deduced from the Qur'an and the *Sunnah*, which contain the divine will as revealed to the Prophet (PBUH), and by application of other principles of *'uṣūl*. Thus in practical terms *fiqh* means the total sum of legal decisions and opinions written by Muslim jurists, which are available in the manuals of *fiqh* of all Muslim jurists. *Fiqh* is also called *Sharī'ah* because it is meant to represent the intention of the revealed will of Allah in a detailed and applied way. The science of *fiqh* in a general sense includes both the *fiqh* literature and *'uṣūl*.[7]

Law in the Islamic sense is a set of value-oriented guidelines directed toward the divine purposes of Allah. Islamic law therefore is primarily normative rather than prescriptive and is designed for moral education as well as for legal enforcement.

Law in the western sense is a different concept. It is the body of rules and directions accepted and approved for enforcement by nations. This approval is achieved in many ways. These could be treatise, legislation, custom, and moral and religious commitment or any combination thereof.

Conceptual clarity in studying and comparing the *Sharī'ah* rules as a whole, or that part of the *Sharī'ah* rules which concern the field of international relations, with modern Western law, is necessary in order to single out the areas of strengths and weaknesses and the causes for confusion and stagnation.

In this way it is possible to trace one of the basic problems of the Muslim peoples in modern times, namely, incompatibility of thought and methodology. The problem is not which rule the Muslims should select, approve, or reject, but rather what is wrong with Muslim thought and why the *Sharī'ah* is no longer providing man with rules and regulations that can enable him to exert a more effective control over his human environment and destiny. In Chapter 3, we will elaborate on this problem to show how defects of the traditional Muslim methodology, brought about by social changes, lie at the bottom of the dilemma of modern Muslim thought. This will enable us to deal with the future participation of Muslims in the modern world.

What has been attempted here is simply to shed some light on the nature of the problem and to clarify some confusion caused by faulty comparisons and conceptions. We are attempting to show that the real role assigned to *fiqh* and *siyar* in the mechanism of the classical social system was to provide a basic source of law for the Muslim society.

While making comparison with the modern Western lawmaking process we have to be aware of the different processes involved and the adjustments necessary to promulgate laws in a modern Muslim society.[8]

Before we examine the issue, we would like to quote al-Sarakhsī's definition of the term *siyar*, since this will make clear the kinds of topics with which the Muslim jurisprudence used to deal. It will also make it easier to explain why *siyar* and *fiqh* as a whole did not function in the full sense of the term *law* but rather as just one major source of the Muslim law. Al-Sarakhsī defined *siyar* in the jurisprudential sense as follows:

> *Siyar*. . .describes the conduct of the believers (Muslims) in their relations with the unbelievers of enemy territory as well as with people with whom the believers had made treaties, who may have been temporarily (*Musta'man*—the subject of a state which was at war with a Muslim state and granted safe conduct to enter Muslim territory) or permanently (*Dhimmī*—the non-Muslim subject of a Muslim state) in Muslims' land; with apostates (*Murtaddūn*). . .and with rebels (*Baghūn*). . .[9]

Siyar includes also the rules of civilized intercourse with peoples and states living in friendship with Muslims, which are contrasted in the Qur'an with those in hostility.

When we say that *fiqh* is a source of Muslim law, this should not be confused with the sources of *fiqh* itself, that is, the Qur'an and the *Sunnah*, which together constitute the *Sharī'ah*. *Fiqh* represents the sum of jurisprudential interpretations, deductions, and opinions of the Muslim scholars, the *'ulamā',* and especially of those of the highest rank, the *Mujtahidūn*, who showed marked competence and independence of thought.[10]

Fiqh achieved this position during the Umayyad dynasty following the first forty years of the history of the Islamic state. With the expansion of the Muslim community and state, and with the bloody struggle of the various parties for the control of the state, the elite who concerned themselves with the welfare of the religious, social, and intellectual affairs of the Muslim peoples resumed their guardianship through the field of Muslim legal studies and the other fields of studies of *din* (Islamic way of life).

The early period of Islam, notably that of the prophet and the first four Caliphs (*al-Khulafā' al-Rāshidūn*) as well as the companions of the Prophet, was considered the ideal period when many legal precedents were set. Starting with the Umayyads, however, the acts and procedures of the government took into consideration other factors besides the opinion of jurists. The peoples of the various lands conquered by Islam, under the influence of their pre-Islamic customs, acted differently in many ways, thus departing from the standards set by both government and the jurists.

The *fiqh* of the *Sunni* (the true followers) Muslims or *al-jamhūr* (the majority), as we know it today, is contained in the four legal schools: the Ḥanafī, the Mālikī, the Shafi'ī, and the Ḥanbalī. These schools are generally accepted as a single group possessing similar Islamic attitudes. Nevertheless, although these schools may be unified on the basic principles of Islam (for instance, that the pillars of Islam are five, not four or six) and may also be unified on basic philosophical and theological isues, they do not take a unified position on all legal opinions.

Some examples from the area of international relations (*siyar*) will demonstrate how far from the truth is the impression that works of the classical Jihad and *siyar* constitute, even today, an Islamic law among nations and offer a sort of unified classical legal code.[11] These examples show how the different schools could differ on basic issues concerning life and death. Where one school would express approval of the death sentence, or even demand it, in a particular case, another would not hesitate to claim the right to life and safety for the same accused individual. On some other issues, it would not be unusual to see almost all possible attitudes expressed by the four schools. We have to keep in mind, however, that these sharp differences between schools did not necessarily result from different theoretical abstractions. As we shall see in Chapter 3, these schools partially agreed and partially differed on the issue of the bases (*'uṣūl*). From *'uṣūl* are derived the source and methods used to derive legal opinions. All of the schools agreed on the Qur'an and *Sunnah* in all respects. They also agreed on *'ijmā'* (consensus) as a source and method but differed on the scope of application.

The issue revolved around the question of consensus by whom? Is it the consensus of the "companions of the Prophet" only or all of the Madinis or all those who "bind and loose" (in this context, elites and leaders of public opinion) or all the *'ulamā'* or *'ummah* (nation)?[12] The disagreement was even sharper when it came to the *istihsan* (juristic preference) of the Ḥanafi school of jurisprudence. The Shafi'ī refused absolutely to include it among the *'uṣūl*.

These differences were sharpened due to the underlying nature of *'usul*. The sources and methods do not involve a systematic and comprehensive theorization. They merely constitute individual employment of the deductive method through the Qur'an and the *Sunnah* in order to handle specific issues and practices. This is the case because there already was a concrete social system, laid down by the Prophet (PBUH), within which the jurists were satisfied to work.

More specifically, the following examples of *Sunni* Muslim jurisprudential opinion illustrate how far opinions could differ.

1. Is *Jihād* (working or fighting in the cause of Allah) an obligation to wage an offensive war or an obligation to defend Islam?

Al-Thawrī and 'Abū-Hanīfa take a similar position in dealing with this question, while al-Sarakhsī, the Ḥanafi jurist, takes an opposite position in conformity with the Shafi'ī school.[13]

Al-Thawrī says:

> Fighting against the associators (nonbelievers, i.e., those who associate others with God's divinity) is not an obligation unless they start the fight; then it is an obligation to fight back against them...

Abū-Ḥanīfa says:

> *Jihād* is a duty on Muslims but they are not required to (fight) unless they are needed.

Al-Sarakhsī says:

> To sum up, the command of *Jihād* and fighting (to Muslims) had been revealed in stages. . . (the final stage being) the absolute order to fight (nonbelievers) . . .this means an obligation, but this obligation is meant to exalt the religion (of Islam) and to subdue the associators.

Al-Shafi'ī says:

> Allah made the *Jihād* an obligation after it had been a matter of choice.

Consequently,

> *Jihād* is an obligation which every capable man (*Kuf*) [must] practice until two things are achieved: one, there are sufficient forces to face the enemies of Islam, and, two, enough

> Muslim forces carry on the *Jihad* until all polytheists turn to Islam and all the People of the Book give the *Jizyah* [the tax equivalent non-Muslim subjects pay to the Muslim state].[14] If enough Muslim forces fulfill this obligation, then the sin of those Muslims who do not join in *Jihād* will not be counted.[15]

Are the non-Muslim enemy's subjects (*al-ḥarbī*) subject to Muslim legal punishment (*ḥudūd*) for a crime once they have been granted safe conduct or protection (*'amān*) to enter Muslim territory?

One recognized authority, Al-Awza'ī, says that they are not subject to Muslim legal punishment.

In answering a question about adultery or theft committed by an enemy subject who carries a safe conduct, Abu-Ḥanīfah says:

> He is not liable to the prescribed punishment (*al-Ḥadd*), but he is responsible for returning what he has stolen."

Thus, he escapes punishment altogether for adultery.

> Al-Shafi'ī says:
>
> When the enemy subjects enter the Muslims' land and commit crimes, they are subject to Muslim legal punishment. Their treatment is of two kinds: one which does not entail human rights will be pardoned, . . . [the other] which entails human rights will be subject to (punishment).[16]

3. The third example concerns the punishment of a Muslim who intentionally kills a *mu'ahid* (a non-Muslim subject).

> The blood money of a Jew or a Christian or a Magian is the same as that of a Muslim. If a Muslim kills any one of those, then he is liable to execution (*Qawd*).
>
> Al-Shafi'ī says:
> A *Mu'min* (believer) would not be executed for killing a nonbeliever. The blood money of a Jew or a Christian is one third of that of a Muslim whereas the blood money of a Magian is eight hundred Dirhams (money unit).[17]

4. The fourth example concerns the question of sparing the life of non-Muslims and accepting the *jizyah* instead.

At least three positions have been taken by the different schools of Sunni jurisprudence. The Shafi'ī school and Ḥanbalī school claim that the *jizyah* is acceptable only from the People of the Book and the Magians. It is not acceptable from any of the polytheists. The Hanafi school and Mālikī school state that *jizyah* is acceptable from all non-Muslims except the Arab polytheists. Another secondary opinion, however, is attributed to Malik. He also shares the position of Awza'ī and Thawri who maintain that *jizyah* is acceptable from all.[18] By way of contrast, the last position offers amnesty to polytheists, thus sparing their lives, while the first position denies them this privilege.

5. Should human lives be spared by widening or narrowing the categories of people whose lives are not subject to killing in war?

> Mālik and 'Abu-Ḥanifal say that:
>
> People who are blind, mad or very old [should not be killed]. People who belong to monasteries (Ahl al-Ṣwāmi') should be left with some of their possessions which are enough for them to live on.[19]

Al-Thawrī and al-Awza'ī narrow the category down to "only very old people should not be killed."[20]

Al-Shafi'ī, in the more authentic position attributed to him, says: "all these categories [of people] may be killed."[21]

On this subject, Ibn Rushd (Averroes) writes:

> The reason for their differences is the [apparent] contradiction between some of the *'āthār* (traditions) and the general meanings of [both] the book [Qur'an] and the sayings of the Prophet [PBUH].

The reason for their differences is their different positions with regard to the reason for the killing. Those who think the reason for killing is that state of nonbelief, did not make any exception. Those who think the reason for killing nonbelievers is the ability to fight did make exception for those who are unable to fight, or who do not engage in hostilities, such as plowmen and servants. This rule is justified on the basis of the Prophet's prohibition against killing woman, even though they were non-believers.[22]

A contemporary Islamic writer expresses the issue involved in such arguments when he points out that jurists contradict themselves when they sanction compulsion-in-religion (in the case of apostates) and at the same time hold the position that free choice is a condition for assuming any responsibility.[23]

Another Muslim writer notes that if one compares all the works on *fiqh*, the conclusions arrived at by one jurist could be the opposite of those of another. The differences reach the point where a man's life could be in jeopardy according to the ruling of one jurist and be saved according to the ruling of another; property is rightfully possessed according to one jurist and is denied by another; a relationship agreeable to one is prohibited by another.[24]

The same thing had been observed long before by Ibn al-Muqaffa'. He suggested to the Khalifah al-Mansūr that all these jurisprudential opinions be put together in a book with their supporting evidence and arguments. Then the Khalīfah would decide which one to authorize, so that all judgment would be uniform and correct.[25]

It has been said that al-Mansur tried to persuade Malik to authorize his opinions in legal matters as laws for the state. Although Malik wrote a book on the *Sunnah* and jurisprudence, *al-Muwaṭṭa'* (The Accessible), he objected to any such authorization.[26]

Throughout Muslim history the *'ulamā'* served as *Sharī'ah* court judges and provided *fatāwā* (legal and/or religious pronouncements). At times, this legislative function was partly undertaken by the Ottoman sultans, who used to issue orders and administrative regulations and either would appoint themselves or someone else to deal with matters of political and administrative interests.[27]

The parts of *fiqh* manuals dealing with the question of international relations – the chapters on *al-Jihād* and related matters such as *al-jizyah* and *al-siyar* – actually deal with matters that are highly political and can hardly be looked upon as simply enforcements or the carrying out of opinions of the *'ulamā',* who had beome more and more removed from the center of power and decision making.[28]

Putting the pieces together, we may say that *fiqh*, as a whole, is an integral part of classic Muslim thought during the height of Islamic civilization known as the High Caliphate, generally extending from 750-1100 A.C. It was the most unifying and articulate element of the traditional way of life, serving to develop and regulate a highly successful society and civilization in terms of economic, political, social, moral, and legal needs. *Fiqh* and *siyar* are part of the methods and attitudes of the policymaking process, and it is as such that they should now be considered as a major source of Islamic law and not as the law itself.

Identifying *fiqh* as such will help to explain why contemporary

Muslims feel the urge to reexamine the works of *fiqh* in the light of modern needs and challenges in conformity with the spirit and goals of the *Sharī'ah*. This is what is referred to as "reopening the door of *'ijtihād*" (the juristic independent judgment). This view will help in solving some conceptual difficulties concerning the position of the *'ulamā'* in framing modern Muslim legislation.

The opinions of Muslim jurists are not and never have been law in the modern sense of the term; they were merely a source of law. The importance of *fiqh* was due, in turn, to its sources, the Qur'an and the *Sunnah*, with their tremendous influence on Muslims' psychology. Also, the propriety, suitability, or convenience of the opinion relative to Muslims' needs lent weight to this source.

The executive, legislative, and judicial functions of Muslim government during the High Caliphate or classical period were not well defined or systematically carried out. The relationship between these branches of government differed from one time to another, from one dynasty to another, and even from one caliph or sultan to another. In modern times, with the massive change in the structure and organization of the Muslim social system and the pressing need for far more precise and effective organization of the social system and government, modern Muslim political authority has begun to commit itself to the Islamic ideals and goals, develop its political base effectively along the same lines, and reorganize and systemize the functions of the government. This can never be achieved without reforming the educational system and the constitutional system, incorporating both Islamic goals and values, and modern needs and functions.

Certain assumptions for further thought proceed from this situation: the *'ulamā'* and Muslim jurists will participate and influence the modern legislator and provide him with ideas and opinions; but since juristic opinions would no longer be confused with laws, confusion, contradiction, and intolerance on the part of many sections of Muslim society would be likely to diminish. Hence, the traditional mechanism of government would function much more easily.

In Chapter 2, the Islamic works of *fiqh* and *siyar* concerning *jihād* will be analyzed. Our purpose is to find out and understand the Muslim framework of the subject and its dynamism and the extent to which Muslims' positive participation in the field of international relations is possible.

FOOTNOTES FOR CHAPTER 1

[1] The Muslim world here refers to all people who call themselves Muslims and associate themselves with Islamic religion and heritage, wherever they may happen to reside.

[2] In references to the Qur'ān, either one of the following two translations will be used unless otherwise stated: 'Abdullah Yūsuf 'Alī, *The Holy Qur'ān: Text, Translation and Commentary* (Washington, D.C.: American International Printing Company, 1945), and Muhammad Marmaduke Pickthall, *The Meaning of the Glorious Kor'ān* (New York: New American Library, (n.d.). See W. Montgomery Watt, *Muhammad: Prophet and Statesman* (London: Oxford University Press, 1961), pp. 242-243.

[3] See Appendix, note 1.

[4] *Ijtihād* is the use of human reason in the elaboration of the Islamic Law.

[5] N. J. Coulson, *A History of Islamic Law*, pp. 75, 80-81, 152-154, 196-199, 211-217, 220-223. See also M. Khadduri, "From Religion to National Law," in *Modernization of the Arab World*, ed. J. Thompson and R. Reischauer (New York: Van Nostrand, 1966), p. 41.

[6] See Muhammad Hamidullah, *The Muslim Conduct of State* (5th rev. ed.; Lahore, Pakistan: S. H. Muhammad Ashraf, 1963), pp. vii-viii and 3-10; Majīd Khaddūrī, *War and Peace in the Law of Islām* (Baltimore: Johns Hopkins University Press, 1952) pp. 251-295, and Majīd Khaddūrī, "Indroduction" to the Classical Work of Siyar by (Muhammad al-) Shaybānī in *The Islamic Law of Nations* (Baltimore: Johns Hopkins University Press, 1966), pp. 63-68.

[7] See Appendix, note 2.

[8] Ibid.

[9] M. Khadduri, "Introduction" to al-Shaybānī, *The Islamic Law of Nations*, p. 40, quoting Shams al-Dīn Muhammad ibn Ahmad ibn Sahl al-Sarakhsī, *Kitāb al-Mabṣūṭ* (The Detailed Work of Jurisprudence) (Cairo: 1906), p. 2.

[10] See Appendix, note 3.

[11] In this connection, M. Khadduri, *War and Peace*, and M. Hamiddullah, *The Muslim Conduct of State*, are good examples. See also A. Khallaf, *Tārīkh al-Tashr'i*, pp. 23-49 and 65-82, and S. Ramadan, *Three Major Problems Confronting the World of Islam* (Tacoma Park, Md.: Crescent Publications, n.d.), pp. 1-6.

[12] Muhammad Abū-Zahrah, *Mālik: Ḥayātuh, wa 'Aṣruh- 'Arā'uhu wa Fiqhuh* (Mālik: His Life, His Age, His Opinions and Jurisprudence (Cairo: Dār al-Fikr al- 'Arabī, 1963), pp. 322-335, 352-360.

[13] Al-Shāfi'ī, *Al-Umm*, vol. IV, pp. 84-85 and 90, and al-Shaybānī, *Sharḥ al-Siyar*, vol. I, p. 188.

[14] The word *jizyah* is derived from the 'Arabic verb *jaza*, meaning, to fulfill or pay back.

[15] Al-Shāfi'ī, *Al-Umm*, vol. IV, p. 90

[16] Ibid., vol. VII, pp. 325-326.

[17] Ibid., vol. VII, pp. 290-291.

[18] Ibn Qudāmah, *Al-Mughnī*, vol. IX, pp. 194-195 and 319-324, and Wahbah al-Zuḥāylī, *Athār al-Ḥarb fī al-Fiqh al-Islāmī: Dirāsah Muqāranah* (The Effects of War in the Islamic Jurisprudence: A Comparative Study) (2nd ed.; Damascus: Al-Maktabah al Hadīthah, 1965), pp. 712-715.

[19] Ibn Rushd, *Bidāyat al-Mujtahid*, vol. I, pp. 310-311.

[20] id.

[21] id.

[22] id.

[23] 'Abdul Mut'āl-Sa'īdī, *Al-Hurrīyyah al-Dīniyyah fī al-Islām* (Religious Freedom in Islam) (2nd ed.; Cairo: Dār al-Fikr al- 'Arabī, n.d.), p. 46.

[24] Muhammad Fatḥī 'Uthmān, *Dāwlat al-Fikrah al Latī Aqāmaha Rasūl al-Islām, 'Aqib al-Hijrah: Tajrubah Mubakkirah li'al Dawlah al-Iyduyūlūjiyyah fi al-Tārikh* (The Ideological State Which the Messenger of Islam Established after the Immigration: An Early Attempt for an Ideological State in History) (Kuwait: Al-Dār al-Kuwaytiyyah, 1968), p. 83.

[25] Subḥī Mahmasānī. *Al- 'Awda' al-Tashrī'iyyah fi al- Duwal al- 'Arabiyyah: Māḍiha wa Hāḍiraha* (Legal Systems in the Arab States: Past and Present) (3rd rev. ed., Beirūt: Dār al- 'iḥm li al-Malāyin, 1965, 1965) pp. 158.59.

[26] 'Uthmān, ibid.

[27] See H. A. R. Gibb, *Studies on the Civilization of Islam*, ed. Stanford J. Shaw and William R. Polk (Boston: Beacon Press, 1962), pp. 7-14, 148-149. H. A. R. Gibb, "Religion and Politics in Christianity and Islām," ed. J. Procter, *Islam and International Relations* (New York: Frederick A. Praeger, 1965), pp. 10-12. S. Mahmaṣānī, *Al- 'Awda' al-Tashrī'iyyah*, pp. 174-175. Thomas Naff, "The Setting and Rationale of Ot'toman Diplomacy in the Reign of Selim III (1789-1807)," pp. 3-4, unpublished paper made available to me by the author.

[28] See Ibn Qudāmah, *Aḥkām Ahl al-Ḍimmah*, vol. IX, pp. 178 and 319. Al-Shāfi'ī, *Al-Umm*, vol. IV, pp. 82, 155, 170; and T. Naff, "The Setting of Ot'toman Diplomacy," p. 17.

Chapter 2

The Classical Theory and Ensuing Developments

I. THE CLASSICAL THEORY OF SIYAR

The classical theory of *siyar* and *jihād* discussed here covers the sum of Muslim juristic opinions during the period of Islamic civilization or High Caliphate on issues of Muslim external relations in works of major Muslim jurists and thinkers such as al-Shaybani, al-Shafi'ī, al-Mawardī, al-Ghazālī, and Ibn Taymiyah.

A. *NATURE OF CLASSICAL MUSLIM THEORY*

Before we get involved in any analysis of the classical Muslim theory of relations among nations, it is essential that we identify what kind of a theory it is, especially since the word "theory" has already been used to convey various meanings in the field of international relations.

In Chapter 1, we have shown that the classical theory is a normative one. Basically, it rests on the authority of divine sources (Qur'an and *Sunnah*) and offers sets of values and standards which indicate how political actors ought to behave. As a matter of fact, the classical theory, with its diversity of opinions, presents, through the works of *fiqh*, the basic historical outlook of the Muslims vis-a-vis their friends and foes and non-Muslim minorities based on the ideological foundation of the Islamic mission.[1] This does not mean that Muslim rulers (caliphs and sultans) in all cases followed the classical theory to the letter. But due to the accepted authority of that theory it was accorded great respect in shaping Muslim attitudes, policies, and actions for a long time.

Islamic works can be considered either as primary or documentary materials or as secondary materials. This depends on the kind of material sought, because for historical studies, the basic works of *fiqh*, *sīrah* (the biography of the Prophet, (PBUH)), history, such as those by Ibn Hishām, al-Ṭabarī, and al-Waqidī, are primary source and documentary materials. For the analysis of the content of Islamic thought, faith, and ideology, the Qur'an and the basic elements of the *Sunnah* serve as the source and documentary materials, while works of *fiqh*, along with other works, serve as secondary materials. In assesing the content of the classical theory of external relations, works of *fiqh* will serve as a primary source, while in discussing the Islamic framework (Chapter 4) *fiqh* materials will serve as a secondary source and the Qur'an and *Sunnah* will serve as a primary source.

B. *BASIC DEFINITIONS*

We have already stated that Islamic studies in the field of international relations are full of conceptual confusion due to the failure to identify the function of *fiqh* as a source of law and due to its role and significance in Muslim social life as the articulate reflection of Muslim intellectuals. In this way *fiqh* did not represent the actual policies or regulations of the Muslim state, as the analysis of the internal relationships discussed earlier has shown. Some contemporary writers have reached erroneous conclusions simply because they did not realize the close relationship between the thinking of the jurists and the concrete social system laid down by the Prophet (PBUH).

This makes it extremely difficult to generalize the various opinions put forth by different jurists. If any generalization is to be attempted at all, it has to be done with utmost care. Thus, to obtain a real picture of High Caliphate thought and to rectify some faulty conclusions, we must take a closer look at the basic terms and definitions pertaining to international relations as preferred by Muslim jurists at the time.

1. Jihād, Dār al-Islām, Dār al- 'Aḥd and Dār al-Ḥarb

These are four interrelated terms in Muslim thought and jurisprudence pertaining to the external relations of the classical Muslim society.

Jihād - In fulfilling his duties to promote and fulfill the cause of Islam, the Muslim should do his best to rectify wrongs. He must do so by his own actions; if he cannot, he must speak out against them; if he cannot he must oppose them in his heart. *Jihād* is not only an outward act, it is also an inward one to strengthen one's own self and correct one's own mistakes. This rule amply illustrates that *jihād* does not necessarily involve waging a war (offensive or defensive). Different jurists have taken different positions in interpreting it, as will be shown in the succeeding discussion.

Dār al-Islam refers to territories in which Muslims are free and secure.[2]

Dār al- 'Aḥd, alternatively call *Dār al-Ṣulh*. This term was coined by al-Shafi'ī to indicate non-Muslim territories involved in treaty agreements giving sovereignty to a Muslim state but maintaining local autonomy. These agreements were considered to extend Muslim jurisdiction with some tributory payment related to the land (*kharāj*), payable to a Muslim state to meet the *jizyah* stipulations, according to Shafi'i.[3]

Dār al-Ḥarb is the opposite of *Dār al-Islām*, and refers primarily to non-Muslim territories hostile to Muslims and dangerous to their freedom and security.

Some writers, notably Majid Khadduri, have been responsible for a certain amount of confusion resulting from their tendency to be overly selective in their use of interpretations of some jurists while neglecting others. Khadduri states that *jihād* was enjoined by God upon all believers to slay the polytheists wherever they may be found, in accordance with the Prophet's utterance "to fight polytheists until they say: 'there is no god by God.'" Khadduri alleges that "in Islamic legal theory, the *Jihād* was a permanent obligation upon the believers to be carried out by a continuous process of warfare, psychological and political, even if not strictly military," until *Dār al-Islam* overcomes *Dār al-Ḥarb*. Moreover, he mentions that the "law of Islam" allows only brief spans of peace, guaranteed by a treaty, "not exceeeding ten years in duration."[4]

Taking Khadduri's last point first, namely, the concept of a maximum duration of ten years for peace treaties, it seems that he depended for this point on al-Shafi'is strict position[5] but ignored the equally authoritative opinion of Abū-Ḥanīfa. Ibn Qudāmah quotes Abū-Hanīfa's argument on this point: "Since a peace treaty is a contract allowed for ten [years] then it is permissible to extend it in the same way as a contract [which has no such time restriction]... Muslims' interest can be [served] in peace more so than in war... the time period being specified in ten years [unit] means that it (also) applies to longer periods."[6]

'Ibn Qudāmah and Ibn Rushd attributed to Mālik, 'Abū-Ḥanīfa, and, according to one opinion, Ibn Ḥanbal, the notion that the duration of a peace treaty could be unlimited depending on the interests of the Muslim state.[7] This illustrates the diversity of opinions of the jurists. In such matters, no one opinion could be singled out to have represented the Islamic law.

With regard to Khadduri's point concerning polytheists, the scope of this term, and Muslims intolerance of their existence, he admits that "Polytheism seems to have been confined narrowly to paganism, with no implied concept of a supreme deity."[8] There is hardly a consensus on this definition. Again, 'Abū-Ḥanīfa understands the term, as referred to in the Qur'an and Sunnah, to mean only *Arab* polytheists. In an opinion attributed to Mālik, the same term is confined to only one Arab tribe, namely, Quraysh.[9] Al-Awza'ī, al-Thawrī and Mālik, in another opinion attributed to him,[10] considered the term, as referred to in the Qur'an and *Sunnah*, in the historical context, maintaining that the term was no longer applicable to pagans. This position sheds light on the degree of tolerance the jurists allowed and illustrates the point that a jurist's opinion can be very far from a consensus of the Muslims.

Khadduri states that *jihād*, in Islamic legal theory, was "a permanent obligation upon the believers to be carried out by a continuous process."[11] He supports this point by quoting from the Qur'an and the Prophet's *Sunnah*. Such a quotation from the Qur'an and *Sunnah* torn out of its context could easily mislead the reader who is aware of the supreme and final authority of these Islamic sources by making him believe that his understanding of *jihād* represents a simple and noncontroversial issue in Muslim jurisprudence.[12] Thus the reader could be left with the impression that Muslim jurists reached a consensus on *jihād*, an all-out, virtually permanent war, through which Islam could be forced on most of humanity or, as Khadduri puts it, quoting the Prophet (PBUH), "fight polytheists until they say: 'there is no god but God.'"

This is, indeed, not the stand of all Muslim jurists. Many of them have tolerated those pagans who stuck to their beliefs. Upon paying *jizyah*, they were not only to be left to pursue their life in peace but also to be protected by the Muslim state. 'Abū-Ḥanīfa, for example, held that *jizyah* should be accepted from all polytheists except Arab pagans.[13] In an opinion attributed to Malik, *jizyah* was accepted from all polytheists except from the Quraysh. Furthermore, al-Awza'ī, al-

Thawrī, and Mālik advocated the opinion that *jizyah* is acceptable from all polytheists without exception.[14]

Khadduri's understanding and portrayal of the truce duration and of polytheism are not much different from his understanding and portrayal of *jihād* and of neutrality in Islam. This is not surprising since he relied basically on one juristic opinion, that of al-Shafi'ī. Again, Khadduri's conclusions pertaining to *jihād* and neutrality would have been valid had there been a consensus of opinion among Muslim jurists. As in the case of truce duration and tolerance toward polytheists, there is no consensus of opinion toward the nature of *jihād* and the presence of neutrality.

'Ibn Rushd, better known in the West as Averroes, summarized a few of the various opinions of Muslim jurists on the issues of peace and war in Islam:

> Some of those who approved of peace whenever the *Imām* finds it in [Muslims'] interest are: Mālik, al-Shafi'ī and Abū Hanīfa. Al-Shafi'ī [only] does not approve of a peace duration, longer than the period which the Prophet, peace be upon him upon him, made with the non-believers. . .the reason for their differences in approving of peace without necessity is the apparent contradiction between His. . .saying(s)." "Then, when the sacred months have passed, slay the idolators wherever ye find them," "fight those who believe not in God nor the Last Day," and His. . .saying," if they incline to peace, incline thou also to it and trust in God." Those who considered that the verse of fighting. . .is abrogating to the verse of peace, did not approve of peace except for necessity. Those who considered that the verse of peace is limiting to that [verse of fighting] did approve of peace if the Imam saw so.[15]

This amply demonstrates that jurists approve peace with non-Muslims without necessity and for unlimited duration.

Besides 'Abū-Ḥanīfa's favorable position toward peace, al-Sarakhsī puts forth the position of al-Thawrī, shared by many other juristic authorities such as 'Ibn 'Umar, 'Atā', 'Amr ibn Dīnār, and Ibn Shibrimah: "Fighting the idolators is not an obligation unless the initiative comes from them. Then, they must be fought infulfillment of His [Allah] obvious saying 'if they fight you, kill them,' and His saying 'and fight all the idolators as they fight you all.'"[16]

Finally, Khadduri's impression of the absence of the concept of neutrality in Islam stems, to a large degree, from his understanding of *jihād*.[17] Since his understanding of *jihād* was shown not to be universally held by all jurists, it must follow that his conclusions pertaining to the concept of neutrality, which is inextricably connected with *jihād*, were not universally held either.[18] Moreover, his interpretation of historical cases as neutralization rather than neutrality may not hold true. In fact, Ḥamīdullah and al-Zuhaylī have reached quite different conclusions. Through their study of the Qur'ān and *Sunnah*, they have interpreted the same historical cases as evidence for neutrality in Islam.[19]

The lesson to be learned from the above discourse is simply that one should be extremely careful when quoting the basic Islamic sources of Qur'an and *Sunnah* and generalizing about Muslim classical thought. This would not only help one avoid any misrepresentation but would also help one attain a better understanding of Muslims' mentality and its relationship to modern thinking and institutions in the area of international relations.

Jihād, as the duty to pursue what is true and right, includes protection of the human rights of life, belief, honor, family, education, and the *Khilāfah* common and private properties. The highest purpose of *jihād* is to change one's own life so that one will pursue these rights in submission to Allah. The second highest purpose is to defend these rights of others. *Jihād* in this second sense is also the pursuit of justice for everyone, always, everywhere; and the substance of justice is human rights.

At this point conceptually speaking, it is very important for us to realize that one cannot deny the existence of any political institution in Islam by the mere fact that it was not historically dominant. The rise of any political institution is a result of the interaction between a doctrine and its environment. If there were no need or practical possibility for a particular institution at one time, then this should not be taken as conclusive evidence of the impossibility of its coming into existence in different circumstances.

2. Al- 'Ahd and Al- 'Amān

A host of terms in the Arabic language commonly mean agreement or treaty: *'adh* (pledge), *hudnah* or *muwāda'ah* (truce), *mu'ahadah* (treaty), *mīthāq* (covenant or pact), *ṣulḥ* (peace treaty), and *ḥilf* (alliance) are a few examples.[20]

Legally speaking, *'ahd* indicates consent on lawful matters and the obligation to fulfill the terms of a contract by the respective parties. Jurists advise termination of the *'ahd* either in case of breach of agreement and unilateral renunciation by the other party, and/or in case the terms of the agreement are known to violate *al-shar'* (lawful standards). The content of the agreement and the concerned juristical school determine the legality or illegality of the *'ahd* in question. For example, if the political authority concluded a truce for more than ten years, there would be no automatic juristic fiat concerning its legality. While Shafi'ī would invalidate it for the extra period beyond ten years, other's such as Ḥanafī jurists, would disagree with Shafi'ī's opinion. The act of pronouncing the renunciation of the agreement on the Muslim side is called *nabdh*. Muslim jurists do not agree to any unilateral renunciation of the *'ahd* on the part of the Muslims merely on the basis of suspecting that the other party will breach the *'ahd*. Such an action has to be based on a clear case of breach of agreement. With the exception of the Ḥanafī school, jurists do not approve of Muslims initiating the breach of any lawful agreement. If the other party did breach the agreement, with or without being aware of its act, the Muslim party has to inform the other party of the termination of the agreement on the part of the Muslims except if the other party attacks the Muslims first.[21]

Because of their attitude toward *jihād* as a means of spreading Islam, some Hanafis would advise the political authority to renounce a truce unilaterally whenever circumstances change to the Muslims' favor. Since they believe that the interest of Islam is best served by undertaking *jihād*, it behooves the *'imām*, as circumstances change, to renounce the truce (*yanbudh 'ilayhim*) unilaterally. Other jurists, however, do not agree with this interpretation of *nabdh* because it constitutes a breach of an agreement. To them, Muslims' interest is a consideration at the time of concluding the agreement but not after that.[22] The *'ahd* was a major diplomatic vehicle which jurists discussed and utilized in order to regulate various aspects of foreign affairs such as peace agreements. Along with *'amān* (safe conduct or pledge of security) and *dhimmah* (constitutional agreement with non-Muslim minorities), the *'ahd* was also used to facilitate political, cultural, and social communications as well as regulate trade with non-Muslim peoples and territories.

Al- 'Amān: While political issues of truce, peace, and constitutional agreements with non-Muslims were reserved to the political authorities, professional, economic, and trade matters were, according to classical jurisprudence, permitted to individual Muslims men and women, via *'amān*, to decide and conduct on their own. The majority of jurists consider this the right of individual adult Muslims.[23]

With the exception of the Ḥanbali, jurists tended to favor the non-Muslims while they were in Muslim lands with regard to their economic interests, social practices, and criminal offenses.[24] They demanded that Muslims be fair and ethical with non-Muslims when the latter entered Muslim territories under the pact of *'amān*. With *aman*, communication and exchange were made very easy between Muslim and non-Muslim territories.

3. Al-Mushrikūn, al-Dhimmah, and al-Jizyah

The word *mushrikūn* derives from the word *shirk*. Literally, it means making partners; religiously, it refers to the attribution of partners or associates to God. In many places in the Qur'an and *Sunnah*, this term connotes investing associates and partners with God's divinity. The verses and traditions pertaining to the Muslims' attitudes and conduct in their relations with different groups of *mushrikūn* are most important to this discussion.

In their attempt to settle the intricate issues of who the *mishrikūn* are and who fits in what category, the jurists sharply differed. Theoretically, their differences were most serious. The absence of theoretical analysis in classical jurisprudence led to a lack of understanding as to what precisely the term *mushrikūn* meant. The verying definitions given to this term led, in turn, to conceptual contradictions.

Jurists classified *mushrikūn* into two basic categories: the People of the Book and the pagans. According to different jurists, each category would include or exclude some non-Muslim groups. The People of the Book (*'Ahl al-Kitāb*) would, in all cases, include the Jews and the Christians. Some jurists went into lengthy discussions as to which specific groups were Jews or Christians.[25] The Magians (Zoroastrians) were treated as People of the Book, either on the assumption that they did have a revealed book or because of the Prophet's tradition ordering their being treated as People of the Book. The People of the Book were allowed and guaranteed freedom of faith upon the payment of *jizyah*.

The term *mushrikūn* could either be stretched to include all non-Muslims except People of the Book or be limited according to the different schools of classical jurisprudence to mean the Arab pagans or only the Arab tribe of Quraysh. The jurists also differed on how to treat pagans. Some would give them no choice other than to accept Islam. If they refused, they should be fought. Others would accept *jizyah* from them, thus treating them as the People of the Book.

The position of forcing some groups of *mushrikūn* to convert to Islam and the administering of capital punishment for apostasy was, unless it is correctly understood, bound to result in tense relations with non-Muslim communities. The methodology of abrogation enabled some jurists to put some Qur'anic verses relating to basic conceptions into a deep sleep. Modern interpreters have tried to bring these verses and the concepts to which they relate back into active duty. They have reintroduced the issue of apostasy and peace, but they have lacked consistency and methodological systematization and have therefore failed to bring about a comprehensive conceptual treatment of these interrelated issues.

Al-Dhimmah: In classical jurisprudence, this term is defined as a sort of permanent agreement between Muslim political authorities and non-Muslim subjects which provides protection for Muslims and peaceful internal relations with the non-Muslim subjects. In return the latter accepted Islamic rule and paid the *jizyah* as a substitution for being drafted into the army. Jurists were fully aware that, in turn, the Muslim state was obliged not only sincerely to tolerate the non-Muslims' faith and religious practices and laws but also to provide them with protection of their lives and properties: "*Their blood is as our blood* and their possessions are as ours."[26]

Generally, it is obvious that there was no compulsion in religion. To those jurists who advocated *jihad* as a permanent duty to be initiated by Muslims, *al-Dhimmah* enabled Muslims to reach out to non-Muslims. Upon realizing the positive meaning of Islam with its social justice, the non-Muslims would be in a better position to judge Islam. Those who were determined to keep their faith, however, could do so.

The conceptual confusion about *jihād* led to confusion on the part of some jurists as to the meaning and significance of *al-dhimmah* and *al-jizyah*. 'Ibn al-Qayyim al-Jawziyyah (1291–1351 A.C.) agreed that since *al-dhimmah* agreements required non-Muslims to pay *jizyah*, these agreements were intended to punish the non-believers. This opinion reflected the prevailing tense relationship between Muslims and others.

'Ibn al-Qayyim's position can be explained on three grounds: first, the cummulative effect of centuries of tension in communal relationships within the Muslims' territories[27]; second, the effects of the Mongol and Crusaders' invasions; and third, the general confusion in understanding the theoretical bases of Islam.

In their understanding of the early Muslim history, the jurists seemed to be impressed more by the conflicts and animosity between Muslims and non-Muslims than by other elements of Islam. Jurists therefore neglected the other elements, which relate to the real meaning of the Islamic mission. For instance, in discussing the relationships between Muslims and non-Muslins, the jurists unduly focused on the word *ṣaghir¯ (Qur'an 9:29), which means vanquished or overpowered. It was mentioned in the Qur'an in the context of hostilities between Muslims and non-Muslims. At the same time, the jurists overlooked the significance of the al-dhimmah* agreement between the Prophet (PBUH) and the Christians of Najran and the constitutional agreement (*Ṣaḥīfat al-Mad¯inah*) between the Prophet (PBUH) and the Jewish tribes of Madīnah. These agreements, and not the word *ṣaghirūn* alone, should have been taken to portray the state of affairs of the Muslims' relations with non-Muslims.[28]

'Ibn al-Qayyim's opinion illustrates this absence of a comprehensive theoretical conceptualization of the idea of Muslim society. Classical jurists committed this mistake because of their partial and descriptive study of Islam through the system laid down by the Prophet (PBUH) (literal sense of *Sunnah*), which, in turn, led them to think of micro rather than macro aspects of the social system. This point will be pursued further in the next chapter.

Al-Jizyah: The above discussion has shown that *al-jizyah* is an integral part of the *dhimmah* agreements. In this sense, *jizyah* is a sort of taxation of non-Muslim subjects in return for the services rendered by the state.

The term *al-jizyah* has been used, however, to connote more than taxation of *al-dhimmah*. In the case of *muwāda'ah* (truce), *jizyah* could be paid in order to cease fighting. Its payment indicated the serious desire on the part of the enemy to cease hostilities against Dar al-Islam. As such, it did not necessitate offering protection or extending Muslim law. In this sense, *al-jizyah* can be looked upon as a tribute. In the case of *'ahd*, which requires extension of Muslim jurisprudence but not necessarily protection, *al-jizyah* is a payment related to land and is called *kharaj*.[29]

Many aspects of *al-jizyah* were discussed earlier in this chapter. Now the amount of *al-jizyah* will be discussed. Some jurists, guided by the Prophet's tradition, opted to fix the maximum and the minimum allowable. Others specified only the minimum, while still others left the amount to the discretion of the political authority.[30]

Jizyah was generally collectible only from breadwinners. The poor, women, children, the aged, monks, the blind, etcetera, were not liable, but still some argued that some of these categories were liable to pay *al-jizyah*. Unlike *zakat* (the tax collected from every Muslim person except the poor), *al-jizyah* was not allocated for specific purposes. It was left to the political authority to decide how to put the money to use.[31] This can explain the lack of enthusiam on the part of some Muslim rulers upon seeing converts joining Islam. They viewed it as loss of forthcoming governmental revenues.

At this point it is suitable to raise some questions pertaining to the nature of the Islamic law and the concept of equality among nations in Muslim external relationships. Some writers have dealt with these questions in haste and confusion. It is claimed that Islamic law, unlike modern Western law, is personal and not territorial. It is also claimed that the Islamic theory and law of nations, as well as those of medieval Christianity, would not provide for the modern concept of equality among sovereign nations, which is at the base of a true international system.

In many ways the argument is confused and arbitrary. It is plausible only if it is logically sound to mix the actual historical relations with some classical juristic opinions and/or with some synoptic quotations from the Qur'an and the *Sunnah*. Such a process could lead to any desirable conclusion or theory a writer wishes to prove. This may explain the unbridgeable gulf among writers, especially if they subscribe to different ideologies or cultures. In this way, it is easy to view Islam as an outdated rigid set of traditions.

As far as Muslim law is concerned, we can deduce from the above discussions that the classic Muslim thinkers of the High Caliphate worked out a complex system to govern external relations. In a close examination of Muslim thought pertaining to *Dhimmah, Dār al-Islam, Dār al-Ḥarb,* and *Dār al- 'Ahd* we find Muslim concepts of territorial and personal laws working side by side in the direction of a theoretical system of governance that basically is a constitutional or treaty agreement providing for pluralistic arrangements in government structure and decentralization of political power. These Muslim concepts of territorial and personal laws together enabled non-Muslim communities as subjects of Muslim states to enjoy autonomy in running their religious and personal affairs.

In the area of public law, or in the case of conflict of laws, the *Sharī'ah* was applicable. This was the arrangement worked out between the Prophet (PBUH) and the Jewish tribes in the early Madīnah period of the Muslim state. The arrangement with the Christians of Najran (about 10/631), which was effective until the death of the Prophet (PBUH), offered even territorial autonomy and self-government to the people of Najran. The same concepts caused Muslim jurists to require Muslims, while in territories under non-Muslim rule, to abide by the *Sharī'ah* in running their affairs. At the same time Muslims were advised not to violate the laws and practices prevailing in these territories. The jurists were in fact making room for the human and personal elements involved in the process. They would not mind non-Muslims raising pigs and eating pork in Muslim territories, but they would object to non-Muslims engaging in public contracts violating their concern for social justice by such measures as usury (*ribā*).

Just as they would not permit Muslims to violate non-Muslim public law, they would strongly object to Muslims being forced to violate their Islamic personal law. As far as public law is concerned, jurists would object only to Muslims engaging in or being forced to engage in activities not sanctioned by the *Sharī'ah*. In any case, they would advise Muslims to observe their own laws as much as possible without offending foreign authorities. Basically, this kind of arrangement does not conclusively divide the affairs into personal and territorial realms. The modern state system badly needs the introduction of the concept of personal law to accommodate the cultural and religious needs of subjects, especially those of minority status.

Equality is a more difficult problem. We will develop the argument gradually in order to clarify some of the confusion in the field. If we understand the history of the High Caliphate or classical period during which almost all powerful nations engaged in hostilities, and take into account the fact that external relations involve more than one sovereign nation, then clearly it was not the Muslims alone who determined the kind of relationships that prevailed. It is possible that the "hawkish" interpretation of *jihād* played a minor role in bringing about the kinds of relationships that prevailed during this classical period.[32]

At the same time, Muslim thought of the High Caliphate exhibited some 'dovish' tendencies, which could be considered a suitable framework for introducing the notion of equality among nations. These include the authoritative interpretations of *jihād* by such jurists as 'Abū-Ḥanīfa and al-Thawrī. These jurists interpreted *jihad* in defensive terms that could serve as a proper theoretical base for developing a law among nations that defines the relations among them in terms of peace and equality. Although this was the case with one important section of Muslim thought, the underlying nature of the actual relationships among the social systems of the major powers did not allow the fruition of this notion. These powers never accepted the emergence and rise of the Muslim state or its Muslim ideals. They never accepted the concept of free choice of belief and religion of their subjects. They persecuted and punished anyone of their subjects who accepted Islam. Therefore, we could say that at least a notable section of classical Muslim thought during its period of global ascendency was compatible with the notion of equality among nations. This may partially explain the apparent ease with which Muslims have accepted the notion of equality in modern times and still search for ways and means to update the Islamic framework in the field of relations among nations.

The turning point in adopting the notion of equality in relations among nations came with the breakdown of the medieval European Christian social system and the development of Europe's industrial power and its attendant political control of almost all of the world. The new European state system was introduced to the rest of the world, and the latter, faced by superior European power, had no real choice but to adopt it.

With this broad and realistic understanding, there is place neither for accusation nor for exaggerated "claims" either against or for Islam. The Muslim objection that adaptation to the new circumstances might result in loss of identity is also out of place.

4. Khalīfah, 'Amīr al-Mu'minūn, 'Imām, and Sultān

These four terms denote political power and authority in the Muslim state and society. All of them, with the exception of the term *sultan*, were used in a broader than just political sense.

Khalīfah (Caliph): in the general Qur'anic sense, this term is an expression of the concept that man was given the ability to manage and control his world as a trust, through which he achieves what he is worth and thus decides his eternal destiny in the hereafter. With this in mind we can better understand the pronouncement of *Khalīfah* al-Mansur that he was the *khalīfah* of God and His shadow on earth.[33] The *khalīfah*, unlike the pope (the vicar of Christ), is bound by the *Sharī'ah* (Qur'an and *Sunnah*) and has no authority to modify doctrine. His pronouncements only attempt to buttress the power and authority of his office under the *Sharī'ah versus any single person's authority among his subjects.*[34]

In Muslim political thought, *khalīfah* actually indicates the role of the first *khalīfah*, 'Abū-Bakr: *Khalīfat Rasul Allah* (successor of the Prophet as head of the Muslim community). In this sense, the *khalīfah* is supposed to take over leadership of the Muslim society. Of course, the function of prophecy ended with the death of Muhammad (PBUH), and no such function was ever to be associated with the office of the *khalīfah*.

'Imām, in contrast with the term *'Amīr al-Mu'minūn* (the Commander of the Faithful, that is, the caliph), signifies leadership with more emphasis on the spiritual affairs of the community. In this sense, a Muslim leading a congregational prayer or a pious Islamic intellectual authority is also called *'imām*.[35]

Sultān, literally, means power or authority. In a political sense, this word signifies power rather than the spiritual leadership of the community.[36]

It is not our intention to give a complete description of the development of the institution of *khalīfah*. What concerns us here is the role of the jurists in the development of Muslim political thought with regard to power and authority in Islamic society and the issues of political unity.

In many ways, the basic political thought of Muslim jurists concerning the office of the *khalīfah* was idealistic. They showed great concern about the ability of the office of the *khalīfah* to serve the ideological cause of Islam.[37]

The Prophet (PBUH), used all the political powers at his disposal to create and develop the Muslim community and state. At the very moment of the Prophet's death, Muslim society was shaken up by the rebellion of various Arab tribes. At this point, the Muslim elite (with respect to quality, leadership, experience and sacrifice rather than to wealth and class) of Madinah (*al-Muhajirūn*, the Makkan immigrants) used the politial office of the *khalīfah* as an instrument to hold together and consolidate Muslim society. Their rationale was that the appointment of a member of Quraysh, the Prophet's tribe, as the head of state, would help secure allegiance from the entire Arab people.[38] 'Abū-Bakr immediately sent Muslim armies to counter all insurrection on strict orders "to accept nothing from anyone except Islam" and the payment of *zakah* (alms). The Muslim elite sided with 'Abū-Bakr in his effort to solidify the Muslim state.[39]

The civil war which erupted approximately three decades later between 'Ali and Mu'awiyah provides another example of the Islamic elites' stand, which favored a central authority. Basically, the Islamic elite and the jurists were leaning toward 'Ali and his Islamic thoughts; however, some of the groups such as al-Khwārij who initially supported 'Ali were not prepared only to be disciplined and submit to a central authority. Hence, the Umayyads gained the upper hand and the Islamic elite and the jurists eventually supported the Umayyads who were in a stronger position to maintain the centrality and unity of the Muslim state.[40]

Theoretically, Muslim jurists advocated a central idealistic Islamic authority. Out of discretion, at times, they upheld the status quo, which was not up to their level of expectation. Historical lessons led many jurists to believe that drastic reforms leading to revolution might bring about more bloodshed and civil war, which, in turn, would be destructive to Muslim society. Basically, *Sunnī* Muslim juristic authorities, out of necessity and helplessness, supported the office of the *khal īfah*, but they often played the role of loyal opposition.[41] They used all possible arguments to support central governance and to maintian the political unity of the state in the service of the *Sharī'ah*.[42]

When the Turks and Mamluks took over political power, with the attendant weakening of the office of the *khalīfah*, the jurists started turning to the masses in order to maintain the characteristics of an already deep-rooted Islamic identity in the society. Their appeal to the people was to support the cause of Islam and to influence the political authorities in that direction. Traditionally, the authorities claimed loyalty and submission to the *Sharī'ah* to obtain the loyalty of the masses.[43]

The courageous stand Ibn Taymiyyah took in his writings and the position of jurists such as al- 'Izz Ibn 'Abdul-Salām in favor of the *Shar ī'ah* show the role which classic Islamic intellectuals played in the service of Islam and the Muslim peoples.

It is also worth noting that Islamic thought during the High Caliphate tried to reconcile the power struggle between the center and the growing regional units. Muslim jurists gave initial approval to the existence of more than one legitimate independent political unit and authority. Some jurists approved of this when the units were far apart geographically and thus difficult to run under a single administration. Thr jurists no longer paid much attention to the question of the office of the *Khalīfah* when it could no longer be preserved.[44]

C. HISTORICAL AND PSYCHOLOGICAL BACKGROUND OF CLASSIC MUSLIM THOUGHT IN INTERNATIONAL RELATIONS

Many modern writers studying Muslim history tend to look at the immediate physical environment to explain it. For example, they stress economic and demographic factors as the reasons behind the fast-moving territorial expansion of early Islam. This oversimplified approach will inevitably lead us to faulty perceptions and misleading conclusions.[45] The similarities between two situations in terms of physical appearance or circumstances are themselves not enough to determine why various groups and individuals took a specific course of action. Social, psychological, as well as historical factors decide what attitudes shape the life and history of a nation. We must keep this aspect in mind when studying classical Muslim thought if we are to understand correctly its attitudes, methods, and significance.

We have already indicated that the deep religious concerns espoused by the jurists helped in maintaining the Muslim community and state. In studying the history of the office of the *khalīfah* one cannot fail to discern the jurists' public role and involvement in pursuing that goal. In reading the works and history of jurists such as Malik, al-Shafi'i, al-Ghazālī, al-Mawardī, and Ibn-Taymiyyah, one can clearly see the influence of political and social factors upon their work while pursuing their Islamic ideal. It can be seen in their awareness of the importance of a central political authority as an instrument to avoid civil and sectarian conflicts and wars. They showed realistic and flexible attitudes and shifts of position regarding the issues of political power and authority. Their ideological convictions as well as the effect of the immediate social and political factors upon their thinking do not need further discussion here, for writers on the subject have already showed remarkable awareness of these aspects.

What we would like to bring up, however, is the deep-seated psychological influence of the historical experience during the life of the Prophet and the sequence of events that ensued. Without a clear awareness of this aspect, it will be very difficult to understand Muslims' viewpoint in their relationships with non-Muslims. For example, without this awareness we cannot understand the fears such jurists had of the Byzantines: "Can you not see that if you did not fight, Islam would have been destroyed? What would the Byzantines (*al-Rūm*) have done?"[46]

Most Muslim writers consulted here perceived the first generation of Muslims as weak and endangered people in relation to the non-Muslim world. Many Orientalists have handily dismissed this perception as being an apologetic attitude. This simple explanation of a deliberate persecution complex may very well be inaccurate. There is hardly any logical ground for doubting the sincerity of all of these Muslim writers. Analysis of the Muslim psychological make-up may provide further explanation.

The psychological effect of the early Muslim historical experience, as it was recorded in the memory of Muslims, is an important factor in explaining the attitude of Muslims regarding external relations. The same factor explains the excessive use of the concept of abrogation of Qur'anic verses and of historical precedents that tended to provide a less friendly outlook toward non-Muslims. Furthermore, this psychological reaction to hostility and danger contributes to an explanation of the tendency of Muslim intellectuals toward micro rather than macro-analysis of the social system. This last point is reserved for the next chapter, since it is concerned more with the problem of methodology than with the content of thought. The point to be stressed here is that abrogation served to strengthen and legitimize the psychological impact of that historical experience.

The Qur'an, the collections of *ḥadīth*, and the biography of the Prophet (PHUB), give the impression that the conflict during the early Islamic era was between unselfish, justice-seeking, persecuted Muslims and self-centered, corrupt, oppressive non-Muslim authorities. It is hard for Western writers to fathom the psychological effect of the events that took place during the early Islamic era.[47] This, coupled with the repercussions these events had on the relations between Muslims and non-Muslims, makes it imperative to relate some of them. This helps us to understand better not only the events themselves but also Muslims' reaction to non-Muslims, which has basically been one of animosity.

Some of these events and their effects are briefly discussed below. A prolonged economic and social boycott, humiliation, torture, and killing forced the early Muslims to cross the sea to Abyssinia in order to escape from that unbearable plight. The flight of the Prophet (PBUH) to Madinah did not mean the end of the confrontation between Muslims and non-Muslims. The Muslims prayed for God's help when the Quraysh went after Muhammad (PBUH), trying to track him down as he (migrated) to Madīnah.[48] In Madīnah, the pressure and aggression of the Quraysh continued. They contacted Jewish tribes in Madinah and other Arab tribes, recruiting them to help put an end to Muhammad's mission.

> They question thee [O Muhammad] with regard to warfare in the sacred months. Say: Warfare therein is a great [transgression], but to turn [men] from the way of Allah, and to disbelieve in Him, to prevent access to the inviolable place of worship, and to expel its people thence, is a greater [transgression] with Allah; for persecution [oppression] is worse than killing. And they will not cease from fighting against you until they have made you renegades from your religion, if they can. [Qur'an 2:217]

The continuous persecution to which the early Muslims were subjected posed a dilemma: should they wait till the enemy attacks, or should they go out against him? In the case of Badr, they chose the latter although they felt that they were weaker:

> And remember, when ye were few and reckoned feeble in the land, and were in fear lest men should extirpate you, how He gave you refuge and strengthened you with His help, and made provision of good things for you, that haply you might be thankful. [Qur'an 8:26]

> But Allah willed that he should cause the truth to triumph by His words, and to cut off the roots of the disbelievers, that He might cause the truth to triumph and bring vanity to naught, however much the guilty might oppose. [Qur'an 8:7-8]

> When the Lord inspired the angels, [saying]: I am with you. So make those who believe stand firm. I will throw fear into the hearts of those who disbelieve. Then smite the necks and

> smite of them each finger. That is because they opposed Allah and His messenger, and if anyone oppose Allah and His messenger, for him Allah is severe in punishment. That [is the award], so taste it, and [know] that for the disbelievers is the torment of the Fire. [Qur'an 8:12-14]

> Ye [Muslims] slew them not, but Allah slew them, and thou [Muhammad] threwest not when thou didst throw, but Allah threw, that He might test the believers by a fair test from Him. Lo! Allah is the Hearer, Knower. [Qur'an 8:17]

It was difficult for Muslims to feel at ease with the non-Muslims, especially in view of incidents such as *Yawm al-Rajī'* (The Day of *al-Rajī'*) and *Bi'r Ma'ūnah* (The Day of *Bi'r Ma'ūnah*). In both cases, pagan tribes approached the Prophet (PBUH) and asked him to provide them with Muslims to teach them Islam. This proved to be a trick, for as these tribes were returning to their encampments, they attacked and killed their defenseless teachers.[49]

As the sources indicate, the persecution of the Muslim community continued. This time, the tribes of Banū al-Naḍīr along with the Quraysh, and Ghaṭfān of Qays'aylān planned to finish off the Muslim community in Madīnah. This alliance was too strong for the Muslims to confront. They dug a ditch around most of Madīnah in order to hinder the advance of the powerful army. To make things worse, Banū Qurayẓah, Muhammad's ally inside the besieged city of Madīnah, conspired to join the alliance and to attack the Muslims from the rear.[50]

> When they [the non-believing allies] came upon you from above you and from below you, and when eyes grew wild and hearts reached to the throats, and ye were imagining vain thoughts concerning Allah, then were the believers sorely tried and shaken with a mighty shock. And when the hypocrites and those in whose hearts is a disease were saying, "Allah and His messenger promised us naught but delusion . . ." they wished but to flee. [Qur'an 33:10-13]

> Of the believers are men who are true to that which they covenanted with Allah. Some of them have paid their vow by death [in battle], and some of them still are waiting; and they have not altered in the least. [Qur'an 33:23-24]

The siege came to an abrupt end due to a worsening of the weather conditions. The Muslims viewed the failure of the alliance's attack as a manifestation of God's help:

> And Allah repulsed the disbelievers in their wrath; they gained no good. Allah averted their attack from the believers. Allah is Strong, Mighty. And He brought those of the People of the Scriptures who supported them [the allies] down from their strongholds and cast panic into their hearts. Some ye slew and ye made captive some. [Qur'an 33:25-26]

The persecution continued even after the peace treaty of *Ḥudaybiyah* was concluded between the Prophet (PBUH) and the Quraysh. In the sanctuary of Makkah, home of the Quraysh tribe, the Banū Bakr, allies of the Quraysh, massacred Khuza'ah, the Muslims' allies.[51] To the Muslims of that time it appeared that the basic objective of the non-Muslims was simply to take advantage of the situation irrespective of peace agreements. This is expressed in the Qur'anic position on these occasions, which can be seen as a direct reaction to the unrestrained aggressive behavior by non-Muslims:

> How [can there by any treaty for others] when, if they have the upper hand of you, they regard not pact nor honor in respect of you? They satisfy you with their mouths while their hearts refuse. And most of them are wrongdoers. (Qur'an 9:7-8]

> And if they break their pledges after their treaty [hath been made with you] and assail your religion, then fight the heads of disbelief—lo! they have no binding oaths—in order that they may desist. Will ye not fight a folk who broke their solemn pledges, and proposed to drive out the Messenger, and did attack you first? What! Do ye fear them? Now Allah hath more right that ye should fear Him, if you are believers. Fight them! Allah will chastise them at your hand, and He will lay them low and give you victory over them, and He will heal the breasts of folk who are believers. [Qur'an 9:12-14]

> Then, when the sacred months have passed, slay the idolators, wherever ye find them, and take them [captive] and besiege them and prepare for them each ambush. But if they repent and establish worship and pay the poor-due (*zakah*), then leave them their way free. Lo! Allah is Forgiving, Merciful. [Qur'an 9:5]

> How should ye not fight for the Cause of Allah and of the feeble among men and of women and the children who are crying: Our Lord bring us forth from out of this town of which the people are oppressors! Oh, give us from thy presence some protecting friend! Oh, give us from thy presence some defender! [Qur'an 4:75]

> And fight them until persecution is not more, and religion is for Allah. [Qur'an 2:193]

Unless we understand the impact of these historical cases, we will find it very difficult to sympathize with the early Muslims' mistrust of non-Muslims. These are the same Muslims who managed to bring about a tremendous humane transformation in the world of their time.

The process of transformation that the Muslims brought about could hardly have been carried out by narrowminded, warmongering people. The early Muslims were confronted by unceasing aggression and persecution, and the non-Muslim powers' basic attitude of hostility against the Muslim ideals and society never changed. This inevitably left its mark on the thinking of the jurists. Thus, war and fighting became practically an integral and natural part of the relationship with non-Muslims, though some of the jurists did not advocate initiation of fighting by the Muslims. But they did advocate fighting back when the Muslims were attacked.[52]

The psychological effect of the struggle during the early Muslim era and the continuation of the confrontation with the neighboring powers, especially the Byzantines, partly explain the exaggerated usage of the concept of *naskh* (abrogation), especially in the field of external relations. *Naskh* helped the jurists in their effort to gain legitimacy and to rally moral support against the hostile, neighboring non-Muslim powers. It did not help them, however, to think into the future beyond their immediate circumstances.

D. AL-NASKH (Abrogation) MISINTERPRETATION AND MISCONCEPTION

This discipline has and still does play an important role in the field of the *Sharī'ah*, especially in the areas of jurisprudence and commentary on the Qur'an. Undoubtedly, the psychological condition of the Muslim jurists has influenced the way this method of abrogation was applied.

In the area of external affairs the most widely discussed and disputed issue has been the "Verse of the Sword."[53] Influenced by the hostile attitudes on non-Muslims during the early Muslim era, some jurists took an extreme position in interpreting this verse. They claimed that this verse abrogated all preceding verses pertaining to *ṣabr* (patience), *ḥusnā* (persuasion), *la' ikrah* (tolerance), and right to self-determination (*lasta 'alayhim bimusayṭir*).[54] For instance, 'Ibn al- 'Arabī and 'Ibn Salāmah believed that the Verse of the Sword had abrogated a total of 124 verses. Muṣṭafā 'Abū-Zayd says that he found the number of verses that were abrogated, by the same verse, to exceed 140.[55]

It has been shown that jurists have had various opinions concerning the nature of *jihād*.[56] Those who stressed the aggressive nature of *jihād* could only do so by applying abrogation to a wide category of Qur'anic verses. Instead of being concerned with reviving human consciousness for erecting an egalitarian human society, this attitude reduced the Islamic mission to a kind of spiritual totalitarianism. Using abrogation in this manner has indeed narrowed the Qur'anic experience.

If this misconception is removed, then the misinterpretation and deployment of abrogation can be corrected. In this way the damaging effects of the method of abrogation would be eliminated. If the meaning of Islam is restricted to interpretation at the time of the hostilities at the very end of the Prophet's era and the rest of the whole spectrum of Qur'anic and Sunnah texts and the experience of the Makkah and early Madinah periods are ignored, then it will not be possible in the future for mankind to pursue justice or even to survive. Islam has to regain all the dimensions of the Qur'anic experience, which make Islam an ideology and a set of values that deal with man in society. This can be done only by re-examining the meaning of the Qur'anic experience and the place of abrogation within it. This will bring about a fundamental change, which will limit the scope of abrogation and will alter its familiar meaning in Islamic jurisprudence.[57]

E. TOLERANCE AND UNITY: A CLASSICAL LEGACY

To shed more light on classical Muslim thought in matters of external relations, it is necessary to examine more closely two major aspects of classical thought: tolerance and the unity of Muslims.

Earlier in this chapter we introduced and defined the terminology of classical Muslim political thought. But mere introduction and definition are not enough. We must go a step farther and link issues within the framework of Muslim political thought to their counterparts in the modern framework of international relations. We must also analyze these classical issues to see how they pose and relate to contemporary problems in the field of international relations. Unless our readers, expecially those attended to Western thought, go through the process of studying these issues within classical Muslim political thought, they will find internal developments in modern Muslim political thought and will not comprehend the Muslim point of view.

In the Islamic framework, which is basically ideological and personal, the issue of tolerance based on an underlying religious commitment constitutes the basis of the Muslim attitude in external relationships. External relations within the classical framework are relations of Muslims vis-a-vis non-Muslims or vice versa in whatever framework or condition, whether in terms of nations or groups. Even when non-Muslims constitute a minority in a Muslim state, the issue contains some international elements because, it will be recalled, the world for the Muslim is divided into *Dār al-Islam* and *Dār-ar-Ḥarb*. It involves an issue of human rights and an issue of political interest of alien governments and alien organizations. As for the issue of the unity of the Muslim *'ummah*, the modern system of independent nation status within the Muslim world and the many international problems involving inter-Arab and inter-Muslim relationships would be better understood by studying its roots in classical Muslim political thought, particularly as regards the general subject of the relationship of Muslims to non-Muslims, both domestic and foreign.

In this chapter we will discuss the two major issues of tolerance and unity to determine in what ways classical thought in these areas poses a problem in the context of this thesis. Solutions and alternatives will be treated in Chapters 3 and 4.

1. Tolerance and Respect for Personal Dignity

The issue of tolerance by Muslims in classical Muslim political thought touched upon the problem of whom to tolerate as well as how to deal respectfully with the tolerated people. All jurists had agreed that the tolerated people were *'Ahl al-Kitāb* (People of the Book), meaning primarily Christians and Jews, as well as some other groups who could be linked with them directly or indirectly, such as *al-Ṣabi'ūn* (the Sabeans). The Magians (Zoroastrians) were also included based on the authority of the *ḥadīth*.[58]

According to some jurists, Arab pagans were not to be tolerated. They were either to turn to Islam or be fought. This is the straightforward Qur'anic text and the text of the *Sunnah*. The jurists who advocated this position reasoned so on the grounds that the Arab pagans had no Book (Scripture), and since they were the people of the Prophet (PBUH), they had to join Islam. Other peoples, especially if they were pagans, were to be treated, according to some jurists, like the Arab pagans.[59]

It is amazing how far removed these jurists were from the meaning of the early Muslim experience relative to non-Muslims. They took the Qur'anic verses out of context and thus destroyed their significance. The Qur'an and the *Sunnah* ordered an all-out war against the Arab pagans who were always referred to as *mushrikūn* (idolators or associators). Whenever the Qur'an speaks of these Arabs, it stresses their cruelty, treachery, hypocrisy, greed, savagery, etcetera. The Arabs who were the subject of these verses were mainly the Bedouins. They continually attacked and persecuted the Muslims and betrayed the agreements and pledges they made with the Muslims. Thus Islam viewed them generally as savage, uncivilized people who lacked the necessary requirements for responsible and orderly human interaction. The jurists also missed the significance of calling the Jews and Christians "People of the Book." In the Qur'anic context, reading and writing connote knowledge and civilization. Readers of the Qur'an cannot miss the favorable position that the People of the Book, Christians and Jews, enjoy in terms of knowledge and civilization, in contrast to Al- 'Arāb (the Bedouin).

A close examination of all Qur'anic verses with regard to non-Muslims from the beginning in Makkah to the end in Madinah reveals that the Islamic attitude toward non-Muslims is far more balanced than is indicated by the classical jurists.[60] Islam developed an attitude of all-out war only against the Adnani Bedouin and their Qurayshi leadership in their opposition to Islam.[61] This hostile Islamic attitude toward the "savage" Arabs came about because Bedouin were considered to be in a stage of social development not capable of any human responsibility or orderly interaction. The "savage" pagans, pursuing in many ways a barbaric course of behavior and life, had to be forced to accept changes that were necessary to put them in the realm of human civilization and orderly social human interaction. A fundamental human change indeed was achieved when Islam introduced basic human rights as Arabia was subdued and started its historic journey of civilization under the tent of Islam.

The jurists who failed to comprehend the Islamic attitude toward the Bedouin are the same jurists who failed to give proper attention to the significance of the agreement made with the Christians of Najran after the conquest of Makkah, when they came in peace to the Prophet (PBUH), and of the treaty with the Jews in what is knows as *Saḥīfat al-Madīnah* (The Covenant of Madīnah).

Even after the long, bloody struggle with the Jewish tribes in Madinah and Khaybar, during which the Jews' political and military power was destroyed, Jews were allowed to live in peace in Madīnah. They were tolerated and were never forced to accept Islam. They were respected to the extent that they were considered still to have enough social ethics and order to allow human responsibility and orderly human interaction.

The classical juristic attitude toward the question of tolerance lost some of its flexibility in dealing with non-Muslim communities owing to its narrow interpretation. Where it could have allowed many creative policies to develop, it became relatively rigid instead and was bound by various historic precedents. This situation came about by excessive employment of abrogation of those Qur'anic verses supporting tolerance and also because of the lack of the early social system.

An issue closely related to the concept of tolerance concerns the payment of *jizyah*. The jurists usually take one Qur'anic verse out of context pertaining to the payment of *jizyah*:

> Fight against such of them who have been given the scripture until they pay the tribute (*jizyah*) readily, being brought low. [Qur'an 9:29]

The bulk of the jurists' emphasis has been on how *saghar* (the act of bringing low) is to be applied, rather than why it must be applied at all. The most reasonable interpretation was that *saghar* of the *Dhimmis* was accomplished with some by their abiding by the Islamic rule and with others by the act of paying the *jizyah*.[62] The first part of this argument is not in line with the spirit of Islam. Islam stands for a better, purer and egalitarian human society. Allah "sent thee (Muhammad) not save as a mercy for the peoples" (21:107). The jurists, in this case, did not project Islam as a mercy and betterment for these people, but as a humiliation. It is very difficult to justify this conclusion unless the verse in question (9:29) is taken out of context. The sequence of verses preceding and following that particular verse cited above does not support the jurists' opinion.

This verse is part of an address to the early Muslims on the subject of confrontation with the aggressive *Mushrikūn* as well as with those People of the Book who shared the *Mushrikūn's* qualities and who, at the time, were fighting the Muslims:

> They want to extinguish Allah's [guiding] light with their utterances: but Allah will not allow [this to pass], for He has willed to spread His light in all its fullness, however hateful this may be to all who deny the truth.
>
> He it is who has sent forth His Apostle with the [task of spreading] guidance and the religion of truth, to the end that He may cause it to prevail over all [false] religion—however hateful this may be to those who ascribe divinity to aught beside Allah.
>
> O you who have attained to faith! Behold, many of the rabbis and monks do indeed wrongfully devour men's possessions and turn [others] away from the path of Allah. [Qur'an 9:32-34]

The whole section ends as follows:

> And wage war on all the idolaters as they are waging war on all of you, and know that Allah is with those who keep their duty [unto Him]. [Qur'an 9:36]

The jurists simply extended a treatment intended for an assumed aggressive, corrupt enemy to include all non-Muslims, regardless of their actual attitudes and of the total meaning and basic objective of Islam to guide and serve man. To accept this major conclusion of the classical jurists we have to forget all about the significance of the constitutional agreements of Madīnah and Najrān. The payment of *jizyah* was divorced from the question of *ṣaghār*. They were completely different issues and served different purposes in dealing with non-Muslims. Finally, it is clear that the question of *ṣaghār* was not intended to apply automatically to all non-Muslims. *Ṣaghār* is an attitude and punishment not for choosing a different belief but for a hostile and treacherous attitude against Muslim peoples in opposition to justice and to the Islamic obligation to protect man's right to safety and freedom of belief.

This brief analysis reveals that the classical framework of political thought directed toward external relationships (relationships with non-Muslims within and without the Muslim state) was in some aspects negative in its attitude and lacked genuine understanding and interest in the long range relations with non-Muslim peoples.

This analysis of the legalistic and rigid attitude partially explains why the spread of Islam after the first two Muslim generations was accomplished mostly by merchants and Ṣūfi teachers in Africa and southeast Asia.

2. The Unity of the 'Ummah

The word *'ummah* is used in the Qur'an in more than one meaning; it has been used to connote excellence, way, length of time, a group, and a people.[63] When the classical jurists dealt with the Islamic *'ummah*, they spoke of the believers vis-a-vis nonbelievers, which is a philosophical or ideological concept. On the other hand, they spoke of *Dār al-Islam* vis-a-vis *Dār al-Ḥarb*, which is a matter of the extent of Muslim rule or jurisdiction and of *khalīfah* in relation to non-Muslim nations. This usage relates to the organizational and constitutional structure of the political authority in the Muslim lands.

Although the early Muslims and the classical jurists were intelligent enough to shift emphasis from one aspect to another in order to face the concrete problems to help the growth and continuity of the Muslim *'ummah* and Islam as a way of life, nonetheless the ambiguity and philosophical aspects led later generations to confusion and contradiction, which contributed to the political collapse and regression of the Muslim world.

The early Muslims did realize the importance of political authority for the establishment and continuity of the Islamic *'ummah*. After the death of the Prophet, the first Muslim "government" of the first *khalīfah*, 'Abū-Bakr, decided to supress the tribal uprising against the central political authority of Madīnah in order to maintain the *'ummah*. The decision was historic, since the issue was both organizational and philosophical. The choice was between anarchy or stability and growth of the nation. This emphasis on the "central" authority helped to nourish and unify the increasingly diverse elements of the Muslim community.

With the vast demographic and geographic expansion of the Muslim polity, which brought different racial and cultural groups under its jurisdiction, political reorganization had to be undertaken. Although this had occurred in practice when the Muslim world was divided into a few independent and semi-independent territories, such classical jurists as 'Abdul-Qāhir al-Baghdādī, al-Māwardī, 'Abū Ya'lā, and al-Ghazālī, who wrote between the eleventh and fourteenth centuries, insisted on a unified supreme central political authority.[64] Although they admitted the existence of a system of multiple sovereignties in the Muslim world, they nevertheless hesitated or refused altogether to help with reorganization and to grant legitimacy to this evolving system.[65] The jurists seemed to have been caught between the concrete model of the simple, single government of the Prophet (PBUH) and the memories of the sad and bitter historical experience of anarchy and civil wars during the reigns of 'Abū Bakr, 'Uthmān, 'Alī, and Mu'āwiyah as well as the civil wars of the Umayyads and the Abbasids such as the war between 'Abdul-Malik ibn Marwān and 'Abdullah 'ibn al-Zubayr and al-Manṣūr and Muhammad al Nafs al-Zakiyyah.

When by the twelfth century the office of the *khalīfah* had, for all practical purposes, disappeared, jurists finally turned to the more fundamental concept of philosophical and ideological rather than political and organizational unity in order to help the cause of Islam and the *'ummah*.[66] Nonetheless they failed to adjust and adapt the political organization to the emerging needs and changes of the Muslim world. As a matter of fact, Muslim writers down to the present have associated power and growth with a central political structure of the Muslim *'ummah*. Their thinking is marked partly by their lack of understanding of the complex issue of power in the world of politics, and by the concrete model of the Prophet (PBUH) and his traditions concerning rebellion and belligerency.[67] These shortcomings continue to be a factor in modern Islamic views on international relations. Most writers, following Western theory, also seem unable to conceive of a position between anarchy and central political authority. Nor, it appears, have they been able to understand the changes that occurred when the Muslim state began to extend far beyond Arab peoples and territories. Their goal has been more Utopian than idealistic, and their attitude more negative—condemning anarchy and disintegration—than positive, utilizing available power and political structures toward a more unified and politically better organized Muslim world. Their approach has lacked consideration of practical and progressive alternatives due to the shortcomings of their negative approach. In spite of their wishes to the contrary, the Muslim world continues to be divided and in a continuous state of conflict.

Unless conceptual confusion is cleared away in these overlapping areas of philosophy and organization, and more serious work is done on thought, functions, and education, the dilemma that troubles inter-Muslim relationships and Muslim unity will never be resolved.

F. HIGHLIGHTS OF THE CLASSICAL THEORY

Looking at the Muslim world as it stretched from the Atlantic to the outskirts of China, we realize, if we do not allow circumstantial details and legalistic arguments to distract our attention from the overall picture, that the rise of Islam and the influence of Islamic thought brought about great revolutionary changes and put into practice a new dimension in human relationships.

Despite the fact that the concept of equality in Islam removed most of the prejudices among Muslims, regardless of race, color, or wealth, its ideal goal of total Islamic equality was thwarted by non-Islamic cultural influences which partially survived in the succeeding Muslim dynasties, and by the partial juristic approach.[68] In regard to the relations between Muslim and non-Muslims, such relations did improve due to the example set by the early Muslim community which granted communal and legal autonomy to non-Muslims, adopted lenient attitudes, provided better defined rules, and showed a more restrained use of victorious power. Here again, however, the concept of equality pertaining to non-Muslims did not go beyond early concrete examples and therefore did not succeed in achieving Islamic ideals.

The limited success of the classic Islamic sense of equality could and should be redirected to reach out to humanity and build relationships on the optimistic foundation of *'Fiṭrah'* (nature, or goodness of human nature) and *Da'wah* (invitation or call, specifically to Islam), rather than on the pessimistic foundation of *Kufr'* (denial of God, disbelief or infidelity), provided of course that the Muslim world and Islamic call (*da'wah*) is in a position to take this optimistic and humane approach. This is not to say that classic Muslims had ever lost touch with the Qur'anic sense of responsibility.

With the partial reestablishment of tribalism under the Umayyad dynasty, which perpetuated its own hostility and destroyed some possible channels of communication, the reader of classical works of jurisprudence cannot help wondering if the Islamic sense of responsibility was not confused with arrogance. The Islamic call for social justice, human equality (equity), and submission to the divine will and directions of the Creator requires the deepest and sharpest sense of responsibility and total absence of human arrogance and egotism, both in internal and external communication.

With the coming of the imperialist powers of Europe in the eighteenth and nineteenth centuries, the classical Muslim attitude toward non-Muslim minorities as well as the actual conditions of these minorities (though most Muslim subjects were in no way better off) were an additional cause for the interference by European powers into the internal affairs of the Muslim states and especially that of the Ottoman Empire.[69]

The classical thought also insisted emphatically on the concept of the unity of the *'ummah*. This attitude has benefited the Muslim peoples in the face of civil wars and foreign attacks, which culminated in serious cultural, political, economic, and military invasions by Europeans in the nineteenth century. The lack of clarity and inability to analyze the concept of the unity of the *'ummah* has backfired in internal struggle, resulting in the absence of effective cooperation and workable institutions.

The major conclusion we derive from our study of classic thought in the field of Muslim international relations is that there.is a great deal to improve and utilize. This calls for a more earnest, organized effort in order to establish the pre-condition for the growth and participation of Muslim peoples.

G. THE COLLAPSE OF CLASSICAL THOUGHT

When writers speak of Muslim classical theory, they do not speak of the Qur'an or the *Sunnah* of the Prophet (PBUH). They usually refer to the Muslim juridical speculations at the height of Muslim civilization during the High Caliphate, primarily the Abbasid period (750-1100 A.C.), which includes major jurists such as the founders of the four Sunnī schools of jurisprudence and other distinguished jurists, including al-Shaybānī and al-Māwardī. Classical Muslim thought later encompassed such major jurists as Ibn-Taymiyyah and Jamāl al-Dīn al-Syuṭī.[70]

Both modern critics and adherents of these schools of thought have generally limited their study and analysis to the conclusions reached by classical jurists regardless of how such conclusions were reached.[71]

Contemporary writers have given little or no attention to the methodology of these jurists and the circumstances under which they worked. Critics have dealt with classical Muslim thought within a modern, Western frame of reference, starting with wrong assumptions and consequently reaching erroneous conclusions. Although the adherents have tried to face modern challenges by continuing to think in terms of old standards, they have failed to comprehend new and constantly changing circumstances. Thus they have tried arbitrarily to reconstruct the Muslim social system in order both to accommodate conflicting demands of the critics and to satisfy the emotions of the Muslims, while actually contributing little to the Muslim cause.

Muslim writers tend to attach great importance to external factors in explaining their problems and shortcomings. It is true that the Western attack on and control of the Muslim world seriously challenged the classical approach, but the Western attack revealed and uncovered rather than caused the decay of Muslim thought, and it was only a matter of time for it to collapse, leaving the Muslim people with nothing but the Qur'an, the *Sunna*, and glorious memories of Muslim achievements. The attacks were fatal because of the state of Muslim thought.[72] Europe, armed with dynamic ideas and efficient methods, based on an empirical and rational approach, confronted the static and rigid Muslim frame of mind, which rested on textual deduction within the limits of the early Muslim model. The Muslims' thinking had lost touch with reality, and they were incapable of regeneration and reorientation in the light of new developments and demands. It had become moot to argue over defensive versus offensive *jihād*, personal versus territorial law, neutrality versus neutralization. The new exigencies demanded the acquisition and employment of new methods and tools.

II. MODERN DEVELOPMENTS: LACK OF METHODOLOGY

When following our line of analysis in trying to explore the background, reasons, and motivations of Muslim thought, one will find the task of analyzing modern developments in Muslim thought in the field of international relations less problematic.

The sharp turns and opposing points of view in the Muslim world today are difficult to understand if one is ignorant of the historical background and circumstances that caused the formation and development of these viewpoints.

Some developments in Muslim thought took place under the actual control or threat of control by non-Muslim Europeans in the twentieth century. These developments took the form either of apology, appealing to the powerful and commanding adversary, or of protest and revolt against the adversary's presence in the Muslims' land. Characteristic of these attitudes was an apologetic appeal to liberalism, overemphasizing peace, freedom, and tolerance, which was promoted by the ruling Muslim aristocracy or Muslim intellectuals who had come in contact with and were under the control of European thought and power, realizing at the same time Muslim weakness and technological backwardness.[73] This was typical of the ruling Ottoman elite and its *Tanzimat* of the nineteenth century, and of the intellectuals who came in contact with the West since Ṭahṭāwī (1801–1873).

The point is not whether the elite and intellectuals were Islamic or un-Islamic in adopting these attitudes. Actually, the nonagressive interpretation of *jihād*, made it easy for them to adapt to the Western control of Muslim nations. The overwhelming European pressure was the immediate source of motivation in adopting this "liberal" attitude. The Muslim intellectual emphasis on peace, cooperation, and tolerance was primarily a psychological weapon to put moral pressure on the foreign oppressors and, in addition, to reform the Muslim nations.

This "liberal" attitude was an attempt to unite the internal front of Muslim and non-Muslim peoples living in the same country into a national front and thus to minimize the manipulation of different religious gruops through the use of communal divisions. Furthermore, this attitude also helped to minimize the shock of the extreme situation of Muslims being ruled by non-Muslims and restrained Muslim peoples from ill-advised confrontations, thus providing the much needed time for Muslims to introduce some basic reforms and to counter European rule. In this light we can understand and explain the thought and position of people such as 'Imān Muhammad 'Abduh of Egypt (d. 1905) in the field of education, *Sharī'ah* law, and theology, as well as his efforts to maintain friendly relations with the British authorities. Of course, it could be argued that 'Abduh's position made the establishment of imperial rule in Egypt much easier for the British.[74]

There was another kind of response to this non-Muslim imperialistic domination and rule. This response aimed at the liberation of the Muslim land. It was organized by the people and their traditional Muslim leadership, such as the *Mahdī* movement in Sudan, the *Jihad* movement of Sayyed 'Aḥmad Barelvī, and the one led by Isma'īl al-Shahīd in India. These movements emphasized the opposite position: Jihad, more or less in terms of classical conceptions of Jihad, in which Muslims are bound to fight evil and aggressive non-Muslims. But the war cry of *jihad* to set the world right was like putting the cart before the horse. Such a call to action was bound to fail because the conditions essential for success, including the development of Muslim thought along contemporary lines, were not present.[75]

The failure of Muslim peoples to attain power and independence in the eighteenth and nineteenth centuries under the traditional leadership of such men as Sayyed Ahmad Barelvi of India, 'Abdul-Qādir al-Jaza'irī of Algeria, and Muhammad al-Mahdī of Sudan through military *jihād* demonstrated the inadequacy of classical thought and leadership in the confrontation with the power technology and secular institutions of modern Europe.

The liberal approach to internal reform of government, to the creation of a free and democratic society, and to a system of international relations of peace and cooperation, especially with the Western powers, also failed.[76] The movement away from the liberal position began early in the twentieth century when the Arabs revolted against their Turkish rulers and joined the allied powers in World War I. They failed, however, to gain the promised independence and fell under direct European occupation in the name of the Mandate System. After World War II, they suffered the loss of Palestine. Some Muslim countries gained independence. These experiences brought disenchantment with Western liberalism, Western institutions, and cooperation with the West. Liberalism failed as the talisman that would bring the blessings of independence from European domination, of stability and prosperity.

Immediately after World War II the growing trend in the foreign affairs of Muslim states was away from peace toward hostile confrontation with the West. Arab countries became involved in the Palestinian question; Muslim Arabs of North Africa rebelled against European occupation; Indonesian Muslims were involved in guerrilla warfare against the Netherlands. All independent Muslim countries joined the United Nations, but they tried to use their membership in the political fight against Western imperialistic powers and to help destroy Europe's imperialistic control over Asia and Africa. With the emergence of the Soviet Union from World War II as a world power, Muslim countries, especially the Arabs, tried to use Soviet economic, technical, and political aid for their cause. These new developments, while speeding up the decline of the liberal approach, introduced to Muslim thought some elements of Marxist theory, notably the concept of wars of liberation (a latter-day form of *jihād*). But Marxist ideological terminology stems from a philosophy that is in conflict with classical Islamic ideology.[77] Islamic ideology is grounded in the basic concept of Muslim believers in one, just, supreme God versus non-Muslims. Marxist ideology is based on the concept of class struggle of the proletariat versus the non-proletarian exploiters. The Marxist influence was of little value to Muslim thought in international relations and Marxist terminology was generally a source of increasing confusion. It was not clear who was to be liberated and why. Marxist terminology came to bear a vague meaning of *jihād* in the Algerian war of liberation and the civil war in Yeman. The introduction of the Marxist influence emphasized the already felt need for social justice, but Marxism helped weaken internal stability by providing an effective rationale for revolution against the old order. Contemporary Muslim jurists and thinkers failed to reestablish Muslim political thought on a basis adequate to meet modern challenges and to help promote effective participation of Muslims in contemporary international affairs. The effects of the alien Western liberal and Marxist thought on Muslim jurists and thinkers failed to bring a genuine growth in Muslim political thought in the area of international relations.

It is worth noting at this juncture that because of the depressed state of Muslim thought in general and the lack of real Muslim power and influence in international affairs, the topic of international relations has a low priority in contemporary Islamic studies.[78]

At this point of discussion, it is necessary to realize that neither peace, tolerance, defensive *jihād*, offensive *jihād* nor the *Jihād* of 'liberation' had provided a successful and satisfactory base for modern Muslim involvement and contribution in the field of international relations. The actual functioning of the international relationships of Muslim peoples and governments is carried out in conformity with the external forms of the modern system without much understanding of the system, and with an almost total lack of active and effective participation. As a result the Muslim peoples have gained very little from the modern system by discussing historical precedents, of neutrality and neutralization, etc., for the problem is much bigger in scope. It is the dilemma of modern Muslim thought.

The Muslims should realize the problems these new developments in Muslim thought present. The question is how can they adapt themselves to new circumstances and make good use of new and alien ideas as well as classical ones.

The grand approach of *Jihād* clearly represents a powerful dynamic Muslim society of the classical period. This approach in its historical framework will be of little help for modern Muslim statesmen. The liberal or the Marxist-socialist approaches are based fundamentally on alien philosophical, historical, and social experiences and frames of reference of the West. Any idea belonging to one of these approaches, unless adjusted to fit with and respond to the inner conscience and personality of the Islamic *'ummah* will result in more inner conflict and confusion, which needless to say, could be very serious to the Muslim nations' capacity to act and respond constructively to existing needs and conditions.

Muslim intellectuals should realize fully that the problem of classical or traditional thought in modern times cannot be argued or understood in relation to any specific or detailed idea. This requires almost a total comprehension and understanding of the modern world which cannot be explained in terms of the classical terms and frame of mind. Thus the problem is elevated to the level of the methodology of generating ideas and solutions and the mechanism of classical Muslim thought in maintaining the social system. The methodology consists of *'uṣūl* and it is clear that Muslims did not re-examine these *'uṣūl* critically for the purpose of re-adjusting the Muslim approach and understanding of the modern world.

The main approach of Islamic thought continues to be legalistic. It has adapted to different methods, for example, *talfiq* (piecing together), only to meet alien standards and to justify historical actions or practices in modern times.[79] Muslim jurists and thinkers have remained sterile in their work because they fail to go back to the origins of Muslim thought (political or otherwise) and reexamine and reform their methods and approaches.[80] Under these conditions no comprehension, systematization, consensus, originality, or productivity is possible. Consequently, it is necessary to examine the problem of methodology (*'uṣūl*) of Muslim thought. New bases and directions for Muslim external relations are possible only after the problems of approach and methodology are satisfactority dealt with.

CHAPTER 2

[1] See Edward Shils, "The Concept and Foundation of Ideology," *International Encyclopedia of the Social Sciences*, ed. David L. Sills (New York: Free Press, 1968), vol. VII, pp. 66-67; and James E. Dougherty and Robert L. Pfaltzgraff, Jr., *Contending Theories of International Relations* (Philadelphia: J.B. Lippincott, 1971), pp. 25-28.

[2] See M. Hamidullah, *Muslim Conduct of State*, pp. 85, 129-131; and W. Al-Zuḥaylī, *Athār al-Ḥarb*, pp. 192-196.

[3] Ibn al-Qayyim, *Aḥkām Ahl al-Dhimmah*, vol. II, pp. 475-490; and al-Shāfi'ī, *Al-Umm*, vol. IV, pp. 103-104.

[4] M. Khadduri, "Introduction" to al-Shaybānī, *The Islamic Law of Nations*, pp. 16-17.

[5] Al-Shāfi'ī, *Al-Umm*, vol. IV, p. 109.

[6] Ibn Qudāmah, *Al-Mughnī*, vol. IX, p. 286. The meaning here is that since a treaty is a contract, it can be negotiated without time limits or on the basis of renewable time periods.

[7] Ibn Qudāmah, id.; Ibn Rushd, *Bidāyat al-Mujtahid*, vol. I, pp. 313-313; and W. Al-Zuḥaylī, *'Athār al-Harb*, pp. 675-678.

[8] M. Khadduri, *War and Peace*, pp. 74-75.

[9] Ibn Qudāmah, *Al-Mughnī*, vol. IX, p. 195.

[10] Id.

[11] M. Khadduri, "Introduction" to Al-Shaybānī, *The Islamic Law of Nations*, p. 16; and M. Khaddūrī, *War and Peace*, pp. 55-56.

[12] Ibn Rushd, *Bidāyat al-Mujtahid*, vol. I, pp. 310-311.

[13] Abu-Hanīfah was the founder of the Hanafī school of jurisprudence and teacher of al-Shaybānī, the author of the classic work of *Al-Siyar, Kitāb al-Siyar al-Kabīr* (The Detailed Work of al-Siyar) and taught also the famous commentator on that work, al-Sarakhsī.

[14] Ibn Qudāmah, *Al-Mughnī*, vol. IX, p. 193; and W. Al-Zuhaylī, *'Athār al-Ḥarb*, pp. 712-715.

[15] Ibn Rushd, *Bidāyat al-Mujtahid*, vol. I, p. 313.

[16] Ibn Qudāmah, *Al-Mughnī*, vol. IX, pp. 286-287; Al-Shaybānī, *Al-Siyar*, vol. I, pp. 190-191; and W. Al-Zuhaylī, *'Athār al-Ḥarb*, pp. 86-87.

[17] M. Khaddūrī, *War and Peace*, pp. 251-267, M. Khaddūrī, "Introduction" to Al-Shaybānī, *The Islamic Law of Nations*, pp. 18-19.

[18] For the text of the opposing point of view of Al-Thawrī and Abū-Hanīfah vis-a-vis Al Sarkhsī and Al-Shāfi'ī, see above. See also M. al-Ṭabarī, *Jāmi' al-Bayān*, vol. II, pp. 189-190.

[19] M. Hamidullah, *Muslim Conduct of State*, pp. 285-300; and W. Al-Zuhaylī, *'Athār al-Ḥarb*, pp. 197-220.

[20] Ibn Qayyim al-Jawziyyah, *Aḥkām ahl-Dhimmah*, vol. II, p. 475; Ibn Qudāmah, *Al-Mughnī*, vol. IX, pp. 284-292; Al-Shafi'ī, *Al-Umm*, vol. IV, pp. 109-114.

[21] See Al-Imām al-Fakhr al-Rāzī, *Al-Tafsīr al Kabīr* (The Big Commentary on the Qur'ān) (Cairo: Abdul-Rahmān Muhammad, 1938), vol. XV, pp. 182-183; Al-Shafi'ī, *Al-Umm*, vol. IV, pp. 107-109; Al-Shaybānī, *Al-Siyar*, vol. I, pp. 190-191; and Abū-Ja'far Muhammad Ibn Jazir al-Ṭabarī, *Jamu 'al-Bayān 'an Ta'wil 'Ayi al-Qur'ān (The Master of Clarity in Interpretation of Qur'ān (2nd ed.; Cairo: Sharikat Maktabat wa Maṭba'at Muṣṭafā al-Ḥalabī*, 1945), vol. X, pp. 26-27.

[22] Al-Shafi'ī, *Al-Umm*, vol. IV, p. 107; Al-Shaybānī, *Sharh al-Siyar*, pp. 187-191; W. Al-Zuhaylī, *'Athār al-Ḥarb*, pp. 358-362.

[23] See Ibn Qudamah, *Al-Mughnī*, vol. IX, pp. 226-233, 312; and 313; Mālik, *Al Mudawwanah*, vol. II, pp. 41-42. M. Khaddūrī, "Introduction" to *The Islamic Law of Nations*, p. 53. Al-Shāfi'ī, *Al-Umm*, vol. IV, pp. 145-146, 196-197; Al-Shaybānī, *al-Siyar*, vol. I, p. 306; and W. Al-Zuhāylī', *'Athār al-Ḥarb*, pp. 220-344.

[24] M. Khadduri, *War and Peace*, pp. 170-174; Ibn Rushd, *Bidāyat al-Mujtahid*, vol. I, pp. 308-309; and Al-Shāfi'ī, *Al-Umm*, vol. IV, pp. 196-197, 290-291, and 325-326.
[25] Ibn Qudāmah, *Al-Mughnī*, vol. IX, pp. 194-195.
[26] Ibn-Qudāmah, *Al-Mughnī*, vol. IX, pp. 271-272; Al-Imām Muhammad ibn Ismā'īl al-Kahl *Subul al-Salām: Sharḥ Bulūgh al-Murām min Adillat al-Aḥkām* (The Ways of Peace: A Commentary on the Attainment of the Desired Support [of Qur'ān and *Sunnah*] of the Islamic Rules) (Cairo: Al-Maktabah al-Tijāriyyah al-Kubrā, n.d.), vol. IV, p. 65.
[27] Subḥī al-Ṣāliḥ; "Editorial Introduction" to the work of Ibn al-Qayyim, *Aḥkām Ahl al-Dhimmah*, vol. I, pp. 8-9, 17; Ibn al-Qayyim, *Aḥkām Ahl-al-Dhimmah*, vol. I, pp. 23-25; M. Khaddūrī, *War and Peace*, pp. 176-177; Ibn Rushd, *Bidāyat al-Mujtahid*, vol. I, p. 328; Ibn Qadāmah, *Al-Mughnī*, vol. IX, pp. 285-289; and Al-Shāfi'ī, *Al-Umm*, vol. IV, pp. 110-112.
[28] See Ibn al-Qayyim, *Aḥkām Ahl al-Dhimmah*, vol. II, pp. 22-25; and Al-Shāfi'ī, *Al-Umm*, vol. IV, pp. 97-99.
[29] Al-Farra, *Al-Aṣhkām*, pp. 153-209; and al-Shāfi'ī, *Al-Umm*, vol. IV, pp. 103-104.
[30] Ibn Rushd, *Bidāyat al-Mujtahid*, vol. I, p. 327.
[31] Ibid., vol. I, pp. 326-327, 329.
[32] The following examples illustrate the juristic difference on the issue of *jihād*: 1. "Fighting against non-Muslims is not an obligation unless [the non-Muslims] started [the war]; then it is an obligation to fight them. . ." (Al-Shaybānī, *Al-Siyar*, vol. I, p. 187); 2. "If the Muslims have enough strength, I would advise that not a year should pass in which (the *imām*] has not [sent] an army or an attack (*ghārah*) into the non-Muslim territories bordering the Muslim [territory] against each direction. Without harming the Muslims. . . and the minimum allowed that no [whole] year should pass without [the *imām*] sending an expedition [against non-Muslim territories], so that *jihād* would not be hindered any year without a serious excuse" (al-Shāfi'ī, *Al-Umm*) vol. IV, p. 90; see also Ibn Rushd, *Bidāyat al-Mujtahid*, vol. I, p. 313.
[33] Sir Thomas W. Arnold, *The Caliphate*, with a concluding chapter by Sulbia G. Haim (New York: Barnes Noble, 1965), p. 51; see also Al-Farra, *Al Aḥkām al-Sulṭāniyyah*.
[34] 'Abbās Mahmud al 'Aqqād, *Ḥaqā'iqi al-Islām wa Abāṭil Khuṣumih* (The Facts of Islam and the Allegations of Its Adversaries) (3rd ed.; (Cairo: Dār al-Qalam, 1966, pp. 236-253). Abū-al-A'lā al-Maudūdī, *Naẓariyyat al-Islām wa Hadyuh* (The Islamic Theory and Guidance), translated from Urdu by Jalīl Hasan al-Iṣlaḥī (Beirūt: Dār al-Fikr, 1967), pp. 48-52; Abū-Y Ya'qūb ibn Ibrāhīm Ḥabīb Ibn Khunāys al-Anṣārī (731-798), "Muqaddimat Kitāb al-Kharāj," in *Nusūs al-Fikr al-Siyāsī al-Islāmī: al-Imāmah 'ind Ahl al-Sunnah* (Readings in Islamic Political Theory: The Sunni Doctrine of the Imāmah), ed. Yūsuf Ibish (Beirūt: Dār al-Ṭalī'ah, 1966), pp. 11-14; A. Hourānī, *'Arab Thought*, pp. 14-15; E. J. Rosenthal, *Political Thought in Medieval Islām* (Cambridge: At the University Press, 1958), pp. 21-27; Muhammad Abū-Zahrah, *Al-Mujtama'al-Insānī fi al-Islām* (Human Society under Islam) (Beirut: Dār al-Fikr, n.d.), pp. 167-170; Al-Qarafī, *Al Iḥkām*, pp. 84-97; Ibn-Kathīr, *Tafsīr al Qur'ān*, vol. I, pp. 70-72; vol. II, pp. 199-200; and vol. III, pp. 522-524; T. W. Arnold, *The Caliphate*, pp. 10-22, 52-57, 170, and 195-197.
[35] See Ibn Kathīr, *Tafsīr al-Qur'ān, vol. III, p. 330.*
[36] See E. J. Rosenthal, *Political Thought in Medieval Islām*, pp. 8, 38-39, 54, 241-242, and 244ff.; see also an Arabic dictionary article on *salata* in such works as Muhammad ibn Abū-Bakr al-Rāzī, *Muktār al-Ṣiḥāḥ* (Cairo: Sharikat wa Maṭba'at Muṣṣafā al-Bābī al-Halabi Wa Awladuh, 1950), p. 330.
[37] See E. J. Rosenthal, *Political Thought in Medieval Islām*, p. 27; H. A. R. Gibb, *The Civilization of Islām*, pp. 148-149; and T. W. Arnold, *The Caliphate*, pp. 11, 25.
[38] Ibn Hishām, *Al-Sīrah*, vol. II, pp. 657-660; and 'Izz al-Din Abī al-Hassan 'Alī ibn Abī al-Karam Muhammad ibn 'Abdil Karīm Ibn 'Abdil Wāḥid al-Shaybānī, better known as Ibn al-

Athir, *Al-Kāmil fi al-Tārikh*; (The Comprehensive [Study] of History) (Beirūt: Dar Beirut li 'al-Ṭibā'h wa al-Nashr, 1965), vol. II, p. 327.
[39] Muhammad Hamidullah, *Majmu'ah al Wathā'iq al-Siyasiyyah li'al 'Ahd al-Nabawi wa al-Khilafa al-Rāshidah* (Political Detriments Concerning the Period of the Prophet and the Rightly Guided Caliphs) (3rd rev. ed., Beirūt: Dār al-Irshād li'al-Ṭiba'h wa al-Nashr wa al-Taw'zi, 1959), pp. 29, 287-305.
[40] See H. A. R. Gibb, *Civilization of Islam*, pp. 7-14.
[41] See T. W. Arnold, *The Caliphate*, p. 25.
[42] E. I. J. Rosenthal, *Political Thought in Medieval Islām*, pp. 27-47.
[43] See E. I. J. Rosenthal, *Political Thought in Medieval Islam*, pp. 27, 32-35, 51; H. A. R. Gibb, *Civilization of Islam*, pp. 4-22, 141-149, 151-164; Muhammad Ḍiya'al-Din al-Rayyis, *Al-Naẓariyyāt al-Siyasiyyah al-Islāmiyyah* (Islamic Political Theories) (4th ed.; Cairo: Dār al-Ma'ārif, 1967), pp. 71, 92-112; Yūsuf Ibish, *Nuṣūṣ al-Fikr al-Suyāsi al-Islāmi: Al-Imāmah 'Inda al-Sunnah* (The Text of Islamic Political Thought: The Caliphate According to the Sunni Muslims) (Beirūt: Dār al-Ṭali'ah, 1966).
[44] Imām al-Ḥaramayn, 'Abdul-Malik ibn 'Abdullah ibn Ḥayawayh al-Juwayni (1028-1085), "Faṣl fi' Aqd al-Imamah li-Shakhṣayn (Chapter entitled "Giving Allegiance to Two Imams"), in Y. Ibish (ed.), *Nuṣūṣ al-Fikr al-Siyāsi al-Islāmi*, p. 279.
[45] Arnold Toynbee, *Civilization on Trial* and *The World and the West* (Cleveland: World Publishing Co., 1958), p. 325; Francesco Gabrielli, *Muḥammad and the Conquests of Islam*, translated from Italian by Virginia Luling and Rosamund Linell (New York: McGraw-Hill, 1968), pp. 103-115; J. Hell, *Al-Ḥaḍārah al- 'Arabiyyah* (Arab Civilization), translated from German by I. al- 'Adawi and edited by H. Mu'nis (Cairo: Maktabat al-Anglu al-Maṣriyyah, 1956), pp. 12-14; John L. Lamonte, "Al-Ḥarb al-Ṣalibiyyah" (Crusade and *Jihād*), in *Dirāsāt Islāmiyyah*, ed. Nuqulla Ziyādah (Beirūt: Dār al-Andalus, 1960), pp. 103-140; and T. W. Arnold, *The Caliphate*, pp. 23-24; Wilfred Cantwell Smith, *Islām in Modern History* (Princeton, N. J., Princeton University Press, 1957), pp. 6-35.
[46] Attributed to Aḥmad ibn Ḥanbal. This quotation is in Ibn al-Qayyim, *Al-Mughni*, vol. IX, p. 183. Similar feelings were expressed by Malik ibn Anas al-Aṣbuḥi, *Al-Mudwanah*, vol. IV, p. 5.
[47] See Bernard Lewis, *The Arabs in History* (New York: Harper & Row, 1960), pp. 42-48; Carl Brockelman, *History of the Islāmic peoples*, translated by Joel Carmichael and Moshe Perlman (New York: Enpriarn Books edition [Alien Property Custodian], 1960), pp. 22-25; Norman Daniel, *Islām and the West* (Edinburgh: Edinburgh University Press, 1960), pp. 229-307; and W. Montgomery Watt, *What Is Islām?* (New York: Frederick A. Praeger, 1968), p. 8.
[48] It is necessary to point out that besides the historical accounts, such as that of Abū-Muhammad Abdul Malik ibn Hishām (d. 218 A.H.), *al-Sirah al-Nabawiyyah*, or Ibn al-Athir's *al-Kāmil fi al-Tārikh*, al-Qur'ān, and the *Hadith*, the six canonicals of Bukhāri (d. 256 A.H.), Muslim (d. 261 A.H.), Abdū-Dāwūd (d. 275 A.H.), al-Tirmiḍhi (d.270 A.H.), al-Nasa'i (d. 303 A.H.), and Ibn-Mājah (d. 275 A.H.) are of substantial help as historical sources. See also 'Izz al-Din Abi al-Hassan 'Ali ibn Abi al-Karam al-Shaybāni (Ibn al-Athir, d. 630 A.H.), *Al-Kāmil fi al-T*
(The Complete [Work] of History).
[49] Ibn Hishām, *Al-Sirah*, vol. II, pp. 169-185.
[50] Ibid., pp. 214-233.
[51] Ibid., pp. 389-398.
[52] See Ibn Rushd, *Bidāyat al-Mujtahid*, vol. I, p. 313.
[53] The Verse of the Sword is: "Then, when the sacred months have pased, slay the idolators wherever ye find them and take them (captive) and besiege them and prepare for them each

ambush. But if they repent and establish worship and pay the poor-due then leave their way free. Lo! Allah is Forgiving, Merciful." See Abī al-Qāsim Hibatullah ibn Salāmah (d. 410 A.H.), *Al-Nāsikh wa al-Mansūkh* (The Abrogator and the Abrogated) (2nd ed.; Al-Ḥalabī wa Awl¯ bi-Misr: Mahmūd Naṣṣār al-Ḥalalu wa Shurakāh, Khulafa, 1967), p. 51.

[54] Muhammad 'Abdul- 'Azīm al-Zarqānī, *Manāḥ il al- 'Arfān fi'Ulūm al-Qur'ān* (Sources of Knowledge in the Sciences of Qur'ān) (Cairo: Dar 'Iḥya' al-Kutub al- 'Arababiyyah, 'Isā al-B¯ al-Ḥalabī wa Shirakāh, n.d.), vol. II, p. 156; Muṣṭafā Abū-Zayd, *Al-Nāsikh wa al-Mansūkh: Dirāsah Tashri'iyyah, Tarīkhiyah Naqdiyyah* (The Abrogator and the Abrogated: A Juristic, Historical and Critical Study) (Cairo: Dār al-Fikr al- 'Arabī, 1963), vol. I, pp. 289-501, vol. II, pp. 503-583.

[55] See al-Imām Badral-Dīn Muhammad Ibn 'Abdullah al-Zarakshī, *Al-Burhān fī 'ulūm al-Qur'ān* (Proof in The Sciences of Qur'ān), ed. Muhammad alu-al-Faḍl Ibrāhīm (Cairo: Dār Iḥya' al-Kutub al- 'Arabiyyah, 'Isā al-Bābī al-Ḥalabī wa Shurakāh, 1957), vol. II, p. 40; Abū-Zāyd, *Al-Nāsikh wa al-Mansūkh,* vol. II, p. 508.

[56] For further examples of the early jurists' difference of opinion on *jihād*, see works of commentary on the Qur'ān of ibn Kathīr al-Qurashī al-Dimashqī, *Tafsīr al-Qur'ān,* vol. I, pp. 310-311; vol. II, pp. 322, 336-337; and of *al-Ṭabarī,* vol. II, 198-199, 332-335; vol. III, pp. 14-21; vol. IX, pp. 153-155; vol. X, pp. 33-34.

[57] This attempt to deal objectively with Muslim thought and its research methods should not be interpreted by Muslim intellectuals in any way other than to draw their attention to strategic factors that prevented Muslim thought from reaching a broader and more basic understanding of the Qur'ānic experience. The intention is the betterment of the conditions of Muslims in the modern world. This broader understanding is an alternative to the formalistic, superficial, and narrow type of intellectual life in which the Muslim world of today is entrapped.

[58] See Ibn Qudāmah, *Al-Mughnī*, vol. IX, pp. 194-195; and al-Shāfi'i, *Al-Umm*, vol. IV, pp. 94-97.

[59] Ibid., vol. IX, p. 323.

[60] See A. M. al-Sa'idī, *Al-Ḥurrīyyah al-Dīnīyyah,* pp. 19-173; Abū al 'Alā al-Mawdūdī, *Al-Isl¯ fī Muwajahat al-Taḥaddiyāt al-Mu'aṣirah* (Islam in Confrontation with Contemporary Challenges), Khalīl Aḥmad al-Hamīdī (trans.) (Kuwait: Dār al-Qalam, 1971), pp. 39-62 and 171-189; and Muhammad Fatḥī 'Uthmān, *Al-Fikr al-Islāmī wa al-Taṭawwur* (Islamic Thought and [Modern] Development) (2d. rev. ed.; Kuwait: Al-Dār al-Kuwaitiyyah, 1969), pp. 254-279.

[61] See Ibn Hishām, *Al-Sīrah*, vol. I, pp. 264-490; and vol. II, pp. 169-190, 308-328, 389-425, and 543-560.

[62]See Ibn al-Qayyim, *Aḥkām ahl-al-Dhimmah*, vol. I, pp. 16-18; and Al-Shāfi'ī, *Al-Umm*, vol. IV, pp. 99-101.

[63] For the different usage of the term *'ummah* in the Qur'ān, see the following verses: 16:120, 42:8, 43:23, 13:45, 11:8, 7:159, 7:164, 28:23, 3:104, 16:92, 23:34, 35:24, 2:134, and 23:52.

[64] See 'Abdul-Qāhir ibn Ṭāhir al Tamīmī al-Baghdādī (A.H. 1038), *Aḥkām al-Imāmah wa Shurūṭ al-Za'amah'* (Rules of Imamah and Qualifications for Leadership), in *Nuṣūṣ al-Fikr al-Siyāsī al-Islāmī*, pp. 126-262. See also Abū-Hāmid Muhammad ibn Muhammad al-Ghazālī (d. 1111), "Fī al-Imāmah," in *Nuṣūṣ al-Fikr al-Islāmī*, ed. Y. Ibish, p. 279.

[65] See Imām al-Ḥaramāyn 'Abdul-Mālik ibn 'Abdullah ibn Hayawayh, surnamed; al-Juwaynī (d. C.E. 1085) "Faṣlun fī 'Aqd al-Imāmah li-Shakhṣayn" (Regarding Appointment of Two Persons for Imāmah), in *Nuṣūṣ al Fikr al-Siyāsī al-Islāmī*, p. 279.

[66] Ibn Taymiyyah, *Al-Siyāsah al-Shar'iyyah*, pp. 5, 42, 136, 138, 143.

[67] See al-Farra', *Fasl: Shurūṭ Ṭā'at al-Imām,* (The Relinquishment of Loyalty to the Imam), in *Nuṣūṣ al-Fikr al-Siyāsī al-Islāmī*, pp. 216-218.

[68] See Appendix, note 4.

[69] See Appendix, note 5.

[70] See N.J. Coulson, *A History of Islāmic Law*, pp. 75-85 and 202-203; M. Khaddūri, "From Religious to National Law" in *Modernization*, ed. J.H. Thompson and R.D. Reischauer, pp. 40-41; M.Y. Mūsa, *Al-Fiqh al-Islāmi*, pp. 27-61; and S. Ramadan, *Islamic Law*, pp. 27-30.
[71] See Fāyez A. Sayegh, "Islām and Neutralism," in *Islam and International Relations*, ed. J.H. Procter, pp. 90-93; M. Khaddūri, *War and Peace*, pp. 268-296; Said Ramaḍān, *Islāmic Law: Its Scope and Equity* (London: P. R. Macmillan Ltd., 1961); and W. al-Zuḥayli, *Athār al-Ḥarb fi al-Fiqh*.
[72] See Hisham Sharabi, "Islam and Modernization in the Arab World," in *Modernization*, ed. J. N. Thompson and R. D. Reischauer (eds.), pp. 32-34; T. Naff, "The Setting and Rationale of Ot'toman Diplomacy in the Reign of Selim III (1789-1807)," p. 28; and W. M. Watt, *What Is Islām*, p. 225.
[73] See Appendix, note 6.
[74]Id.
[75] See Mas'ūd al-Nadawi, *Tārikh al-Da'wah al-Islāmiyyah fi al-Hind* (The History of the Call for Islam in India) (Beirūt: Dār al- 'Arabiyyah, n.d.), pp. 163-177, 265-280; Shakib Arslān (1286-1366/1869-1946), *Limādhā Ta'akara al-Muslimūn wa Limādha Taqaddama Ghāyruhum* (Why Muslims Are Declining and Why Others Are Progressing) (Beirūt: Dār Maktabat al-Ḥayāh, 1965), pp. 43-55, 149-161; and W. C. Smith, *Islām in Modern History*, pp. 89-92.
[76] See A. Ḥourāni, *'Arabic Thought*, pp. 341-373; Bernard Lewis, *The Emergence of Modern Turkey* (2nd ed.; London: Oxford University Press, 1968), pp. 124-128; H. A. R. Gibb, "The Reaction in the Middle East against Western Culture," in *The Contemporary Middle East*, ed. B. Rivlin and J. S. Szylionwicz, pp. 132-140; Abū-al-A'lā al-Mawdūdi Hassan al-Bannā and Sayyid Qutb, *Al-Jihād fi Sabil Allāh* (Jihad for the Cause of Allāh) (Beirūt: Al-Utiḥād al- ' li-al-Munaẓ Imāt al-Ṭullābiyyah, 1970), pp. 103-134; M. Khaddūri, *War and Peace*, pp. 294-296; M. al-Mubārak, *Al-Fikr al-Islāmi al-Ḥadith*, pp. 50-131; Nadav Safrān, *Egypt in Research of Political Community* (Cambridge, Mass.: Harvard University Press, 1961), pp. 181-258; N Ḥawātmah, *'Aẓmat al-Thayrah fi al-Janūb al- 'Arabi: 'Arḍun wa Taḥlil* (The Crisis of the Revolution in South Yemen: Analysis and Criticism) (Beirūt: Dār al-Ṭali'ah, 1968), pp. 239-249; T. Naff, "The Setting and Rationale of Ot'toman Diplomacy," pp. 27-28; W. C. Smith, *Islām in Modern History*, pp. 58-89; W. M. Watt, *What Is Islām*, p.225; and W. M. Watt, *Islāmic Political Thought*, pp. 118-119.
[77] See Abdul-Hamid Saddiqi, *Tafsir al-Tarikh* (Interpretation of History), Kāẓim Jawad (trans.) (Kuwait: al-Dār al-Kuwaytiyyah, n.d.), pp. 87-162; A. K. Brohi, *Islām in the Modern World*, compiled and edited under the auspices of Islamic Research Academy of Karachi by Khurshid Ahmad (Karachi: Chiragh-E-Rah Publications, 1968), pp. 69-91; H. A. R. Gibb, "The Reaction in the Middle East Against Western Culture," in *The Contemporary Middle East*, eds. B. Rivilin and J.S. Szylciwicz, pp. 132-149; Jihād Qal'aji, *Al-Islām Aqwā* (Islam Is Stronger) (Beirūt: Dār al-Kitāb al-'Arabi, n.d.), pp. 97-167; Khalifa 'Abdul-Hakim, *Islām and Communism* (3rd ed.; Lahore, Pakistan: Institute of Islāmic Culture, 1962), pp. 43-67; M. Rafi-'Ud-Din, *Ideology of the Future*, 3rd ed. and 411-481; and Muhammad al-Ghazāli, *Al-Islām fi Wajh al-Zaḥf al-Aḥmar* (Islam Fighting Communist Expansion) (Kuwait: Maktabat al-Amal, n.d.), pp. 20-58.
[78] See Appendix, note 7 and 8.
[79] Contemporary Muslim political thought in the field of international relations is not limited to essays related directly to the field. Literature about the biography of the Prophet, for example, is one more important source for this field. It is also worth noting that contemporary Muslim university texts have started making specific reference to international relations, though in most cases the treatment is very brief. See, for example; Muhammad Ḥāfiẓ Ghānim, *Mab al-Qānūn al-Dawlial- 'Ām* (Principles of International Law) (4th ed.; Cairo: Maṭba'at Nahḍat

Masr, 1964), pp. 50-55. Also see 'Alī Manṣūr, *Muqaranāt Bayn al-Sharī'ah al-Islāmiyyah wa al-Qwanīn al Waḍ'iyyah* (Comparative Study between the Islamic *Sharī'ah* and Secular Laws) (Beirūt: Dār al-Fatḥ, 1970), pp. 54-68 and 75-131. The following references are representative of works that one way or another reveal some of the shortcomings mentioned above: Al Sayyid Sābiq, *Fiqh al-Sunnah* (Understanding of the *Sunnah*) (Kuwait: Dār al-Bayān, 1968), vol. XI, pp. 140-235; Muhammad Ahmad Ba-Shumayl, *Banū-Qurayẓah*, pp. 236-283; M. Hamidullah, *Muslim Conduct of State*, pp. vii-viii; W. Zuḥāylī, *'Athār al-Ḥarb*, pp. 14-27.

[80] Most contemporary works on *'uṣūl* are descriptive. Analysis and criticism in most cases are limited to the question of authenticity of the *Sunnah* and a general call for new *ijtihād*. See A. Khallaf, *'Ilm Uṣūl al-Fiqh*, pp. 8-10; A. Khallaf, *Khulāṣat Tārīkh al-Tāshrī'*, pp. 103-104; A. Khallāf, *Maṣādir al-Tasrī' al-Islāmī*, pp. 5-18; Anwar Ahmad Qādirī, *Islāmic Jurisprudence in the Modern World: A Reflection upon Comparative Study of the Law* (Bombay: N. M. Tripathi Pvt. Ltd., 1963), pp. 55-81, 305-324; Faẓlur Rahmān, *Islamic Methodology*, pp. v-viii, 1-84, and 175-191; M. al-Mubārak, *Al-Fikr al-Islāmī al-Ḥadīth*, pp. 7-26, 150-151, and 186-195; M. Y. Mūsa, *Al-Fiqh al-Islāmī*, pp. 175-206; and N. J. Coulson, *A. History of Islamic Law*, pp. 182-218.

Chapter 3

Reform of Methodology

Muslim methodology refers to *'uṣūl*, the formal classical methodology of Muslim jurisprudence. Unlike Western positive law, *'uṣūl* takes the whole of human conduct as its field and is concerned with both internal and external affairs of the Muslim peoples. Classical Muslim methodology provides not only the research method for Muslim thought but also its source material. As was mentioned in Chapter 2, Muslim political thought, including the Islamic theory of international relations, continues to be classical in its approach through the techniques of *taqlīd* and *talfiq*.

In this connection, H.A. Sharabi says:

> The movement of reform in nineteenth century Islam 'awakening', was not an intellectual awakening, but a *reaction* to the military and political threat of Europe. Even after the European impact has been transformed into a cultural challenge, response to it remained largely defensive and negative.

H.A.R. Gibb says:

> It [knowledge] is still dominated by the ideal of authority; and if Western 'authorities' are now recognized alongside Muslim 'authorities,' the result is only to create a confusion of thought....

Mālik Ibn Nabi admits this by stating:

> The Modern [Muslim cultural] movement in fact has no precise understanding of its goals nor of its means. The whole affair is just a passion for new things. Its only way of (generating reform) is to make Muslims imitators and customers of foreign civilization, thus lacking in originality.

In the conclusion of his study of "Islamic Reform," Malcolm H. Kerr states:

> The nationalist sentiments of the present day provide no such moral guideline, or 'regulative principle,' as one writer [Albert Hourani] has put it. . . . Nor can the concern for social justice so explosively conspicuous in the Near East today, quite provide such a principle either, as long as it is primarily an instrument and an expression of nationalism.[1]

A comprehensive understanding of classical Muslim methodology as a generator and filter of Muslim political thought, throughout its history, is a necessary condition for revitalization.[2] An original and adaptable system of political thought is needed for the emergence of a new framework of Muslim international relations capable of answering the needs of present-day Muslim policymakers. In this connection it is worth noting the comments of H.A.R. Gibb:

> The Koran [Qur'an] and the Tradition are not, as it is often said, the basis of Islamic legal speculation, but only its sources. The real foundation is to be sought in the attitude of mind which determined the methods of utilizing these sources.

He also said in another work:

> Every scientific argument must always take the same course and reach the same conclusion, unless you change the same postulates or invent new tools.[3]

I. THE MUSLIM METHODOLOGY: A SPACE-TIME PROBLEM

Before we deal with the problem of space-time in the context of Muslim thought, it is useful to clarify the nature of this problem. The substance and the structure of social institutions at any point of space and time reflect the need and the rationale of a specific society. With progress of time and change of space the substance and structure should reflect these changes. The degree of failure of institutions to change in response to the accumulation of newly emerging needs affects the degree of the problem of space-time. In this context we will deal with Muslim political thought and methodology and its acute problem of relevance to the needs of Muslims in the contemporary world.

Classical Muslim methodology (*'uṣūl*) refers to the basic textual sources and methods used in producing Muslim attitudes in different spheres of life including international relations. These sources are the Qur'an, *Sunnah, 'ijmā'* (consensus), and *ijtihad* (the use of human reason or *'aql*) in elaboration and interpretation of the *Sharī'ah. 'Ijtihād* includes the fourth major source of Muslim thought, the *qiyās* (analogy), along with other supplementary methods such as *al-'istiḥsān* (juristic prefernce), *al-maṣlaḥah or al-maṣāliḥ al-mursalah* (public interest), and *al-'urf* (the customs of a particular society).[4]

Except for the Qur'an, which for the most part expresses itself in terms of general statements as philosophical guidance, including on those matters relating to international relations, we find that the *'usul* reflect the classic Muslim point of view.[5]

The space-time factor is not limited to the content of the *Sunnah* in particular and classical Muslim thought in general, but is also present in the *'uṣūl* themselves, the way they were established and developed. The contemporary traditional narrow examination of the *'uṣūl* on the one hand and the Modernist and Orientalist overemphasis on the question of the authenticity of the *ḥadīth* seem to distract from what seems to us the basic problem of modern Muslim thought.[6] Unless the space-time dimension of the classical methodology is dealt with and proven properly, Muslim political thought is bound to lack productive and original content and methodology, and to continue to be trapped in *taqlīd* and *talfiq*.

A. *THE IMPACT OF THE MAIN 'UṢŪL ON MUSLIM THOUGHT*

Before we discuss the *'uṣūl* of Muslim jurisprudence and the kinds of defects existing in them, we will investigate the function and strategy and fundamental position of the basic *'ul* in shaping Muslim thought and in building and developing Muslim jurisprudence (the *Fiqh*).

Unlike Western positive law and the Western legal system, Islamic jurisprudence takes the whole of human conduct for its field.[7]

> Not only does it regulate in meticulous detail the ritual practice of the faith . . . but many of its precepts are also directed solely at the individual's conscience, inasmuch as certain acts are classified as 'recommended' and 'reprehensible' where performance or omission may be divine approval or disapproval

> but entails no 'legal' sanctions as such... The popular movements demonstrated that the appeal to the Shari'ah can still be an effective instrument to energize the demand for social justice.[8]

No idea or institution can win the legitimacy or acceptance of the Sunni Muslim scholars unless it can pass this traditional methodological test (*'uṣūl*). Ideas and institutions failing to pass this test will continue as foreign objects in the body of Muslim thought, generating inner psychological tensions. These ideas and institutions lack effective rapport within the inner core of the Muslim personality and motivation. To demonstrate this psychological crisis, I shall recall two major issues handled by the competent and recognized Muslim authority, Rashīd Riḍa. The issues were those of apostasy (*Riddah*) and usury (*Ribā*).[9]

In the case of apostasy, Rida applied the Muslim source-material, *'Uṣūl*. He discarded the *'Ijmā'* on the ground that it was not based "on a clear text of the Qur'an. "On the contrary," he argued, "there is a text which forbids all compulsion in religion" and the *'Ijmā'* is, therefore, in contradiction with "a higher *'Aṣl* (the source or method)." Regarding the issue of usury in the case of bank interest, he observed that Muslims are faced with the danger of "economic penetration and domination by the western economic system of capitalism." He therefore evoked the principle of *Ḍarūrah* (necessity) to allow interest to be charged where applicable.

Neither the authority of Riḍa, combined with the authority of Jamal-ud-Dīn al'Afghānī and the Grand *'Imām* Mahmūd Shaltūt of al-Azhar, could permanently settle the issue of interest on the ground of *Ḍarūrah*. The issue of interest is still a source of tension and dispute, leaving the banking system, and in turn the whole economic system, in the Muslim world on shaky grounds. Being uncertain of the Islamic ethics[10] involved, the Muslims have become motivationally weak.

Of course, the answer to such a dilemma is not a formal-legalistic *Fatwa* of: "yes" or "no", "*Ḥālāl*" or "*Ḥārām*." This has been tried and all other possible formal-legalistic positions on the issue of fixed interest rates have been tried. But, then, there are always realities and practicalities which call for workable alternatives. The mere repetition of outdated policies has therefore failed to produce the desirable behavior or to put an end to the restlessness and tension.[11]

Comparing Riḍa's conclusions on apostasy with those on usury, we find that his opinion concerning apostasy has gained firm ground and wide acceptance. In the case of usury, however, the problem was hardly resolved, creating instead more argument and confusion.

One crucial difference between the two issues under discussion, which ought to be noted, is that, while the former did pass a formal test of traditional *'uṣūl*, the latter did not. It is primarily in this context that we can understand the meaning of the uneasy coexistence between modern ideas and institutions and the Muslim personality. The modern ideas and institutions did not filter through and pass the *'uṣūl* test. They remained alien and continued to exist under the pretext of *Ḍarūrah*. The principle of *Talfīq* (piecing together) was utilized in order to create a workable relationship, and the result was a continuing absence of originality in contemporary Muslim thought.

It seems as though much effort has been directed toward the content of Muslim thought, while not enough has been done pertaining to the problem of methodology. This has led to the borrowing of foreign ideas, ideologies and institutions, but these apparently failed to revitalize Muslim thought. Muslim public life has been transformed into a sort of theatre where the intelligentsia seem to be playing the roles of Dr. Jekyll and Mr. Hyde. At times, they appeal to Islamic motivaton, while at others, they yield to foreign pressures and to the temptation chaoticly to introduce alien ideas and institutions. The front row applauds the excellence of the actors, while the masses are left sleeping in the back seats.[12]

The necessary methodological reform was rendered more dificult because both the traditional elite and the modernists have busied themselves with problems of theology and the authencity of the *Sunnah*.

This atmosphere of expediency and confusion among intellectuals began basically as a reaction to the Western military and political threat. This reaction led to a new system of education distinct from the traditional religious system. The result was the formation of two separate groups of intellectuals, the *'Ulamā'* and the *Muthaqqafūn* (secular and professional intellectuals), each pursuing their own separate approach and activity. The widening gap between the theological and philosophical reactions of the traditionalists and the reformists, and the simultaneous borrowing and imitation of foreign ideas, ideologies and institutions by the *Muthaqqafūn* precluded any possible genuine revival of Muslim thought, either in assimilating the already existing stream of new ideas or in the necessary methodological adjustments.[13] Although the door of *'Ijtihād* has been declared to be wide open - even if it was claimed to be otherwise earlier - we fail to detect any effective movement toward the revitalization of the Muslim social system or the regeneration of Muslim thought.[14]

The preceding discussion reveals the broad and important nature of Muslim jurisprudence (*fiqh*) in the traditional system of Muslim thought and the strategic position which *'uṣūl* occupies. The discussion further reveals how failure to understand the function and appreciate the development of *'uṣūl* in the system of Muslim thought underlines the intellectual and psychological crisis of the Muslim peoples.

The next step is to study and investigate these *'uṣūl* in order to acquire a better understanding of their nature, function, the way in which they are still useful, and the manner in which they should be adjusted to fit the requirements of the contemporary Muslim world.

B. THE 'UṢŪL: HISTORICAL BACKGROUND

The *'Uṣūl Istinbat al-Fiqh'* (the source material, principles, and methods for deduction of jurisprudence) consist of four basic *'uṣūl*. The Qur'an and the *Sunnah* are also called *al- 'Aṣlayn* (the Two Sources) since they are the text material of jurisprudence. The Qur'an, the *Sunnah* and 'Ijmā' (consensus) are called *al-Thalāthu al- 'Uṣūl* (the Three Sources), distinguishing them from the fourth source, *Qiyās* (analogy) or the method for deducing juristic opinions, since *Qiyās* belongs to the realm of *'Aql* (reasoning) as applied to the text (the Qur'an and the *Sunnah*).

1. The Qur'an

The direct, revealed Word of Allah is the first source material of Islamic thought and jurisprudence. It is in Arabic and divided into one hundred and fourteen *Suwar* (chapters), containing more than six thousand verses. The Qur'an is a book divinely revealed to the Prophet Muhammad (PBUH) in verses during the latter twenty-three years of his life (d. 632 A.C.), in the two cities of Makkah and Madīnah in Western Arabia. The authenticity of the Qur'an - a written text - is beyond dispute.

Watt noted that it became "clear that the rationally formulated doctrines of the Ash'arites had less power to evoke responses in ordinary men than the pregnant language of the Qur'an itself. Many Muslims have turned back to the Qur'an and to doctrinal formulations of a Hanbalite type."

The Qur'anic values constitute the basis of the *Sharī'ah*. Through direct contact and religious education and practices, the Qur'an shapes the Muslim outlook and conscience.[15]

2. The Sunnah

The *Sunnah* of the Prophet, as Muslim jurists define it, consists of all the authentic reports of pronouncements and acts of the Prophet (PBUH) or such deeds or sayings of other people that had gained his explicit approval. Its subject matter is in large the life and actions of the Prophet (PBUH) and members of his community. The *Sunnah* of the Prophet as is reported in the authentic collections of *Ḥadīth* is the second *'Aṣl* (singular of *'usul*). Muslims believe it is divinely-inspired, though in meaning and not in letter as in the case of the Qur'an. The *Sunnah* basically is meant to supplement and to help interpret the Qur'an. This position has been firmly secured for the *Sunnah* of the Prophet (PBUH) by al-Shafi'ī in his classic work, "Al-Risalah" (The Message).[16]

The most famous and accepted collections of *Sunnah* (*Ḥadīth*) are the six "*siḥāh* " (authentic ones). The "*Saḥiḥayn*" are the two authentic collections of al-Bukhārī (194-250 A.H.) and Muslim (202-261 A.H.), which are widely accepted by *Sunnī* jurists and *'Ulamā'* as the most precise and authentic collections. The other four "*Siḥāḥ*" are the four "*Sunan*" of 'Ibn Mājah, 'Abū-Dawūd, al-Tirmidhī and al-Nasā'ī. The "Muwaṭṭa' " of Mālik stands, insofar as the *Sunnah* part of it is concerned, on almost the same footing in terms of authenticity, like the other six, but is not regarded as a collection of *Sunnah* as such because it was composed primarily as a work of jurisprudence. These are by no means all the collections of *Sunnah*. There are many others, but they are not considered as authentic as these seven collections. From the above information we can deduce that, in Muslim thought, the *Sunnah* is considered divinely-inspired and it contains a wealth of source materials.

The subject of *Sunnah* is a lengthy, difficult and controversial one. In fact, the controversy starts with the very word *Sunnah*. What does it mean? Does it refer to the *Sunnah* of the community (the living *Sun-*

nah), or only to the *Sunnah* of the Prophet (PBUH)'? How is the *Sunnah* of the Prophet related to the Qur'an and to the living *Sunnah* of the Muslim community? How authentic and precise is the *Sunnah*? When was the *Sunnah* documented in writing? How much of it has been preserved? How have the political and theological tensions and struggles affected its authenticity? What are the right criteria to be applied to the *Sunnah*? Should criticisms be applied to the form or to the content, or to both? How far can man apply reason to measure divine revelation?[17] These are some of the more important questions raised since the *Fitnah* (civil war) which was started by the killing of 'Uthmān, the third Khalīfah (656 A.C.).

Apparently, the question of *Sunnah* seemed to have been settled by classical Islam. This was the result of al-Shafi'ī's argument in his "Risalah" on behalf of the *Sunnah* of the Prophet[18] and also because of the tremendous efforts made by Muslim scholars in sifting the *Sunnah*.[19] Besides, there was another major reason why the issue of *Sunnah* after al-Shafi'ī seemed to slip into the backstage as an unimportant controversial problem. The reason was that by the time of al-Shafi'ī Islamic jurisprudence had already been established, its major legal issues had been settled, and the framework of jurisprudence had been laid down, so controversy about *Sunnah* no longer had serious practical implications. This makes us realize that the concern with authenticity and other related questions represented not merely academic and religious concerns but practical, political and human interests.

The approach to the problem of *Sunnah* depended on the methodology applied and the competence of the scholars in the field.[20] The authenticity of the *Sunnah* has been settled and its significance as a part of the *Sunnī* Muslims frame of mind has been permanently established. Other schools of thought, such as the Ẓahiriyyah of the famous 'Ibn Ḥazm al'Andalusī, either disappeared or slipped away to far-off regions or into minority groups as in the case of the *Shī'ah* school of thought.

When we understand the new developments and challenges that the Muslim world has had to undergo and to face during the last few centuries, we can understand why the issue of the authenticity of the *Ḥadīth* has been raised again. For the modernists and some reformists, this was primarily a way to do away with an outdated traditional legal opinion. We will show why practically all possible positions on the issue of authenticity of the *Ḥadīth*, its rejection, acceptance or sifting have failed to revive either the creativity or the productivity of Muslim thought. To achieve this we have to make explicit the basic assumptions involved in the traditional Muslim frame of thought and in the basic changes in the Muslim world, and the basic issues involved in the renewed issue of the authenticity of the *Sunnah*.

To really understand the subject of the *Sunnah*, one must wade through a huge pile of material. But in order to understand how nearly futile the issue of the authenticity of the *Ḥadīth* is, it is sufficient to glance at two contradictory works on the same subject, the famous work of the late Joseph Schacht, *The Origins of Muhammadan Jurisprudence*, and the work of M.M. Azmi, which was supervised by the late A.J. Arberry, *Studies in Early Ḥadīth Literature*. Arberry wrote in the forward of Azmi's work, "In this field of *Sunnah* Dr. Azmi has done a pioneer work of the highest value and exact standards of scholarship."

Two short quotations from each of the above-mentioned works make the picture clear and help us in this work turn away from what is seemingly a futile effort and instead look ahead for new answers and directions.

In the Epilogue of the work, Schacht says:[21]

> The idea we have gained of the formative period is thoroughly different from the fiction which asserted itself from the early third century A.H. onward.

In what Azmi[22] calls his final conclusion, he says:

> The examples supplied by Schacht tend to refute his own theory. The phenomena of *isnad*, the number of transmitters belonging to scores of provinces, make the theory of 'projecting back' artificial creations and similar statements almost impossible to accept . . . Traditionalists have taken the utmost care to check errors and discrepancies with sincerity.[23]

3. The Qiyās (Analogy)

We cannot understand the wide usage of *qiyās* and the emergence of the many supplementary *'uṣūl* unless we understand the implicit assumptions of the classic period of Islam. The classical thought of the Abbasid Empire which was the major power in the world of the High Caliphate, was basically content with the social system and achievements of the model laid down by the Prophet (PBUH). Thus the role assigned to both Muslim thought and Muslim methodology was the maintenance of the basic model.[24] *Qiyās* meant to seek similarity between new situations and early practices, especially those of the Prophet (PBUH). Classical Muslim thought also succeeded in producing a few supplementary methods, notably that of *al-maṣlaḥah*, make up for the growing number of new situations that were difficult to deal with by the direct application of textual material or by analogy with that material. An example of the use of *maṣlaḥah*, not only when there is no text (*nass*) for reference in ruling on a specific situation but also as a principle used to override a text or consensus (*'ijmā'*) considered to be inconvenient or unsuitable, was given by 'Abu-Ḥāmid al-Ghazālī in his work *al-Mustaṣfā* (Selected Works). He ruled that it is proper to kill Muslims who were used in captivity to shield dangerous non-Muslim enemies against a Muslim attack. The public interest (*maṣlaḥah*) necessitated the ruling contrary to the *naṣṣ* and *'ijmā'* prohibiting the killing of a Muslim.[25] The further classical Muslim jurists drew away from the time of the Prophet (PBUH), the more they used and successfully elaborated the method of *maṣlaḥah*, as in the case of the Ḥanbalī jurists in their concept of *siyāsah shar'iyyah* (Islamic public policy).[26] With the passing of time and the accumulation of internal and external changes, Muslims could no longer work within the framework of the classical model, which required only the simple maintenance of the existing social system. Modern challenges make new demands on the Muslim methodology. The basic requirement now is to generate original thought commensurate with the needs of internal and external affairs that does not run counter to the basic intents and values of Islam.

II. THE SUNNAH AND THE SPACE-TIME DIMENSION

Contemporary criticism and dissatisfaction with traditional Muslim thought in the field of international relations usually concentrates on the *Sunnah*[27]. Traditions that seem to present harsh and/or outdated practices against non-Muslims usually lend themselves to such disapproval. The standards against which these criticisms are measured are mostly ideological Western concepts and utopias; the examples are customarily drawn from such issues as *jizyah*, tactics in foreign relations, and warfare with non-Muslims. Traditionalists and apologists have tried to defend the *Sunnah* and Muslim jurisprudence by attacking unfavorable examples of Western practice, such as racial discrimination and modern imperialism. The situation was frustrating for the critics, who were often Westernized, and for the apologists alike.

This contemporary Muslim dissatisfaction with traditional thought in the face of the Muslim failure in modern times to prevent Western encroachments and Muslims' failure to match Western material achievements could explain to a great extent the efforts by modernists to prove the fallibility of the *Sunnah*, thereby toppling the structure of traditionalist thought built on the *Sunnah*. The failure of the modernists, in their turn, to make Muslim political thought more responsive to the needs of the times has resulted in an even more detailed questioning of the *Sunnah* and its relevance to Muslim dilemmas, especially as regards international relations. Excessive concern with the authenticity of the *Ḥadīth* only points up the need to free modern Muslim thought from the negative and inhibiting influences of the traditional Muslim social system, involving space-time elements of a millenium ago. It is important to establish that this element of space-time in the *Ḥadīth* is one of the most important sources of Muslim political thought.

A few examples of the *Ḥadīth* from the field of *siyar* (relations among nations) and related matters reflect elements of space and time.

> Anas reported God's Messenger as saying "Go in God's name, trusting in God, and adhering to the religion of God's Messenger. Do not kill a decrepit old man, or a young infant or a woman. Do not be dishonest about booty, but collect your spoils, do right and act well, for God loves those who do well." 'Abū Dawūd transmitted it.[28]

> 'Alī told that God's Messenger had in his hand an Arab bow, and on seeing a man with a Persian bow in his hand he said, "What is this? Throw it away. Keep (*'Alaykum*) to this and such like and to spears with shafts, for God will help you to support the religion with them and establish you in the land." 'Ibn Mājah transmitted it.[29]

> 'Abū 'Usayd reported the Prophet (PBUH) as saying to them at the Battle of Badr when they drew up in lines to meet Quraish, "When they come near you shoot arrows at them." A version states "When they come near you shoot at them but do not use all your arrows." Bukharī transmitted it.[30]

Looking carefully at these traditions (the whole of classical and traditional political thought has been built upon them), we can see clearly that these are instructions pertaining to the running of a medieval war in the context of a medieval social system, and any reference to them overlooking the space-time context is misleading. To make any meaningful use of this kind of traditions we have to understand the underlying value aspect involved in such pronouncements, as distinguished from the concrete physical and cultural aspects.

It is understandable for the classical jurists to have engaged in literal analysis, a word-for-word and an issue-for-issue comparison and analogy in their arguments along the lines of these traditions, but when contemporary jurists function in the same manner and even repeat the old instructions word for word, there is obviously a lack of comprehension of the changes that have taken place.[31] Today, the repetition of old instructions that forbid killing women, children, etcetera, in war, show clearly that modern jurists are not aware of the implications of modern warfare and modern weapons.[32] These kinds of instructions are of no help to the administrators of modern warfare and mean little to them. Often the choice of the kinds of weapons to use, whether it be conventional or nuclear bombs or even exotic weapons, no longer exists. It is often difficult to single out civilians. Under the techniques of modern warfare, the question is no longer whom one should kill or not kill, but how many one should kill, and what constitutes "over-killing."

It is understandable that al-Shafi'ī, in dealing with foreign relations, advises the Muslim rulers to attack the *mushrikūn* in their country at least once a year if not more often, and not to accept a truce for more than ten years in analogy with the *Sunnah* of the Prophet (PBUH), since the latter was engaged with his enemy in a battle at least once a year and did not accept a truce for more than ten years.[33] But no statesman could accept this kind of analogy and understanding under the existing extremely dangerous conditions of warfare and the fragile international system of today or in the foreseeable future.

'Imām 'Ibn Kathīr tells us in his work of *Tafsīr* (commentary on the Qur'an):

> When the Messenger of God, peace be upon him, arrived at Makkah, he and his Companions had suffered badly from Yathrib's [Madina's] fever and it had exhausted them. The *Mushrikūn* said that the People [the Muslims] who would be arriving here were people who were exhausted from Yathrib's fever and they were as a result in a bad condition. The

Mushrikūn were seated near the [Black] Stone. God made known to His Prophet what the *Mushrikūn* had said. The Prophet ordered his Companions to walk half-running [in the area where the *Mushrikūn* could see them] in the first three circumambulations [of the Ka'abah] to show the *Mushrikūn* their endurance, and ordered them to walk between the two corners where the *Mushrikūn* could not see them. The Prophet spared his Companions half the running (*Yarmulū*) in all the circumambulations in his fear for their exhaustion. The *Mushrikūn* said, " Are these the people whom we thought the fever had exhausted? These are stronger than so and so." Transmitted in the two Sihah from the tradition of Ḥammād 'Ibn Zaydabah.[34]

For that reason it is a command of the *Sunnah* (practiced even today) that Muslims walk half-running in the first three rounds of *ṭawāf*, the circling of the Ka'abah in Makkah.

It is clear that in this case what has been considered tradition (*Sunnah*) out of love, respect and adherence to the Propeht (PBUH), which is good for that purpose, was in fact tactics used by the Prophet (PBUH) in order to deceive the enemy, who were waiting for the first available opportunity to destroy the Muslim army. This example shows to what extent the Prophet was responding to the circumstances around him. The effect of the time-place element is not always so evident or simple, and in order to overcome the limitations of this time-place element, much more sophistication is needed in analysis.

The real problem underlying the *Sunnah*, and with it *'uṣūl* and the whole of traditional Muslim political thought, is the failure to comprehend the time-place influence on them. This element must be present in one way or another with all instructions concerning the carrying out of any concrete system. This kind of *Sunnah* and instructions, except for their noble goals, should not be extended beyond their space-time limitations. Such an attitude could not exist except for extreme conservatism, shortsightedness and an unawareness of new realities. The lesson we learn from these examples is that *Qiyās* in areas of social interactions should be total and comprehensive wherever applicable. A long loss of time and a radical change of place may leave little practical room for the method of partial and case to case *qiyās*.

III. CONCRETE EXAMPLES GIVEN IN THE QUR'ĀN

The Qur'an is not exactly like the *Sunnah*, as we noted before, For the most part, it expresses itself in general statements as philosophical and ideological guidelines. These verses of a general nature form the foundation of Muslim outlook and belief. The Qur'an has played, and continues to play, a major role in forming and maintaining values in the Muslim conscience and social system. Nonetheless, when the Qur'an speaks in terms of specific cases or gives concrete examples, it, like most of the *Sunnah*, involves a space-time element. In these instances, readers ought to be extremely careful in deducing generalities, especially in the field of external relationships, where Muslims do not have full control over events. Simple and direct deductions from Islamic textual materials, without properly accounting for changes involving the space-time element of the early Muslim period, is a retrogressive practice. The classical jurists could indulge in such practices because the social system of the classical period remained basically unchanged through the entire period. Both the early Muslim period and the classical Muslim period consisted of largely agrarian societies. For the most part, Muslims in the classical period governed the great powers and civilization and controlled the classical world.

This situation is clearly illustrated by the following examples which include a basic concept in the field of international relations, power. Allah says in the Qur'an:

> O Apostle [Muhammad]! Rouse the believers to the fight. If there are twenty among you, patient and persevering, they will vanquish two hundred; if a hundred, they will vanquish a thousand of the unbelievers, for these are a people without understanding. For the present, God hath lightened your [task], for He knoweth that there is a weak spot in you; but [even so], if there are a hundred of you, patient and persevering, they will vanquish two hundred, and if a thousand, they will vanquish two thousand, with the leave of God; for God is with those who patiently persevere. [Qur'an 8:66]

It is clear that these verses are instructions to the Prophet regarding mobilization and preparation for fighting. The verses clearly state the ratio of 1:10 and then 1:2 as the number of Muslim soldiers who would be able to defeat the number of enemy soldiers. The verses also speak of qualities–faith, patience, and perseverance. The important point here, however, is that some basic assumptions regarding the ratio of Muslims capable of fighting nonbelievers can be valid only if other factors, such as skills, techniques, and equipment continue to remain constant. The passage makes this point quite clear: after certain factors change ("for the present . . . He knoweth that there is a weak spot in you . . ."), the ratio correspondingly changes drastically from 1:10 to 1:2. Thus the reader or the jurist should be aware of the meaning of any change and of its effect on the strategy of confrontation with the enemy. Furthermore, it is evident that if commentators or jurists ignore the implicit assumptions involved in such verses, or draw heavily on merely the ratio in commenting on the above verses, they are in danger of committing a grave mistake and distorting the illustration or example given in the Qur'an, as has happened at times.

With this, let us compare what a jurist of the late second century A.H. (eighth century A.C.) and a jurist of the late fourteenth century A.H. (twentieth century A.C.) say on the subject.

The famous jurist al-Shafi'i (767–820 A.C.) says:

> [When the verse was revealed] Ibn 'Abbas told us that "If there are twenty among you, patient and persevering, they will vanquish two hundred," Allah made it a duty that they [the Muslims] should not flee [from the battlefield against] two hundred. Allah the Most Supreme revealed: "For the present, Allah hath lightened your [task], for He knoweth that there is a weak spot in you; but [even so], if there are a hundred of you, patient and persevering, they will vanquish two hundred." Allah made it a duty that they should not flee from two hundred of their enemy's soldiers, and this is as Ibn 'Abbas said: "By Allah's will, with the [clear] revealed text (*Naṣṣ*) there is no need for interpretation . . . When the Muslims go to the battlefield and find their enemy double their number, they are not allowed by Allah (*Ḥurrima 'Alayhim*) to turn away from them . . . Even if the number of Mushrikin is more than double, I would not like them to turn away, but it would not call for the anger of Allah (*Sukhṭ*)."[35]

From this quotation, we cannot fail to observe that al-Shafi'ī emphasized almost entirely the number of fighters. As mentioned before, considering al-Shafi'ī's time, it is not surprising that he came to such an understanding. Conditions then were still comparable to those of the Prophet's time. Another early jurist, Mālik Ibn Anas, did realize in a vague way that the real issue involved in the verses was the concept of power rather than the number of fighters.[36] One twentieth-century jurist has quoted Mālik to this effect.

Al-Sayyid Sābiq, writing in the second half of the twentieth century on the same subject, has taken the same line.[37] To make the picture clear, we will quote most of the parts dealing with the problem. The title of the section is, "Fleeing from the double (number of enemies)."

> Previously [in the work] it has been mentioned that it is not permissible (*Yaḥrum*) to flee, while advancing toward [the enemy] except in two cases: turning to fight in a different direction (*Taḥarruf*) or joining another group of the Muslim army. [What is left for us] is to say that it is allowed (*Yajūz*) to flee during the battle if the enemy is more than double, but if it [the enemy] is double or less, then fleeing is not allowed (*Yaḥrumu*). Allah the Most Supreme says: "For the present, God hath lightened your [task]... ."
>
> He [the author] of "Al-Muhadhab" says: "If their number is more than double that of the Muslims, fleeing is allowed. But if they think that it is most probable that they will not perish, then it is better (*al-Afḍal*) that they stand fast (*al-Thabāt*). But if they think that it is most probable that they will perish, then there are two ways. The first: They are obliged to leave because Allah says, 'And be not cast by your own hands to ruin'. " [2:195] The second: It is recommemded (*Mustaḥabb*) but not a duty, because if they are killed they gain martyrdom.
>
> If the number of non-believers is not more than double of the Muslims, if they do not foresee the probability of destruction, they are not allowed to flee, but if they foresee the probability of destruction, there are two ways (*Wajhān*). [The first]: [Fleeing] is not allowed because Allah the Supreme says, It [fleeing] is not allowed and they [the jurists] said [this] is the right [position] because of the apparent [meaning] of the verse... [The second]: The opinion of Ibn al-Mājishūn, related from Mālik Ibn Anas is that: "Weakness is not a matter of numbers but is a [lack] of power, and it is allowed that one for one [the Muslim] flee if [his enemy] has a better horse or sword and stronger [body], and this the most apparent."[57]

This is all that this writer has said on the subject, and we see that it is hard to find in it any scientific analysis or research on the conceptual meaning or application of power at the present time, either by him or other Muslim writers of the twentieth century.

How much does—or can—this contemporary traditional writer's work mean to a twentieth-century statesman? Are such writings irrelevant to the modern world?

With such a level of scholarship on the contemporary meaning of power, it would not be surprising if a Muslim were to conclude that either power is a matter of numbers or, clinging to a traditional belief, that Muslims automatically will be victorious even if they are weaker than their enemy.

The most elemental principle of strategy has always been that one can attain victory only if one is more powerful than one's adversary in the broadest meaning of power (*quwwah*). Contemporary analyses show clearly that power is a broad concept that includes all elements of human life: military, technological, economic, psychological, moral, and spiritual.

'Ibn Rushd made a mistake in treating power exclusively as a materialistic equation when he summarized the opinion of Mālik Ibn Anas by saying: "[Double] is to be considered in terms of power, (in the widest sense) not in the number of fighters," but Mālik did not use the term *quwwah*. This kind of comparison of power could not hold true and be logically valid unless the concept of power in the mind of Mālik were not limited to physical power. If the power, most broadly construed, of the enemy is double or more than double that of the Muslims, then obviously the Muslims will ultimately be defeated. The crucial element here is the word "power," including tangibles and intangibles. The wording of Mālik, however, may imply a physical meaning in terms of equipment by his latter reference only to the excellence of the enemy's sword and horse. If the enemy were better equipped in sword and horse, thereby possessing greater physical power, a Muslim, according to Mālik, was not obliged anymore to fight him man to man. As mentioned it is only logical that the more powerful will be victorious and the weak will be vanquished,[38] but the key to applying this truism is the definition of power to include both the physical sense and the widest non-physical sense of this term.

Another result of this lack of awareness of the space-time element involved in such verses of the Qur'an is the classical concept of permanent abrogation (*naskh*). Due to this concept, the different principles and values behind the Islamic experience in Makkah and early Madī inah are forgotten due to disuse. All that mattered was the last position of the late Madinah period, which in most cases fit the situation of a powerful and established society and states such as that of the Ummayyads and the Abbasids. The previous eras were gone and therefore historically were abrogated. Contemporary Muslim jurists, though trying to reinterpret many cases of *naskh*, seem to accept the same concept of permanent *naskh*, overlooking the space-time element involved in the old concept of *naskh*. In their thinking, no attempt was made to disavow the concept, only to reinterpret it. The Verse of the Sword ('Āyat al-Sayf) is a good example of a *naskh* argument that abrogates all previous principles. The Verse of the Sword, according to most dependable interpretations, is "And fight the pagans all together as they fight you all together" (Quran 9:36).[39] Al-Sarakhsī, commenting on al-Shaybāni's *Siyar*, says:

> To sum up, the command of jihad and fighting [to Muslims] had been revealed in stages . . . [the final stage being] the absolute order to fight non-believers. . . . This involves an obligation, but this obligation is meant to exalt the religion [of Islam] and to subdue the associators.[40]

Al Zuḥaylī has made it clear that most jurists of the second century A.H. (eighth century A.C.) considered war as the rule, not the exception, in the relations between Muslims and non-Muslims because of their exaggeration in using *naskh*.[41] They had not been critical in their understanding of the Qur'an, having stopped at the apparent meaning of each verse without making serious efforts to compare and reconcile the different verses of the Qur'an. Thus, these jurists could claim that a certain verse abrogated other verses. This juristic understanding reflects only the conditions of their time. Al Zuḥaylī thinks that the reason behind the jurists stand was the prevalent need for Muslims at that time to be prepared constantly for battle in order to protect Islam. Under the political circumstances, it is not very difficult to understand why the technique of abrogation served as an aid in providing for a simple and firm position to strengthen the morale of the Muslims when facing their enemies. War was of limited effect. The enemy never accepted the concept of freedom of religion and belief. The safety and security of Muslims made war a necessary and acceptable instrument in the classical relationship between *Dār al-Islam* and *Dār al-Ḥarb*.

In modern times, the international system is trying to provide some alternative to the continuing hostility among nations because it is extremely dangerous to accept war as a legitimate means to resolve political disputes among nations. In maintaining the classical juristic position, Muslim intellectuals have suffered from the classical misuse of the technique of abrogation, which almost did away with the the various values and positions advocated in Makkah and Madīnah to direct and guide Muslims in their relations with non-Muslims. Al Zuḥaylī concludes:

> The position of the [classical] jurists that war is the permanent basis [for international relations] is no authority binding on anyone. It has no support from Qur'an or *Sunnah*. It is only a decision (ruling) of temporary effect.[42]

The Qur'an represents the basic source of values for the Muslim social system and international outlook, and is the basic force shaping the inner conscience and outlook of Muslims throughout the world. Despite the fact that Muslims have by and large failed to live up to the ideal expectations of Islam, it is clear that Muslims, through continuous interaction and contact with the Qur'an, have always been deeply affected by it. Any reform that ignores this fact or suggests otherwise does not show a real awareness of the influence of the Qur'an on Muslims. The time-place element must be taken into account when the Qur'an is used to interpret a contemporary situation.

IV. AL 'IJMĀ' AND THE CHANGING WORLD

'Ijmā' simply means "consensus": As an *'asl* (plural *'uṣūl*), it is meant to be applied in cases where there is no *naṣṣ* (text) from the Qur'an or the *Sunnah* to decide the *ḥukm* (rule). Needless to say, no 'ijmā' could ever oppose the authentic texts of Qur'an and *Sunnah*. When consensus occurs within these limits, it is binding on all Muslims. The only agreement among jurists based on 'ijmā' concerns the prayers being five times a day, the obligation of *zakah*, etcetera. These subjects, however, are backed by the Qur'an and *Sunnah* and the *'ijmā'* of the companions of the Prophet (PBUH); they are, in fact, common knowledge. Beyond these fundamentals, no absolute consensus has been reached on any issue. There is continued controversy in the different schools of jurisprudence.[43]

Some writers seem to be optimistic about the possibility of using the technique of ijma' to develop modern Muslim jurisprudence.[44] But if we understand the real problem involved in the existing conditions of traditional thought, especially in the 'usul aspect, we realize that the problem lies not only in attaining consensus, per se, but also in an intellectual attitude that had not yet produced a creative and effective methodology. The ideas and institutions inherent in this methodology may or may not call for 'ijmā'.

The traditionalists consider *'ijmā'* the consensus of all *Mujtahidūn*, which in the contemporary world boils down to the consensus of the authoritative *'ulamā'.* This view is no longer satisfactory. The *'ulamā'* no longer necessarily represent the main stream of Muslim intellectual and public involvement. Their system of education does not reflect the changes that are occuring in the world today. Their opinions therefore often only add to the already existing confusion.

It is clear that the simple, traditional concept of *'ijmā'* is no longer suitable for a non-classical social system. Law and policymaking, especially in the field of international relations, involve complex techniques and considerations that are not susceptible to the old application of *'ijmā'.*

It is also clear that *'ijmā'* on different subjects now requires the consensus of other segments of society. The application of ijma' can no longer be the exclusive prerogative of the professional *'Ulamā'.* Moreover, in a rapidly changing world, the concept of permanent ijma', particularly as regards the fluid area of international relations, is neither practical nor possible because of the space-time factor.

V. BASIC SHORTCOMINGS: LACK OF EMPIRICISM AND SYSTEMIZATION

We have already shown that classical as well as contemporary Muslim jurists and thinkers for the most part overlooked the concept of space-time as it was involved in the structure and application to classical Muslim methodology. There are two additional shortcomings inherent in that methodology: the failure to gather empirical data and concomitantly the failure to employ a rigorously systematic approach.

A. LACK OF EMPIRICISM

From the very beginning of *'uṣūl*, we find Muslim jurists looking upon deduction from the Islamic texts as their main method in acquiring knowledge and in maintaining the social system according to the *Sharī'ah*, both in internal and in external matters. They called it *'uṣūl 'istinbāṭ al-fiqh* (the sources of deducting jurisprudence).[45] In the physical sciences such as medicine, mathematics, and geography, however, Muslims drew on both, text and reason. They were empirical, experimental and applied both induction and deduction. Social sciences, such as political science, psychology, sociology, and social psychology, were absent basically because of the absence of empiricism and the lack of systematic induction and investigation of man and his social nature and reality. The notable exception was the eighth (fourteenth) century scholar, Ibn Khaldūn (1332-1406 C.E.), who marks the real beginning of modern social sciences.

Two main reasons for this uneven classical Muslim growth are worth noting. The first was, as we already mentioned, the general satisfaction with the existing social system laid down by the Prophet (PBUH) and strengthened by the religious texts. The second reason seems to be the failure of the ninth century Mu'tazilla movement to deal properly with the question of reason (*'aql*) and revelation (*waḥy*) in an Islamic context. As a result, they could not establish a permanent basis for the evolution of a rational philosophy in Islam.[46]

There was a general reaction in the ninth and tenth centuries against the alien Greek philosophy and the Islamically improper position of Mu'tazilla on the relation between reason and revelation. This reaction put an end to the Mu'tazilla experiment and simultaneously brought the demise of empiricism and systematic investigation in the field of Islamic social studies.[47] *Tahāfut al-Falāsifah* (Refutation of the Philosophers) of al-Ghazali (450-505 A.H.) in the fifth (twelfth) century is a landmark in the battle against rationalism.

This attitude is reflected in the orthodox educational program, in which the text was emphasized and not much attention was paid to developing systematic rational knowledge pertaining to law and social structure.[48] This attitude, which does not really conform to the Qur'anic attitude concerning *shahādah* (the humanly comprehensible), was easily accepted by those who were isolated from the passage of changing situations, or were conservative or interested in maintaining the status quo. The result was a lack of proper input and feedback into Muslim social studies and decision-making process, and an absence of even the concept of organized social sciences. For these reasons *siyar*, continued to be a formalistic field of study rather than a dynamic Islamic empirical study of international relations.

It is not true that jurists, in approaching the Islamic text, proceed only by divine guidance; in the process they have to draw on their acquired understanding and knowledge. No one could really engage in such an activity with a blank mind. Lack of rigorous application of empiricism through both deduction and induction and other methods of scientific research in the field of the social sciences is bound to result in grave errors and misunderstandings. It is mainly under the influence of Western challenges, discoveries and scientific methodology that Muslims have hastily reinterpreted their texts in the face of these new realities. Nevertheless, they have failed to establish serious integrated studies and systematic research in the areas of law and social science, including that of international relations. At present the Muslim system of education still lacks originality in this direction and is only a poor imitation of an alien educational system.

Three examples from the field of international relations will suffice to show how the lack of an empirical approach affects Muslim social studies and the growth of the Islamic social system.

The first example has already been mentioned, that of the ratio between the number of Muslim and non-Muslim combatants mentioned in Qur'an 8:66. An empirical, systematic, conceptual study of the problem of power would help us to understand better the reason for giving the specific numbers in the Qur'anic verse. Close examination of the verse reveals a component of power other than that of mere number of fighters. The number of fighters is only one aspect of an army's power. As a matter of fact, for reasons due to changes in the component of power of the early Muslims, the Qur'an reduced the ratio of Muslim fighters from 1:10 to 1:2. Modern wars are more complicated and have many other components of power, depending on the type of confrontation, from guerrilla warfare to massive mechanized warfare to total nuclear destruction.

The second example is the formal legal discussion on the right of the army to cut down trees, destroy houses, and kill cattle. Let us listen to the way Ibn Rushd put the case:

> The reason for their [the jurists'] differences [about the cutting down of trees, the destruction of houses, and the killing of cattle by fighting armies] is [the difference between] what

> Abū-Bakr did and what the Prophet did. It is proven that the Prophet burned the Banū al-Naḍīr's palm trees. It has also been proven true that Abū-Bakr is said not to have cut trees or destroyed inhabited [homes]. Whoever thought that Abū-Bakr acted contrary to the Prophet's precedent, assumed he did so for one of two reasons: either he knew of an abrogation, or Abū-Bakr thought that the action against the Banū al-Nadir was a special case. As for the jurists' conflict [against Banū al-Naḍīr], whichever reason they assume for Abū-Bakr's action, they agree with Abū-Bakr's stand. And whoever depends [only] on what the Prophet did, he would not accept either the saying or the action of anyone [else] as an authority. [In this case] he would allow cutting down the trees. What made Mālik differentiate between animals and trees [was that he saw] in killing animals [an act of] mutilation, and mutilation is prohibited, and it was not reported that the Prophet, peace be upon him, had killed animals. That is the limit allowed [for Muslims] in injuring the non-believers in their persons and their possessions.[49]

To this stand al-Sarakhsī answered:

> But we say: If [it] is allowed [in war] to kill human beings (*al-Nufūs*), and that is a matter of greater magnitude, then destruction of buildings and cutting down trees is obviously allowed.[50]

Of course the whole literal argument, as we see it, is now no longer relevant. In modern wars massive destruction is inevitable. The important thing here is that the argument constitutes a poor input in terms of empirical and rational understanding of war as well as a lack of feedback on the concept of war strategy and other major issues essential in each battle. Looking back, we can see that neither the Prophet nor Abū-Bakr intended in their commandments either to produce a war manual which officers must consult for daily orders or to limit Muslim decision makers' freedom in dealing with foreign powers according to changing circumstances.

It seems apparent that both the Prophet (PBUH) and Abū-Bakr within the Islamic framework were doing something which they saw as necessary in the situation each faced. In the case of Banū al-Naḍir, the Prophet (PBUH), facing a hostile tribe standing behind their fortresses, had to destroy their source of livelihood in order to force them to come out and surrender. Under their command were water wells and dates, a long-lasting source of food. Using a strategy of destruction, the Prophet (PBUH) freed his army to face the imminent danger of the Quraish and other Arab tribes. What Abu-Bakr faced was a different situation. He sent his army to a vast land with the basically non-hostile peoples of Syria and Iraq who were controlled by unpopular powers, the Romans and the Persians. Destruction of the source of living of friendly people is a foolish policy which will alienate the people and turn them toward the enemy. Of course, this argument does not nullify but rather reinforces the higher Qur'anic values and ethics against corruption and excess or waste of all kinds including killing (*'adam al-'ifsād wa 'adam al- 'isrāf*). Nothing may be killed or injured needlessly. These basic values and principles of Islam no doubt guided both the Prophet (PBUH) and Abū-Bakr in achieving victory and saving human lives. There is no need for any further literary and arbitrary explanation by the jurists.

The third example is the role of the technique of *naskh* in cases such as the Verse of the Sword *('Āyat al-Sayf)*, which has caused contemporary Muslim scholars wrongly to accuse the classic jurists of unconsciously compromising by subordinating their understanding to their immediate needs.[51] It is very difficult to understand why many contemporary Muslim jurists have committed such an error unless one has some insight into the immediate circumstances under which the classic jurists lived. Those circumstances influenced their understanding of the horizontal dimension of the Qur'anic experience from the very beginning in Makkah to the final end in Madīnah. The classical period of Muslim history was basically an extension of the late Madīnah period (7-11/628-632) when Muslims held a position of superiority and strength vis-a-vis all their non-Muslim adversaries. The formative period for the establishment of jurisprudence and its *'uṣūl*, under the Umayyad and early Abbasid dynasties (sixth - ninth century A.C.), was a victorious experience similar to that of the last stage of Madīnah. The approach of most jurists perhaps understandably was simply to negate the early experience in Makkah and early Madīnah through the technique of abrogation. No doubt a serious analytical and empirical study of the development of the Islamic movement in Makkah and Madīnah and the development of the Muslim–non-Muslim relations in Arabia could have led to a different understanding and employment of the *naskh* technique and different deductions from the Qur'anic verses.

The foregoing examples are understandable in the context of coeval knowledge and needs. But to continue the same attitude and methodological framework in the present is not justifiable and is antithetical to Muslim interests.

Islamic countries need a new framework for Muslim social thought, one that is based on a systematic and objective investigation of the social aspects of human life. Only then is the achievement of a viable modern system of philosophical and moral, Islamic values possible. Together with fulfilment of this need, inductive and deductive methods must be rigorously applied to Muslim social studies. It is not surprising that *'ijtihād* (original juristic opinions) ceased by the end of the fourth century A.H. (eleventh century A.C.) because the source material was the same, the method of deduction was the same, and no fresh input and feedback through new and continuous empirical investigations were available in the fields of jurisprudence and social studies.[52] Unless Islamic social sciences and humanities are genuinely established along with its textual bases through empiricism, and unless both induction and deduction are applied in these fields, *'ijtihād* must, for all practical purposes, continue to be considered as closed and Muslim thought will lack dynamism and productivity.

B. LACK OF OVERALL SYSTEMIZATION

In discussing Qur'anic exegesis, Shahīd Isma'īl R. al-Farūqī touched upon the problem of systemization in works of older jurists and commentators when he said:

> It is needless to point out that our ancestors completed remarkable studies constituting a tremendous wealth of insight, though none of them followed this method [axiological systemization]. We can not do without their work nor can we afford to overlook the insight of their research or the wisdom of their vision . . . [though] none of them achieved the axiological systemization we need today.[53]

Fazlur Rahman agrees with this, although he sees it in a different context.

> A most fundamental and striking feature of our *Fiqh* is that

> its various parts and legal points and enunciations do not actually tie up with one another to make it (a really) well-knit system. . . . Indeed, even a casual student cannot fail to notice this "atomicity" of *Fiqh*, this, in effect, intellectually unrelated development of almost all its enunciations. Therefore rather than being a system, it is a huge mass of atoms, each atom being a kind of system in itself. Broadly speaking, *Fiqh* constitutes materials for a legal system, but is not a legal system itself. We do not, however, deny that *Fiqh* is endowed with a sufficiently definite character which marks it out from other legal systems. . . its Islamicity; what we deny is that it is a logically connected, intellectually worked out and therefore a closely-enough-knit legal system.[54]

Lack of comprehensive systemization is clearly apparent in classical works of jurisprudence and *siyar* on one or more of the issues already discussed. The need for a comprehensive systematic approach in the fields of law and Islamic social sciences is in a real sense a contemporary Muslim problem.[55] To the classical jurists and scholars the problem hardly existed. Their aim was not to abstract a social system or to revolutionize the existing one; their effort was basically intended to work out, make explicit, and adjust the details and parts of the already existing system. The jurists' work was in many ways logical and systematic within the existing conditions and frame of mind. The contemporary Muslim social system under the new changes, needs, challenges and pressures, has fallen apart and the changes are so tremendous that mere maintenance of an old order is no longer workable or desirable.

Muslim thinkers of the present have to achieve a clear, workable, abstract framework of the Islamic social system and social sciences and their relationship to the external world. The model of the social system laid down by the Prophet (PBUH), and his companions, which constitutes the body of the *Sunnah*, although it constitutes an important aid for understanding and consequently abstracting the values and the basic outlook of Islam, cannot be applied or compared issue by issue with the social system that must be built to meet today's needs, realities, and challenges.

Lack of systemization and empiricism is a problem when Muslim students today use *'uṣūl* in the old way while the old intellectual atmosphere and implicit assumptions are no longer valid or present.[56]

Lack of systemization and empiricism is at present a problem for the modernists as well as for the traditionalists.[57] Imitation of historical systems is as wrong as imitation of a foreign one. Both lack comprehensive understanding of the existing realities of contemporary Muslim peoples and the Muslim world.

Contemporary Muslim thinkers and scholars should realize that ad hoc and accidental reflections on the issues of Muslim social life and system are no longer enough. They have to create Islamic human and social sciences. They have to systematize the goals and methods and their concerns and studies of Islamic life. They have to concern themselves in their studies with the facts of social life and with its nature and interactions as much as with Islamic texts and regulations. They have to create and develop comprehensive inductive and deductive Islamic methodology.

VI. CONCLUSIONS

1. The problem of Muslim political thought in general lies not in the content as much as it lies in the methodology.

2. The problem of the authenticity of the *Sunnah* is basically an expression and reflection of the unhappiness on the part of Muslims with the centuries-old jurisprudence.

3. The problem of *'ijtihād* and the related question of jurisprudence and *siyar* lies in a lack of understanding of the nature of *'uṣūl* and in the absence of necessary adjustment.

4. The *'Uṣūl Istinbāṭ al-Fiqh* (the jurisprudential textual sources and methods for the deduction of Muslim jurisprudence) were devised and developed in response to the needs of maintaining the classical social system of the dynastic period.

5. With the rise of the modern West and emergence of industrial society, the classical frame of analysis is no longer workable or acceptable.

6. *'Uṣūl* can no longer draw on partial analysis; it has to readjust to provide a comprehensive analysis, abstraction and systemization in order to confront the task of rebuilding the Muslim social system and creating Islamic social sciences.

7. The rebuilding of a modern Muslim social system and modern studies in the field of international relations, require conceptualization

and abstraction of values, directions, and basic outlook so that Muslims can resume active participation. *'Uṣūl* has to provide for a genuine, comprehensive, and systematic analysis.

9. Genuine establishment of empirical and systematic studies and research in the field of social sciences and humanities from the Islamic point of view is a necessary step for Muslim intellectuals to provide proper and up-to-date input and feedback in Muslim thought, jurisprudence, *siyar*, and social structure.

10. Deduction and induction, the availabiity of the best possible scientific and objective input, and concern with data feedback are necesary tools in the rebuilding of the social system and in approaching the Islamic source materials of the Qur'an and the *Sunnah*. With these tools Muslim thinkers, scientists, and jurists, in their studies of the source material of Islamic ideology, will be armed with the necessary information and tools; and the process of feeding back the up-dated material will guarantee continuously a realistic understanding of the next developments in the social system and help in planning and directing the growth of Muslim society.

11. The problem of analysis of the *Ḥadīth* is basically not authenticity but the lack of appreciation, proper consideration, and understanding of the effect of space-time on concrete systems.

12. *Qiyās* can no longer be partial or call for an issue-by-issue approach. It has to be systematic, conceptual, abstract, and comprehensive.

13.*'Ijmā'* is not a matter of consensus of a number of experts or jurists. Its meaning and function should be worked out in relation to the legislative function in concrete politial systems, where it may produce a workable relationship between the ideal and the real with maximum possible support and participation on the part of the Muslim peoples.

14. A comprehensive and conceptual understanding of the technique of *naskh*, so as to stop the narrowing down of the rich Islamic and Qur'anic experience into a single historical act on the part of a historically concrete social system, is urgently needed. This has to be done on a systematic and conceptual basis, not a legalistic one.

15. Exposure to the proper Islamic literature and insight into matters of the social system's structure, decision-making procedures, and law will provide Muslims with proper and practical guidelines for their building efforts. Education to this effect is the answer to contemporary Muslims' need for positive participation. Nothing positive can come

out of the controversy about the authenticity of the *Ḥadīth* and other related questions.

The next chapter is a trial application of the reformed methodology suggested in this chapter. We will approach the basic source material of Islam—Qur'an and the *Sunnah*—with the aid of the systems analysis approach, attempting to understand and conceptualize the source materials, especially the *Sunnah*, and to remove the space-time effect from the concrete social system of the early period of Islam, mainly the era of the Prophet (PBUH).

With the proper input and feedback and adequate comprehension and conceptualization of modern challenges in the Muslim world and the international system, these insights may help bring about a more harmonious interaction and more positive participation.

CHAPTER 3

[1] See Appendix, note 8.
[2] See Appendix, note 9.
[3] H.A.R. Gibb, *Muhammadanism: A Historical Survey* (2nd ed.; New York: Oxford University Press, 1962), p. 91.
[4] A. Khallaf, *'Ilm 'Usūl al Fiqh*, p. 149; A. Khallāf, *Māṣadir al Tashrī'*, pp. 19-103; Joseph Schacht, *The Origins of Muhammadan Jurisprudence* (Oxford University Press, 1950), pp. 120-130; Muhammad Abū-Zahrah, *Ibn Ḥanbal: Hayātuh wa 'Aṣruh-uh wa Fiqhuh* (Ibn Ḥanbal: His Life, His Time, His Opinions, and His Jurisprudence) (Cairo: Dār al-Fikr al 'Arabī), pp. 287-332; M. Abū-Zahrah, *Mālik*, pp. 324-358; M. Abū-Zahrah, Tārīkh al-Madhāhib, pp. 73-359; Al-Shāfi'i, *Shafi'i's Risālah*, pp. 288-290; S. Maḥāsanī, *Al-'Awda-al-Tashrī'iyyah*, pp. 150-160; and S. Ramaḍān, *Islāmic Law*, p. 23.
[5] Of the 6,000 verses of the Qur'ān there are between 80 to 500 verses which technically (depending on the definition) meet the criterion of a "legal rule." The remainder consists of broad propositions and a large number of moral precepts of a general nature, relating to such matters as unity of man, freedom of religion, nonaggression, right of self-defense, distribution of wealth, fairness in commerical dealings, etc. See. J.N.D. Anderson and N.J. Coulson, *Islamic Law in Contemporary Cultural Change*, p. 14.
[6] H. Gibb, *Modern Trends in Islam*, p. 124.
[7] J.N.D. Anderson, *Islamic Law in The Modern World* (New York: New York University Press, 1959), p. 4.
[8] H. Gibb, *Muhammadanism*, pp. 191-192, eds. Jerome N.D. Anderson and Norman J. Coulson, *Islamic Law in Contemporary Cultural Change* (London) p. 14.
[9] See A. Hourani, *'Arabic Thought*, pp. 237-238, A. al-Sa'īdī, *Al-Ḥurriyyah al-Dīniyyah*, pp. 30-33, 160-161.
[10] See J.N. Anderson, *Islāmic Law in the Modern World*, p. 3.
[11] For some examples see: 'Abdul-Hādī Ghanāmah, The Interestless Economy in *The Contemporary Aspects of Economic and Social Thinking in Islam*, The Muslim Student Association of the United States and Canada, (Gary, Indiana: The Muslim Student Association of The United States and Canada, 1970), pp. 85-100. See also, 'Abdul-Ḥamīd A. Abū-Sulaymān "The Theory of Economics in Islām: The Economics of 'Tawhīd'" in *The Contemporary Aspects of Economics and Social Thinking in Islām*, The M.S.A., pp. 26-79.
[12] See Mālik ibn Nabī, *Wijhat al- 'Al'ām al-Islāmī*, p. 57; M. al-Bahī, *al-Fikr al-Islāmī*, pp. 490-491. Also, a recent example of what seems contradictory between what is Islamic and what is modern is the jihād bond which has been issued recently in Egypt. Al-Ahrām, The Egyptian daily newspaper (containing statements of Egyptian officials) has a page explaining why the government has to pay interest rates for *jihād* bond. See al-Ahrām, April 17, 1971, p. 3, No. 30798 yr. 97.
[13] H. Gibb, *Modern Trends in Islam*, p. 22, 73, 84, 104, 107; W. Montgomery Watt, *Islāmic Political Thought: The Basic Concepts*, (Edinburgh: Edinburgh University Press, 1968), pp. 128-129.
[14] See Fazlur Rahman, *Islamic Methodology in History* (Karāchī: Central Institute of Islamic Research, 1965), p. 149; H. Gibb, Modern Trends in Islām, pp. 22, 60, 73, 84, 104-105; J. Anderson and N. Coulson, *Islāmic Law in Contemporary Cultural Change*, pp. 49, 54; Mālik ibn Nabī, *Wijhat al- 'Alam al-Islāmī*, pp. 83, 185.
[15] H. Gibb, *Modern Trends in Islām*, pp. 49-50; Ismā'il al Farūqī, "Islam" in *The Great Asian Religions: An Anthology*, compiled by Wing-tset Chan, Ismā'il Rajī al-Farūqī, Joseph M.

Kitagawa & P.T. Ragu, (London: Collier-Macmillan Ltd., 1969), p. 336; Muhammad ibn Idr is al-Shāfi'i, *Islamic Jurisprudence: Shāfi'i Risāla*, translated with an introduction, notes & appendices by Majid Khaddūri, (Baltimore: The John Hopkins Press, 1961), pp. 66-80; Muhammad 'Izat Darwazah, *al-Dustūre al-Qur'āni fi Shu'un al-Ḥayāh*, (The Comprehensive Qur'ānic Constitution in Affairs of Life) (Cairo: Dār Iḥyā' al-Kutub al-'Arabiyyah, 'Isā al-Bābi al-Ḥalabi wa Shurakāh, n.d.) pp. 2-80.

[16] J. Anderson & N. Coulson, *Islamic Law in Contemporary Cultural Change*, pp. 23-24; S. Maḥmasāni, *Al- 'Awda' al-Tahri'iyyah*, pp. 146-148.

[17] See D.S. Margoliouth, *The Early Development of Muhammadanism* (London: Williams & Norgate, 1914), pp. 79-98; Fazlur Raḥmān, *Islāmic Methodology*, pp. 2-84; Joseph Schacht, *The Origins of Muḥammadan Jurisprudence* (Oxford: The Clarendon Press, 1950), pp. 1-5, 11-13, 329; Muḥammad Abū-Zahrah, *Tārikh al-Madhāhub al-Islāmiyyah* (History of Muslim Schools of Thought) (Cairo: Dār al-Fikr al- 'Arabi), vol. II, pp. 66-69.

[18] See J. Anderson and N. Coulson, *Islamic Law in Contemporary Cultural Change*, pp. 22-24; S. al-Maḥmassāni *Al-'Awada' al-Tashri'iyyah*, p. 146.

[19] See H. Gibb, *Muḥammadanism*, p. 85; Muḥammad Ḥamidullah, *The Earliest Extensive Work on the Ḥadith: Saḥifah Hammam ibn Munablih*, trans. Muḥammad Raḥimuddin (5th rev. ed.; Paris: Centre Cultural Islamique, 1961), pp. 1-69; Muḥammad Muṣṭafā Azmi, *Studies in Early Ḥadith Literature with a Critical Edition of Some Early Texts* (Beirūt: Al-Maktab Al-Islāmi, 1968), pp. 246-247, 260-268, and 289-292; S. Mahmassāni, *Al-'Awda' al-Tashri'iyyah*, pp. 147-149.

[20] Abū-Bākr Muḥammad ibn Mūsa ibn Ḥāzim al-Ḥamadhāni (d. 584 A.H.) *Kitab al-I'tibār fi al-Nāskh wa al-Mansūkh min al- 'Athar* (Book of Lessons about the Abrogator and Abrogated of The Traditions) Rātib al-Ḥakimi (ed.) (Hums, Syria: Maṭba'at al-Andalus, 1966), p. 29. 200-201, 218-219. See Ṣalaḥ al-Din al-Munajjid and Yūsuf Q. Khuri (ed.), *Fatawa al-Emām Muhammad Rashid Riḍā* (Juristic Opinions of Imām Muḥammad Rashid Riḍā) (Beirūt: Dār al-Kitāb al-Jadid, 1970).

[21] J. Schacht, *The Origins*, p. 329.

[22] M. Azmi, *Studies in Early Ḥadith Literature with a Critical Edition of Some Early Texts* (Beirūt: Al Maktab al-Islāmi, 1968), p. 247.

[23] 'Abdul-Wahhāb Khallaf, *'Ilm 'Usūl al-Fiqh* (The Science of The Source-Method of Jurisprudence) (8th ed.; Kuwait: Al Dār al-Kuwaytiyyah, 1968), p. 45; M. Abū-Zahrah, *Mālik*, pp. 322-341; S. Mahmasāni, *Al-'Awada al-Tashri'iyyah*, p. 150.

[24] Imām Ibn Kathir (774/1372) described the role assigned to the *Sunnah* in the classical jurisprudence when he said: "If some said, what is the best way of interpreting the Qur'ān? [The answer] is that the most valid (*sah*) method is to interpret Qur'ān with Qur'ān. What is general in one place has (usually) been explained in another place. If [this is not the case and] you were unable to do that, then go to the *Sunnah*. It is [a material] which explains Qur'ān and makes it clear. [Not only that] but Imām Abū-'Abdullah Muḥammad Ibn Idris al-Shāfi'i, may Allah the most Supreme grant his soul mercy, [also] said that all the decisions of the Messenger of Allāh were from what he understood from the Qur'ān... and whenever we could not find the interpretation [of Qur'ānic materials] in the Qur'ān [itself] nor in the *Sunnah*, then we turned to the interpretation (*'aqwal*) of the Companions [of the Prophet] because they know better. . . ." See Ibn Kathir, *Tafsir al-Qur'ān*, vol. I, p. 7.

[25] See A. Khallaf, *Maṣādir al-Tashri'*, pp. 101-102. Also see Al-Farra', *Al-Aḥkām*, pp. 37, 43, and 49; Ibn Qudāmah, *Al-Mughni*, pp. 204-205; W. al-Zuḥayli, *Nadhariyāt al-Ḍarūrah*, pp. 163, 168, and 243.

[26] See M. Abū-Zahrah, *Ibn Ḥanbal*, pp. 218-331.

[27] J. N. D. Anderson and N. J. Coulson, *Islamic Law in Contemporary Cultural Change*, pp.

23-24; S. Maḥmāsanī, *Al- 'Awda'al-Tahrī'iyyah*, pp. 146-148.

[28] [Waliyyal-Dīn Muḥammad Ibn 'Abdullah al-Khaṭib al- 'Umarī al-Tabrīzī], *Mishkāt al-Maṣābiḥ* [sic]. Translated with explanatory notes by James Robson (Lahore; Pakistan: Sh. Muḥammad Ashraf, 1963), vol. III, 838.

[29] Ibid., vol. III, p. 825.

[30] Ibid., vol. III, pp. 821, 837, and 838; Al-Shaybānī, *Al-Siyar al-Kabīr*, vol. I, p. 87.

[31] See Ibn Rushd, *Bidayāt Al-Mijtahid*, vol. I, pp. 311-312; Mālik ibn Anas, *Al-Mudawanah*, vol. III, p. 8; and Al-Shaybānī, *Al-Siyar al-Kabīr*, vol. I, p. 42.

[32] See Muḥammad Abū-Zahrah, *Al- 'Alaqat Al-Dawliyyah fī al-Islām* (International Relations in Islam) (Cairo: Al-Dār al-Qawmiyyah li al-Ṭibā'ah wa al-Nashr, 1964), p. 43; S. Sabiq, *Fiqh al-Sunnah*, vol. XI, pp. 48-49, 129-132; and B. Sābiq, *Fiqh al-Sunnah*, vol. XI, pp. 92-94, 127, 132-139.

[33] See Al-Shāfi'ī, *Al-Umm*, vol. IV, pp. 90-91; and Ibn Rushd, *Bidāyat al-Mujtahid*, vol. I, pp. 313-314.

[34] Ibn Kathīr, *Tafsīr Al-Qur'ān*, vol. IV, p. 202. The reader should be aware that the question of time and place in Islam and throughout this thesis deals with questions of social relationships and systems. This has nothing to do with the question of *Ibādah, Sha'āir* and *Dhikr* (worship).

[35] Al-Shāfi'ī, *Al- 'Umm*, vol. IV, p. 92.

[36] Ibn Rushd, *Bidāyat al-Mujtahid*, vol. I, p. 313.

[37] Al-Sayyid Sābiq, *Fiqh al-Sunnah*, vol. XI, pp. 127-128.

[38] It is worth mentioning the lack of proper treatment of the concept and factors of power in Muslim works. I could not find Muslim works devoted to an investigation of the subject *per se*.

[39] See Abū-Zayd, *Al-Nāskh fī al Qur'ān*, pp. 11, 504; Al-Zuḥaylī, *'Athar al-Ḥarb*, p. 56.

[40] Al-Shaybānī, *Al-Siyar al-Kabīr*, vol. I, p. 188.

[41] See W. Al-Zuḥaylī, *'Athar al-Ḥarb*, pp. 130-131.

[42] Ibid., p. 135.

[43] M. Abu-Zahrah, *Mālik*, pp. 324-325; and M. Abū-Zahrah, *Tārīkh al-Madhāhib*, pp. 73, 359.

[44] A. Khallab, *'Ilm 'Usūl al-Fiqh*, p. 149, and S. Maḥmassānī, *Al-'Awda al-Tashrī'iyyah* p. 150.

[45] A. Khallaf, 'Ilm *'Usūl al-Fiqh*, pp. 11-12; and M. Abū-Zahrah, *Ibn Ḥanbal*, p. 205.

[46] See E. I. J. Rosenthal, *Political Thought*, pp. 114-115; Ignaz Goldzieher, "Mawqif Ahl al-Sunnah bi' Iza 'Ulūm al- 'Awa'il" (The Attitude of the Orthodox Muslims toward the Knowledge of Ancient Peoples), in *Al-Turāth al-Yunānī fī al Haḍārah al-Islāmiyyah: Dirāsāt li Kibār al-Mustashriqīn* (The Greek Heritage in the Islamic Civilization: Studies of most Important Orientalists) (3rd ed.; Cairo: Dār al-Nahḍah al- 'Arabiyyah, 1965), pp. 123-172; Abū-Zahrah, *Fī Ẓil al-Islām*, pp. 17-30; and T.J. Boer, *Tarīkh al-Falsafah fī al-Islām* (History of Philosophy in Islam), translated from German by Muhammad 'Abdul-Hādī Abū-Riḍah (4th ed.; Cairo: Lajnat al-Ta'līf wa al-Tarjamah wa al-Nashr, 1957), pp. 95-125.

[47] A. Ḥourani, *'Arabic Thought*, p. 18; H.A.R. Gibb, *Islamic Civilization*, pp. 10-14, 148-149; and W. Watt, *Islamic Thought*, pp. 162-164.

[48] See Fazlur Rahman, *Islamic Methodology*, pp. 168-179, and M. F. 'Uthmān, *Al-Fikr al-Islāmī wa al-Tatawwur*, pp. 535-547.

[49] Al-Shaybānī, *Al-Siyar al-Kabīr*, vol. I, p. 43.

[50] Ibn Rushd, *Bidāyat al-Mujtahid*, vol. I, pp. 311-312.

[51] M. Abū-Zayd, *Al-Nāskh*, vol. II, pp. 506-508; and W. Al-Ẓuhāylī, *'Athar al-Ḥarb*, pp. 79-81, 108, 113, 135-138, 192.

[53] See H. A. R. Gibb, *Modern Trends in Islam*, p. 124.

[53] Isma'il Rajī Al Faruqī, "Towards a New Methodology for Qur'ānic Exegesis," *Islamic Studies*, (March 1962), p. 47.

[54] Fazlur Rahman, *Islamic Methodology*, p. 184; see also M. A. al-Zarqa, *Al-Fiqh al-Islāmī*, pp. 1-5.

[55] N. J. Coulson, *A History of Islamic Law*, pp. 1-7 and 220-221.

[56] See Appendix, note 9.

[57] See A. Khallaf, *'Uṣūl al-Fiqh*, pp. 20-96; Muḥammad Yūsuf Mūsā, *Al-Fiqh al-Islāmī Madkhalun li Dirāsatih, Niẓām al-Mu'amalāt fīh* (The Islamic Jurisprudence: An Introduction of Its Study, The System of Interaction According to It), (3rd ed.; Cairo: Dār al-Kutub al-Hadīthah, 1958), pp. 48, 65-84, 127-142; S. Mahmassānī, *Al-Awda al-Tashrī'iyyah*, pp. 90-108; S. Ramadan, *Islāmic Law*, pp. 11-12 and 184; also see H.A.R. Gibb, *Modern Trends in Islām*, pp. 73, 84, 107, 121-124; I. al-Fārūqī, "Toward a New Methodology for Qur'ānic Exegesis," p. 47; N. J. Coulson, *A History of Islāmic Law*, pp. 202-225.

Chapter 4

From Legalistic to Political Thought

In Chapter 2 we reviewed classical Muslim thought and modern developments. If there exists any key word for the crisis of Muslim thought in the field of external affairs today, that word is "irrelevance."

The aggressive attitude involved in the classically militant approach to *jihāh* is clearly irrelevant today to a people who are weak and backward intellectually, politically, and technologically.

The "liberal" approach,[1] which emphasizes thinking in terms of peace, tolerance, and defensiveness, has proved irrelevant in a world facing ever increasing struggles for political, social, and economic liberation. For Muslims, whose energies are needed almost exclusively in the struggle against the conditions, both internal and external, that contribute to their human misery, this approach has proved to be no longer tolerable or useful.

Modern Muslim thought in the field of external affairs is either irrelevant to the reality of the Muslim psychology and conscience or to the reality of the world in which the Muslims live. It is erroneous to assume that Muslim psychology, consciousness, history, lands, and peoples are shapeless. Muslims must learn how to adjust to modern challenges and institutions, and to respond and accommodate them within the general Muslim outlook. By the same token, Muslims have to realize the necessity of adjusting to strategies and policies that fit the different parts of Muslim lands and Muslim peoples at different times. For example, what could be applied to the Turks in the fourteenth and fifteenth centuries is different from what could be applied to them in the nineteenth century. By the same token, policies that fit the Pakistanis, the Iranians, or the Turks of today are different from policies that fit, for example, the Egyptians or the Syrians.

The need for the adoption of systematic empirical approaches in the social sciences, as a prerequisite to the creation of a new practical Islamic framework in the highly political field of international relations, has been emphasized in Chapters 2 and 3. Legitmacy for this approach in Islamic thought is possible only in reference to the early Islamic sources. To achieve this goal, we must, as a first step, apply the systematic empirical approach to the Prophet's external policies in the state of Madīnah. This will help to eliminate the traditional legalistic interpretation of those policies. The second step is to correct some major defects in the traditional Muslim concept of the relationship between God and man. The third step is to develop a basic workable Islamic framework in the field of external relations that frees the Muslim policymaker from the space-time elements involved in the traditional approach. In this way, the policy maker will be better able to deal with the changing realities of the contemporary world. The final step is to test this framework against some major contemporary Muslim foreign policies. We have to bear in mind that the success of an ideological framework is measured by its compatibility with the basic assumptions of that ideology, on the one hand, and its utility to the policymaker, on the other. We will start with the first step, namely, a projection back to the Prophet's attitude and policies as regards external relations.

A. RECONSTRUCTION OF HISTORY: POLITICAL RATIONALE OF THE PROPHET'S EXTERNAL POLICIES

We have already (in Chapter 2) discussed some misconceptions concerning the early Muslims' experience in relation to non-Muslims, which brought about tense relations in the classical period. These misconceptions prevented both the development of a more dynamic federal state system and the acquisition of a broader range of human rights and participation of non-Muslim minorities. Certainly, these misconceptions did not promote an attitude of proper cooperation between Muslims and non-Muslims.

We need not repeat what has already been said to explain how this situation came about in Muslim thought, nor remind the reader that this does not imply that non-Muslims were innocent or that the attitude of non-Muslims toward Muslims was either tolerant or cooperative.

As a result of this attitude of hostility toward cooperation, modern Muslim writers have often been contradictory and apologetic in their efforts to reinterpret Muslim history—thus not utilizing the political significance and rationale of the rich and broad experience of Islam. I propose here to examine four basic issues, frequently referred to but misread by traditionalists, which clearly point up the superior political rather than the purely legalistic rationale of the Prophet (PBUH) in his conduct of foreign affairs. These four issues are:

1. The war prisoners of the battle of Badr.
2. The Muslim expedition against the Jews of Arabia and in particular the Banū-Qurayẓah of Madinah.
3. Lenient policies toward the archenemies of the early Muslims, the Quraysh.
4. Continued respectful tolerance shown to the People of the Book.

A. THE PRISONERS OF WAR OF THE BATTLE OF BADR

The Battle of Badr took place between the Muslims and the tribe of the Quraysh in the second year after the Hijrah (emigration) of the Prophet (PBUH) from Makkah to Madinah.[2] The Muslims, about 300 in number, opposed approximately 1,000 Qurayshi warriors and achieved a decisive victory in which most of the Quraysh leaders were killed or captured. Only two out of about seventy prisoners of war were executed. The remainder were set free upon their paying various amounts of ransom. The Battle of Badr was the first major armed confrontation between the Muslims and the Quraysh and other Arab and Jewish tribes of Arabia. This battle came after twelve years of pressure and severe persecution against the Muslims, many of whom were forced to flee, first to Abyssinia and then to Madīnah.[3]

While the Quraysh tried to persuade the Madīnis to expel the Prophet (PBUH) and his Qurayshi followers, he began to establish and consolidate the Muslim force for the inevitable confrontation.[4] He made an honorable peace arrangement of a federal type (the Madinah Pact) between the Muslims and the Jewish tribes of Madīnah. He established a brotherhood between the *muhājirūn* (emigrants) from Makkah and the *anṣār* (helpers) of Madīnah. He personally sent expeditions to the areas surrounding Madīnah to seek support and to establish peace and security.[5] Ibn Jaḥsh's expedition of surveilance ended with the first attack by Muslims against a Qurayshi caravan. The importance of this expedition is that it led to the march of the Quraysh army toward Madīnah and consequently to the battle of Badr between the Muslims and the Quraysh. The following Qur'anic verse (8:67) was revealed in relation to this occasion:

> It is not for any prophet to have war-prisoners until he hath thoroughly subdued the land.

Legalism led Muslim writers to apologize for this verse by arguing the contrst with another verse, (47:4) which reads as follows:

> Therefore, when ye meet the unbelievers [in fight], smite at their necks; at length, when ye have thoroughly subdued them, bind a bond firmly [on them]; thereafter [is the time for] either generosity or ransom, until the burden of war may may be lifted.[6]

The argument of these writers is that the first verse is "not a permanent legislation" for ruling. It is the second verse that is the permanent and established rule for deciding the fate of prisoners of war. The first is only to blame Muslims for having taken prisoners and to point out that the "real" will of God is not to take prisoners of war.[7]

This is the modern way of applying the old static technique of abrogation. Contemporary writers often take the liberal approach of considering the release of prisoners of war as safe and sound, dismissing the verse of blame for not killing all prisoners of war captured in Badr as something temporary, pertaining only to the period of the establishment of the early Muslim state.[8] The other way in which modern writers look at the issue is by rationalizing it as a legal case of war criminals rather than prisoners of war.[9]

These writers seem to overlook the significance of circumstances in directing punitive measures against adversaries of the Muslims. It is clear that the first verse was revealed at a time of extreme pressure on Muslims, whereas a close examination of the second verse shows that Muslim victory was foreseen.

In order that we may understand the meaning and significance of actions, policies, and pronouncements related to the early period of Madınah, and the circumstances that led to Badr and resulted from it, we must take a closer look at the parts of the *Sūrat al- 'Anfāl* which were revealed in relation to the Battle of Badr.[10]

Interestingly enough, some verses advising the Prophet (PBUH) to take extreme measures in order to protect the Muslim community were inserted (on the Prophet's orders) in *Sūrat al- 'Anfāl* (The Spoils of War) instead of *Sūrat Al- 'Aḥzāb* (The Clans). The latter, it should be realized, refers explicitly to the Battle of the Ditch and the subsequent Battle of Banū Qurayzah, but in the context of a Muslim victory. This shows that the *Sūrat al- 'Anfāl* deals with the pressures facing Muslims in early Madinah only and is meant to guide Muslims facing similar circumstances.[11]

The chapter of *al- 'Anfāl* reveals to the reader the fears of the Muslims due to their lack of manpower, their need for the employment of psychological warfare, and the free hand of the Prophet (PBUH) to employ all suitable actions to counter overwhelmingly superior enemy forces. *Sūrat al- 'Anfāl* also illustrates the Muslim call for co-existence and reconciliation on the condition that the persecution of Muslims and hostility against their religion cease.

The verses concerning war prisoners of Badr specifically reveal employment of the threat of extreme punitive action against the enemy in the battlefield as a restraining device of psychological warfare. The psychological use of threat in this way exlains why the threat was not actually carried out at Badr. The killing of prisoners of war was an extremely rare exception throughout the life of the Prophet (PBUH). It is clear that the verses were to serve political rather than legal ends.

B. BANŪ QURAYẒAH: USE OF EXTREME ACTIONS FOR SECURITY AND PSYCHOLOGICAL ENDS

The Banū Qurayẓah were one of the Jewish tribes residing in Madinah when the Arab tribes of Madinah turned to Islam. Although the Jewish tribes were inferior in number and military capabilities, yet they were, as scholars and craftsmen, culturally and economically superior to their Arab neighbors.[12]

The Banū Qurayẓah were a part of the federal arrangement between the Muslims and the Jewish tribes of Madīnah. This arrangement provided religious freedom, self-government, and a joint military alliance against the Quraysh, the archenemy of the Muslims.[13]

The Quraysh, Ghaṭafān, Qays 'Aylān, and Banū al-Naḍīr formed an alliance, assembled a large army and marched against the Muslims in Madīnah. During the siege of the city, the Banu Qurayẓah revoked their pact with the Muslims and opened negotiations with the attackers. Ḥuyay 'Ibn 'Aḥṭab of the Banū al-Naḍīr, the tribe that had already been expelled from Madīnah for their hostile and subversive activities in collaborating with the Quraysh, was the initiator and mediator of these negotiations. The negotiations failed, however, to meet the demands of the Banū Qurayẓah. After the siege had collapsed, the confrontation between the Muslims and the Banū Qurayẓah brought the execution of all the fighters of the Banū Qurayẓah.

As we saw in Chapter 2, the whole episode of the Battle of the Ditch and the great alliance against Madīnah was a nightmare to the Muslims. The Prophet (PBUH) offered the tribe of Ghaṭafān a third of Madīnah's yearly crops if they would withdraw and relieve some of the pressure against the Muslims. The Qur'an eloquently describes this pressure against the Muslims and their fear of total destruction.

Writers have emphasized either the moral and legal implications of the Banū Qurayẓah's treacherous breach of their agreement with the Muslims, or the propaganda of the religious and political war which the Jewish rabbis waged against Islam, or the alleged desire of the Muslims to confiscate Jewish wealth.[14] After many centuries, writers seem to have overlooked the Qur'an's and the Prophet's perceptions of the extreme danger in such an alliance and the psychological impact on the Muslims of the withdrawal of the Jews from the alliance as a motivation for the Muslims to take exceptional and extreme measures. The significance of the extreme action taken against the tribe of the Banū Qurayẓah lies in the attempt on the part of the Muslims to avert similar alliances in the future. No other reasoning can really explain the strong punitive actions against the Banū Qurayẓah.

If the reason were a matter of wealth, it does not explain why other wealthy Jewish and Arab tribes were not as severely dealt with as the Banū Qurayẓah. If the reason, as others claim, was the Jews' breach of the treaty and their subversive activity, one need only point out that other Jewish and Arab tribes before and after the Battle of the Ditch had been accused of the same act, including the Banū al-Naḍīr and the Quraysh. It is interesting to note that after the Battle of Uḥud, the Banū al-Naḍir were expelled from Madinah, while after the Treaty of Ḥudaybiyah (with the Quraysh) the Jewish tribes of Khaybar only had to pay a tribute of half their crops, which put an end to their financial and political power; furthermore, one year later the Quraysh the arch-enemy of the Muslims, upon surrender, were honorably set free. The political reasons for the differing treatment of the Quraysh and the Jewish tribes of Khaybar will be discussed under the next heading.

Although Islam continued to build distinct religious practices (such as fasting in the month of *Ramaḍān* and *zakah* or the giving of charity), it never questioned the right of the followers of the earlier scriptures (Jews and Christians) to uphold and practice their religions. The whole issue of the difference in punitive action against the enemy was simply political and signifies the political flexibility and realism which, in my judgement, the early Islamic framework exhibited. This is not to say that the Islamic framework of external relations is free from moral restraints. A look at the Qur'an and the *Sunnah* of the Prophet (PBUH) will easily show the fallacy of such a claim. The variance of punitive measures implies that political decisions involving the major interests of the Muslim government and community have to be realistic and flexibile within the limits of the Islamic framework. This framework, although asserting moral principles and attitudes, does not narrowly and blindly predetermine and rigidly restrict political leaders and actions.

Increasing Arab-Jewish treachery and attacks, and the fresh memory of the extremely dangerous role of the Banū al-Naḍīr who had been expelled and set free, exerted overwhelming pressure on the Muslim community and gave rise to a fear of total destruction. The Prophet (PBUH) therefore now had to use political and military means available to destroy the overwhelming power of the enemy in order to secure the Muslims' existence. It was clear that the Prophet (PBUH) could no longer tolerate the settlement of the Banū Qurayẓah in Madīnah; nor could he afford to set them free and add to the strength of his enemy under these extreme cirucmstances.[15]

Despite the fact that military and political confrontations forced extreme actions, the Islamic stand based on both religious and practical grounds, on allowing non-Muslim minorities to co-exist was never denied. On the contrary, the Prophet (PBUH) was firmly determined to hold this stand througout his life. His victories simply brought about the assertion of his moral but realistic attitude toward external relations. As a matter of fact, he managed throughout to make the strict fulfillment of agreements a condition for establishing any external relationship, thus exerting a moral superiority for his side over his adversaries.[16] Moral commitment and successful planning and execution of foreign policies both are necessary for the success of ideologically oriented societies. The employment of these elements of policymaking by the Prophet (PBUH) helps to explain his great success. There is no doubt that the lack of moral commitment in contemporary international affairs constitutes a source of danger for world peace.

The significance of policy variations in banishment and retaliation, in a dynamic response to the basic interests and needs of the Muslim state in relation to its environment, is reinforced by further examination of other political and military activities performed during the last ten years of the Prophet's life as head of the Muslim community and state at Madīnah. He ordered some missions to eliminate the enemy's leadership, notably the mission to kill K'ab 'Ibn al- 'Ashraf of the Banū al-Naḍīr.[17]

Muslim writers paid much attention to the justification of these wars and missions in purely legal terms, but gave very little attention to their political and strategic significance.

Since the Prophet (PBUH) and the early Muslims presented a new way of life, they expected a very unfavorable response from the Quraysh and other Arab tribes. Thus, they had to be on the defensive. The moral justification of the Muslim response can be easily made, but that does not explain the strategy of the response.

From the very beginning at Madinah, the Prophet aimed to interrupt the major economic interests of the Quraysh. He planned his battles as surprise attacks and even advised Abu Basir to form a guerrilla approach against the Quraysh lines of communication. Missions to eliminate the enemy's political leadership were directed at groups that built alliances against the Muslims. The element of surprise, the guerrilla attacks, the threat of extreme punishments, and harsh punitive measures and reprisals all succeeded in terrifying the enemy, causing disorder in their ranks and bringing many of them to side with the Muslims.

It is this kind of realism, with its wide margin of political maneuverability, rather than legalism and formalism, that explains the Prophet's successful conduct of external affairs.

C. QURAYSH: THE HONORED VANQUISHED

After Khaybar, the Prophet (PBUH) finally put an end to the hostile Jewish power in Madīnah and the surrounding area, stopping their valuable political and financial aid to the anxious, disabled, and exhausted Quraysh.

With the failure of the Quraysh to live up to the peace agreement between themselves and the Prophet (PBUH) and after they committed a massacre in Makkah itself when their allies (Banū Bakr) fell upon the *Khuza'ah*, the Prophet (PBUH) took the opportunity to carry out a surprise master plan against Makkah.[18] His psychological warfare succeeded in bringing Makkah and the Quraysh to surrender.[19] There were no military reprisals, no destruction, and no punishment, even after all the bitter memories and the long nightmare of persecution of Muslims at the hands of the Quraysh. On the contrary, the Prophet (PBUH) took all measures to ensure the safety of Makkah and all its inhabitants. He did everything in his power to win their hearts and gain their support. He was now master of Arabia and found it possible and fruitful to follow a policy of leniency and far-reaching generosity toward the Quraysh and other tribes such as the Hawazin of Ta'if.[20] The decision had also clear political motives. The Muslims were now strong and secure, and, moreover, new plans were already taking shape. After Khaybar, the Prophet (PBUH) had realized the inevitability of armed conflict with the great powers of Byzantium and Persia when the first bloody conflict had materialized at Mu'tah between the Muslims and Roman troops.

With Arabia and the dominant Quraysh tribe on his side, the Prophet was able to turn north toward the stronghold of Byzantium in northern Arabia. These involvements against northern neighbors also had the advantage of maintaining the cohesion and enthusiasm of the Arab tribes. Armed conflict was inevitable, regardless of any academic argument about whether the new Muslim state should expand.[21]

Upon returning to Madīnah from the peaceful conquest of Makkah, the Prophet (PBUH) , in response to the hostile Roman attitude and actions toward Muslims, led the largest Muslim army of his time north toward Tabūk on the borders of Palestine. This was the last time he led his army before his death. Usamah's expedition was the last Muslim expedition ordered out before he died. Although it was ready before the Prophet's death, it moved toward its destination in the north only upon renewed orders from the newly appointed *khalīfah* after the Prophet's death. Later events proved the political wisdom of the Prophet (PBUH) in consolidating the Muslims' power in Arabia before getting involved in armed conflict with the two hostile empires bordering on the north.

D. FREEDOM OF RELIGION AND BELIEF

The fourth issue, freedom of religion and belief, is still an important source of confusion and contradiction in contemporary Muslim political thought. The traditional approach contributes to the atmosphere of fear and suspicion between Muslim and non-Muslim peoples. It minimizes communication and makes interaction and cooperation more difficult. The traditional position stems from classical interpretation of the early sources on the issues of apostasy (*riddah*), the historical case of the forced Islamization of Arab pagans, and the imposition of the poll tax (*jizyah*) on non-Muslims. Once more, these issues reveal the traditional approach to be an obstacle to introducing a constructive Islamic approach to relationships between Muslims and non-Muslims in the Muslim world today and in a modern Islamic framework in the field of international relations.

Muslim reformists and modernists, such as 'Abduh, Riḍa, 'Azzām, al-Ṣa'idī, and many others, made strenuous efforts to resolve this problem, but it is still not clear conceptually.[22] Apart from other factors, the issue of freedom of belief in Muslim societies has to be made conceptually very clear.[23] For Muslim societies, the issue is not an internal one alone, but touches on an important ideological aspect of their relations with other states and peoples. Clarification is essential if the Muslim society is to be a truly open one in which civil rights are guaranteed and available to all members of the society in a reciprocal relationship between rights and duties, along pluralistic lines free from religious and sectarian biases. Loyalty and commitment to the welfare of all people and their different systems of law is the only guarantee for the sincere exercise of rights and duties of individuals and groups. Freedom of ideology and religion assisted by peaceful and orderly means of practice and expression, is necessary for healthy, stable, expanding, and progressive societies.

In Chapter 2 we discussed the classical issue of *jizyah* and the People of the Book. We would like to emphasize here that the overall Islamic framework starts ideologically from a genuine concern for one's fellow man.[24] All Muslims, particularly intellectuals, need to focus on this basic emphasis. The fundamental Islamic attitude concerning relations among human beings is expressed in the Qur'an and *Sunnah* in terms of love (*tawaddūhum*), help (*tuḥsinū*), gentleness (*allatī hiya aḥsan*) and protection (*dhimmah*).

This attitude, however, should not be confused with situations of confrontation, particularly that of the historical confrontation faced by the early Muslims in Arabia. It was the Prophet (PBUH) himself who drew up the honorable agreement of *jizyah* with the friendly Christian tribes of Najran and before that the Madinah Pact with the Jewish tribes of Madīnah, and it was the same Prophet (PBUH) who waged a war of life and death against some of the same Jewish tribes who sought the destruction of the Muslim community. These confrontations were situational and tactical, and do not destroy the bases of Islamic ideology. Qur'anic references and the detailed accounts of the *Sunnah* and the *Sirah* (history of the life-time of the Prophet (PBUH)) are aids in revealing the realistic rational approach of Islam. These details are matters of historical record that signify the pragmatic Islamic policies undertaken by the Prophet (PBUH) in order to secure the safety and success of the Muslim mission.

The issue of all-out war against the Arab pagan tribes unless they turned to Islam cannot be understood as ideological oppression. This decision came after the establishment of the Muslim state at Madinah and after about twenty-two years of persecution and war. It is not acceptable to say, as do the traditionalists, that the Prophet (PBUH) had to force them to Islam because the verse concerning *jizyah* of the Peoples of the Book was not revealed at the time the Prophet (PBUH) gave the order of forced Islamization against the Arab Bedouins.[25] The Prophet (PBUH) never tried at any time to convert the Jewish tribes of Madinah and the Arab Christians of Najran by force. The forced Islamization was a decision, after the experience of about twenty years, to protect the human rights of Muslims and Arab peoples alike. The Islamization of the wild Bedouin tribes of the Arabian Peninsula was to provide them with the framework for an orderly social system and intertribal interaction.[26] The change proved to be sincere, responsible, correct and in the best interest of the Arabs especially in defending their human rights. Contrary to the cultural legacy of other tribal peoples such as the Mongolians and Germans, the primitive Arab tribe, because of their exposure to the discipling and rehabilitating effects of Islam, became the carriers of culture and builders of civilization. The Arabs, along with other Muslim peoples, established the greatest civilization up to that time in human history and contributed a great share to the continuity and growth of human culture. Allah (SWT) says:

> Those who believe, then reject faith, then believe [again] and [again] reject faith and go on increasing in unbelief, God will not forgive them nor guide them on the way. [Qur'an 4:137]
>
> And they observe toward the believers neither pact nor honor.

> These are the transgressors. And if they repent and establish worship and pay *zakah*, then they are your brothers in religion. We detail our revelations for a people who have knowledge. [Qur'an 9:10-11]

> The desert Arabs say, "We believe." Say, "Ye have no faith"; but say ye only, "We have submitted our will to God," for faith has not yet entered your hearts but if ye obey God and His Apostle. [Qur'an 49:14]

> They (the desert Arabs) impress on thee as a favour that they have embraced Islam. Say, 'Count not your Islam as a favour to me: Nay, God has conferred a favour upon you that He has guided you to the Faith. [Qur'an 49:17]

> And hold fast, all together, by the rope which God [stretched out for you], and be not divided among yourselves; and remember with gratitude God's favour on you; for ye were enemies and He joined your hearts in love, so that by His Grace, ye became brothers. [Qur'an 3:103]

If forced Islamization were simply an exercise to show superiority, or a denial of the right of religious freedom, the Prophet (PBUH) had more reasons and time to practice this against the Jewish tribes of Madīnah; however, he never attempted that policy either before or after issuing his orders regarding the Islamization of the Arab tribes. As we mentioned in Chapter 2, the Qur'anic terminology is revealing in this respect. Thus, we can see that the case of the Islamization of the Bedouin pagan tribes of the Peninsula was a case of establishing a necessary civilized framework for human interaction based on human maturity and dignity. Properly understood, it does not destroy but rather reinforces the concept of ideological tolerance and real concern for basic human rights proper for humanity, which is an integral part of the responsibility of the *khalīfah* (vicegerent and custodian on earth).[27]

Apostasy is theoretically the most interesting of the three issues. We find most traditional writers holding the opinion that denial and denunciation of Islam by adult male Muslims is apostasy, and unless they return to Islam they should be executed.[28] The serious problems arising here are twofold: one is the space-time factor, and the second is the conceptual confusion involved in the issue as it has been treated by Muslim writers.

The space-time impact of the issue of apostasy relates to a conspiracy on the part of some Jewish groups to create chaos and confusion in the young Muslim community by using the tactic of apostasy, that is, confessing Islam and then renouncing it as a group. It is worth noting that this conspiracy and its expected consequences were mentioned in the Qur'an:

> A faction of the People of the Book say: Believe in the morning what is revealed to the Believers, but reject it at the end of the day; perchance they may [themselves] turn back. And believe no one unless he follows your religion. [Qur'an 3:72-73]

The question of apostasy is also related to the very serious question of hypocrisy, with which the Qur'an dealt in many lengthy sections and verses. The hypocrites of Madīnah presented a dual problem for the young Muslim community. They helped the enemy, hindered war preparations and action, waged psychological war against the Muslims and helped to destroy their morale. In this connection the Qur'an says:

> Had they gone forth among you, they would have added naught to you save trouble, and would have hurried to and fro among you, seeking to cause sedition among you, and among you there are some who would have listened to them. Allah is aware of the evil-doers. Aforetime they sought to make difficulties for thee until the truth came and the decree of Allah was made manifest although they were loathe (much to their disgust). Of them is he who saith: 'Grant me leave (to stay home) and tempt me not.' Surely it is into temptation (they) have fallen. Lo! Hell is all around the disbelievers. If good befalleth thee (O Muhammad) it afflicteth them, and if calamity befalleth thee, they say: 'We took precaution,' and they turn away well-pleased. Say: 'Naught befalleth us save that which Allah hath decreed for us. He is our protecting Friend.' In Allah let the believers put their trust. Say: 'Can ye await for us aught save one of two good things (victory or death in Allah's way), while we wait for you that Allah will afflict you with a doom from Him at our hands. Wait then! Lo! We are waiting with you.' [Qur'an 9:47-52]

The threat of frightful punishment obviously was to check their activities and the practice of conspiratorial hypocrisy. Hypocrites would be trapped in their role all through their lives. To achieve the same effect of checking hypocrisy and destructive activities the Prophet (PBUH) gave the order to kill Abdullah ibn S'ad ibn Abi Sarh which later was waived at the desperate request of 'Uthman ibn 'Affan. Sa'd had been a scribe to the Prophet (PBUH) when he ran away, declaring his disbelief and claiming pubicly that he had made some changes in his assigned recording. Such conspiracies of hypocrisy or apostasy are extremely serious crimes and the weights and punishments assigned for them have important space-time considerations. These factors play a decisive role in determining their legal punishments.

The conceptual confusion occurs in the early period of Islam, because this political conspiracy took the form of apostasy while the real goal was to destroy the Muslim community. The confusion lies in taking the act for what it appeared to be and not for what it was meant to be. They mistook political conspiracy for an exercise of the human right of freedom of belief and responsibility of choice. The jurists seemed to exercise little analysis concerning the whole question. The word apostasy alone determined their position.

This misunderstanding of the significance of the word apostasy in the Qur'an and the punishment assigned to it in the *Ḥadīth* of the Prophet (PBUH) destroyed in the classical jurisprudence the basis of the Islamic concept of tolerance and human responsibility.

The early Muslim position on apostasy, as we have seen, was directed not against freedom of conscience and belief but toward enforcing the policy of Islamization of the warring Bedouin tribes and toward checking conspiracy.[29] The Islamic position concerning freedom of religion and belief is clearly stated in the Qur'an. Allah says: "Let there be no compulsion in religion" (Qur'an 2:256) and "Dispute ye not with the People of the Book, except with means better [than mere disputing], unless it be with those of them who inflict wrong [and injury]." (Qur'an 29:46)

Islam always showed full confidence in its truth and in the faith of the Muslims. It always strove to achieve and defend the human right to freedom of choice, conscience, responsibility, and belief.

The conceptual confusion regarding freedom of belief in classical and consequently in traditional political thought occured because Muslim scholars did not realize the basic meaning and reason behind the Prophet's policy of Islamizing the untamed desert tribes. These scholars also did not take into account the criminal aspects of the question or the security needs which early Muslims faced in these cases where the Prophet (PBUH) condemned apostasy. This confusion on the part of jurists explains their endless conceptual contradictions and their inappropriate resort to the method of abrogation.

The so-called War of Apostasy against the first *khalīfah*, Abū-Bakr (632–35 A.C.), was not an exercise of freedom of faith or conscience. It was basically an act of ever-renewed Bedouin reaction against all restraints of political and social authority. The issue in that particular act of belligerency against the government of Abū-Bakr was the payment of *zakah* (alms) and the new central political authority of Arabia.

'Ibn al-Qayyim seemed to realize the conceptual significance of the laws issued by the Prophet (PBUH) at Madīnah vis-a-vis this kind of conspiratorial apostasy. He points to the issues involved as a political measure against subversive activity, having nothing to do with the exercise of freedon of faith and conscience.[30] It is very important for Muslims to keep in focus the basic and central value of individual moral responsibility and freedom of belief and conscience in Islam and not to be lost in formal, legalistic, and short-sighted academic arguments about details and textual materials. Ideological freedom is a basic necessity for any constructive, peaceful, and humane ideology, both internally and externally.

II. RECONSTRUCTION OF THE CONTINUUM IN INTERPRETING THE QUR'AN

We have already shown in Chapters 2 and 3 how classic jurists wanted to maintain and live in a social system similar to the one established by the Prophet (PBUH). This is why the classical jurists tended to produce manuals describing detailed Muslim behavior and social institutions to go with them, which at that time were necessary for them.

With the classic method of *Naskh*, we find these jurists tending to narrow the margin of freedom of political action to basically the *Sunnah* of the last period of the state of Madīnah, which is essentially a secure "big power" policy of self-restraint although not without some policy elements of the early Madīnah period of confrontation with the aggressive, tyrannical, and treacherous ruling elites of disbelievers.

The power which the Muslim polity commanded and the weaknesses and decay of its adversaries made it possible for the Muslim *'ummah* to carry on these sorts of policies, although not without deviations whenever the *Sultān* felt the political necessity to do so.

Seeking to narrow the Islamic position to a purely defensive, peaceful and tolerant position, the liberal modernists found the methodology of abrogation is not always helpful and, at times, is a double-edged weapon. Abrogation ends most arguments in conceptual confusion. We have to settle the issue of abrogation, especially the particular cases mentioned and discussed in the Qur'an, and show the significance of the internal structure of the Qur'an. Otherwise, the Qur'an and for that matter the Islamic ideology and institutions will appear to be simply a traditional way of life belonging to classical times.

A. ABROGATION (NASKH)

Looking at the Qur'anic and the early Islamic experience as a whole, we find that it carried the Muslims through eras of major and comprehensive changes. It sought justice and peace for man in this world and in his relationship to the incomprehensible dimensions of the universe and his destiny beyond life and death:

> "Those who spend (of that which Allah hath given them) in ease and adversity, those who control their anger and are forgiving toward mankind: Allah loveth good. And those who, when they do an evil deed or wrong themselves, remember Allah and implore forgiveness for their sins - for who forgiveth sins save only Allah? - and will not knowingly repeat (the wrong) they did, the reward for such will be forgiveness from their Lord, and Gardens underneath which rivers flow - a bountiful reward for (those who) labour." [Qur'an 3:134-136]

This Qur'anic experience dealt with man as an individual as well as in community, and led him from individual and minority status to the level of a society and government, and from humiliation, persecution and weakness to dignity and power. It achieved much in peace as well as in war. Hardly an experience or mood of the human life and mind was not involved in that gigantic historical experience. Seeking to achieve its assigned goals for human life and society, Islam established a basic framework of values, principles and limits which would provide the Muslim leadership a very wide margin for dynamic and creative political planning and action.

Although jurists and scholars quoted the companions of the Prophet (PBUH) on the abrogation of this or that verse, they do not quote the Prophet (PBUH) himself in specifying any verse abrogating any other verse.[31] As a matter of fact, the jurists exerted great effort to prove the very existence of abrogation in the Qur'an.[32] Although they give great importance to the definition of abrogation, even contemporary scholars pay no attention to the framework of abrogation.[33] What we can deduce from their lengthy arguments is that their framework is static, that abrogation is the result of an act which occurred once in history, and that Muslims are trapped in a single position decided by an accident of a course of actions that took place some time back in history. It is understandable for the classic jurists to think of Muslims as a powerful, established society, but contemporary jurists and scholars are in a state of confusion. They either speak in general, vague terms, divorced from the actual problems and challenges facing the Muslim peoples and authorities, or they speak from a position of idealistic fantasy, assuming a powerful, established society and authority. Muslims are no longer in that time or place. Muslim authorities need Islamic political thought and scholarship comprehensive enough to respond creatively to the new realities and challenges of the contemporary world.[34]

It is important to put the concept of abrogation back in proper context and limit it basically to abrogation of the messages and *'āyāt* revealed before the message of Islam was complete. All parts and rules of the message and experience of Islam are valid whenever they are required in the light of changing circumstances in broad human life and experience. The Islamic rules and system always should qualify for unlimited combinations to fit human needs and circumstances in the light of Islamic goals, values, and principles. *Naskh*[35] should be applied only to clear cases suitable for the concept of *naskh* such as the changes of *Qiblah* once and for all from the direction of Bait-al-Maqdis to Makkah.

Muslim intellectuals and authorities have to restore responsible intellectual, political and legislative freedom of maneuverability within the Islamic framework. The Makkan revelations and attitudes are as valid and relevant to human situations and relationships as the early and late Madina period's revelations and attitudes. Gentleness, generosity, forgiveness and humility are as relevant for human society as force and coercion.

Muslims should always be able to resort to *Ḥusnā* (persuasion), *Ṣabr* (patience), as well as *Qitāl* (fighting), psychological as well as physical etc., according to their immediate needs.

Responsible intellectual, political and legislative freedom, which allows a dynamic use of the different phases of the multi-dimensional Qur'anic outlook within the constitutional framework, are always the characteristic of all progressive, dynamic societies. This was also the case with the Prophet (PBUH) and at least with his first two successors, more obviously in the case of the second Khalifah, 'Umar ibn al-Khaṭṭāb. This has to be restored if the enormous time-space gap is ever to be bridged in a constructive manner within the forseeable future. To this end, it is very useful to study and consider the position and the argument of 'Abū-Muslim al- 'Aṣfahānī about the meaning and the proper range of *naskh*.

B. SIGNIFICANCE OF THE INTERNAL SYSTEM OF THE QUR'AN

Readers of Islamic literature in many cases feel that the treatment and quotation from Qur'anic materials are used without reference to the context. This phenomenon, we think, is due to more than one reason. One is what we have already mentioned, that is, the application of a static, occidental approach to abrogation.

The second is failure to recognize and appreciate the internal system of the Qur'an, which has led to: a) over-simpification and generalization of concrete cases mentioned in the Qur'an, thus overlooking some aspects of the time-place dimension involved in some Qur'anic verses, and b) overlooking the internal structure and the Qur'anic sequence of the Qur'anic verses in each section, which leads to focusing on minor details in an argumentative and legalistic way in derogation of the overall Qur'anic framework. This fragmentation leads to blurred Qur'anic vision and loss of well-defined Islamic goals and priorities.

The third reason which we think responsible for this partiality, fragmentation, and lack of comprehensive and systematic way of thinking in understanding, dealing with and quoting the Qur'an is a conceptual misunderstanding of the different roles in Muslim society and government of the judiciary, which judges and disciplines, and of the social institutions, which educate, encourage and protect.

1. Significance of Concrete Cases in the Qur'an

The Qur'an basically is composed of verses revealing general principles, directions and philosophy. But along with these verses, other verses refer to specific cases, elaborate on them, and provide the Muslims involved in these specific cases some specific directions and orders.

Early writers and commentators on the Qur'an used to overlook the significance of the contexts and the characteristics of these verses when they generalized and abstracted meaning and directions from them.

'Āyat al-Sayf' or *'Āyat al-Qitāl'* (The Verse of the Sword or The Verse of Fighting) is a good example to illustrate the problem at hand. The simple classic juristic approach of *Naskh* helped the cause of a war already in progress against the big powers of the north before the death of the Prophet (PBUH). As a matter of fact, this approach has the advantage of a direct and simple explanation. This added tremendous moral power to the war efforts against the stubborn, imperial Roman enemy of the north.

The Verse of the Sword says: ". . . And wage war on all the idolators as they are waging war on all of you . . ." [Qur'an 9:36], and the related verse in the same chapter says: "O ye who believe! Fight those of the disbelievers who are near to you, and let them find harshness in you" [Qur'an 9:123]. These two verses played, in classical jurisprudence, a central role in determining the Islamic position pertaining to the relations among nations. The classic interpretation today is damaging to many aspects of the multi-dimensional Islamic character of the Qur'anic philosophy and does not fit the needs and challenges of the contemporary world.[36]

In the light of the total Qur'anic revelation and experience and contemporary needs and challenges, Muslim scholars should reform their approaches and methods in understanding and interpreting the Qur'an and the Islamic message to man. All concrete cases and examples should be examined closely under full awareness of the time-place dimension to grasp their real significance and emphasis within the value framework revealed throughout the Qur'an and manifested in the early Islamic experience.

Upon closer examination, the above verses of fighting (*Qitāl*) involved a situation where the Muslims were already engaged in an all-out and vicious war against the Quraysh and the allied tribes. The verses instruct the Muslims on the best manner and strategy to deal with this savage enemy and war already in progress. The verses were dealing with a specific situation. They were to complement and not negate the general rules, attitudes and moods of the wider framework and scope of Islam in the field of external relationships.

2. The Internal Structure of the Qur'an

Failure to recognize and appreciate the internal order and structure of the Qur'an, its chapters, sections and verses is one major shortcoming of the classical methodology. It was not uncommon for a scholar to deal with the verses of the Qur'an as entities independent of each other, with little or no regard for the essential concept of the *sūrah* entertaining them, their place and significance in the order of the *sūrah* (chapter) and of the preceding and following surahs. A verse or a part of a verse could be interpreted and analyzed out of context and without regard for its sequence in the *sūrah* and for its relation to the other verses of the *sūrah*. This method made it possible for individuals to force the Qur'an and its verses to appear to yield some of the desirable narrow interpretations they desired. This method made it possible for some of the classical jurists using the concept of *naskh* (abrogation) to use the various verses or part of a verse out of Qur'anic context to fit the time and circumstances of the classical scholars when the Muslims were the greater power on earth, fighting vicious enemies, and war appeared to be a reasonable means to settle political disputes. In the contemporary world this approach is no longer acceptable.

We have to reconsider our methodology in studying and interpreting the Qur'an. We have to appreciate the internal order and structure of the Qur'an. We have to appreciate the way the Qur'an was revealed to the Prophet (PBUH) chapter after chapter and verse after verse according to the manner and the order directed by Allah (SWT).

There obviously was divine purpose in the way the Prophet (PBUH) was guided by Allah (SWT) to arrange every verse and every word of the Qur'an in the place and position assigned to them by the direct order of Allah (SWT).[37]

The following two examples demonstrate this shortcoming of the classical methodology:

The first example deals with the way in which commentators handled the Qur'anic verse which says: "Allah forbiddeth you not with regard to those who fight you not for (your) faith nor drive you out of your home, from dealing kindly and justly with them, for God loveth those who are just" [Qur'an 60:8]. Commentators and jurists have argued whether the Verse of the Sword abrogates this verse (of peace).[38] If we look at the verse in its place in *Sūrat al-Mumtaḥinah*, we find the verse represents a general rule for the Muslims about the manner and the way they should deal with their peaceful non-Muslim relatives and neighbors. They were ordered and encouraged to be friendly, helpful and just with them. The verse differentiates very clearly between the state of peace and the state of war. During war and hostile confrontation with non-Muslim enemies, Muslims should guard against their enemies. They should unite against them and lend them no help or support.[39]

The same *Sūrah* and the verse preceding the verse in discussion teaches the Muslim the reason behind the Islamic manner and general rule of conduct in peace and war toward non-Muslim peoples and shows that war is a passing condition. The whole Qur'anic lesson and direction in *Sūrat al-Mumtaḥinah* started as follows: "It may be that Allah will ordain love between you and those of them with whom ye are at enmity. Allah is Mighty and Allah is Forgiving, Merciful." [Qur'an 60:7]

The second example deals with another verse also in *Surat al-Mumtaḥinah*, which says:

> Say to the Bedouins who lagged behind: "Ye shall be called against a people possessed of great might to fight them, or they shall surrender (Yuslimun) [*Yuslimun could also mean literally 'turn to Islam'*]. If ye obey, God will give you a goodly wage, but if ye turn your backs, as you turned your backs before, He will chastize you with a painful chastisement." [Qur'an 48:16][40]

Looking at major works of *tafsīr* (commentary of the Qur'an) such as al-Ṭabarī, Ibn Kathir and al-Razi, we find that their major concern was not about what kind of attitude and discipline this *ayah* (verse) is trying to build in these peoples. Their major concern basically was to know who those people were who "Possess great might". We find al-Tabari provides us with a long list of the best guesses of many jurists and scholars about these people's identity. He included in that list almost every possible enemy of the Muslims. These commentators listed Persia, Rome (Byzantium), Hawāzin, Gaṭan and Banū Ḥanifāh. Some of these scholars speculated that this verse could be directed against people yet to come. Finally al-Ṭabarī concluded that the verse did not really tell us if any of the guesses made by the different scholars were meant in the verse, and that it was enough to know that the people mentioned in the verse are people who "possess great might."[41] Ibn Kathīr added to the list of guesses, the *Thaqīf*, all the idolators, the Kurds, and people of small eyes, flat noses and flat faces who were interpreted as Turks.[42] Al-Rāzī's comments and analyses though less detailed were not different basically from the other previous commentators.'[43]

It was more relevant to the order and structure of *Sūrat al Fath* to discuss the troubles and dangers facing the Muslims from their external and internal enemies among the hypocrites. The *sūrah* explained at length these dangers and the conduct, discipline, and strategies required from the Muslims to face these dangers. The *sūrah* went to great length in teaching the Bedouins about the proper conduct and discipline expected of them if they were to join the Muslim cause and define and integrate into the Muslim society.

The classical jurists perhaps could afford to pay only limited attention to the internal order and structure of the Qur'an. They might be able, without danger, to limit their interest and analysis of the Qur'an to the narrow and limited issues that seemed to occupy their minds. Muslims and Muslim scholars can no longer continue the same narrow interest and methodology. They have to pay more attention to the basic issues, values and directions revealed in the Qur'an through its internal sequence and structure.

The classic frame of mind and outlook and methodology explains the conclusion reached by 'Ibn Kathīr in commenting on verse 256 of *Sūrat al-Baqarah* (there is no compulsion in religion). He used verse 48 of the widely separated *Sūrat al-Fatḥ* and verse 36 of another distant *Sūrah, al-Tawbah*. 'Ibn Kathīr,[44] commenting on the first part of verse 2:55 says:

> Said some other [jurists], it ['No compulsion in religion'] was abrogated by the Verse of Fighting [Qur'an 9:36], and all nations should be called to join the religion of straightforwardness, the religion of Islam. If someone refused to join, did not surrender or did not pay the Jizyah, he should be fought until killed. This is the meaning of compulsion. Allah says: "You shall be called against a people possesed of great

> might to fight them or they surrender." Allah says: "O Prophet! Strive against the disbelievers and the hypocrites! Be harsh with them."

Muslim scholars need to give greater concern to these aspects and shortcomings of their methodology and its application.[45]

Sayyid Qutb in his commentary on Qur'an, *"Fi Ẓilāl al-Qur'an"* (In the Shades of the Qur'an), tried to introduce the system of paragraphs in writing the Qur'an to show the significance of the internal structure to the student of the Qur'an. This is one of many steps to introduce a more systematic and comprehensive understanding of the Qur'an through this internal system and structure.

III. FROM FANATICISM TO RATIONALISM

The second step in the systematic, emperical approach to develop Muslim thought in the field of international relations is to correct an important traditional misconception of the relationship between God and man. The importance of this misconception is that under certain conditions, it can lead to fanaticism in intercommunal and international relations between Muslims and other peoples.

Fanatics usually assume an extraordinary concern for the decline and corruption of the Muslim social system and develop a strict attitude for dealing with this decline. The intercommunal and international dimension of this fanaticism is an attitude of self righteousness, contempt, and a lack of concern for non-Muslims who are all believed to be deviant toward Muslims. Such attitudes are not only harmful to communication and interaction between Muslims and non-Muslims but are also destructive to the very foundations of the Islamic mission. The Qur'an says: "We sent thee not but as a Mercy for all creatures" [Qur'an 21:107] and "God forbids you [Muslims] not, with regard to those who fight you not for [your] Faith nor drive you out of your homes, from dealing kindly and justly with them: for God loveth those who are just" [Qur'an 60:8].

Two factors on the part of some Muslims can contribute to a misguided fanatical attitude in relations between Muslims and non-Muslims. The first, which we have already mentioned, is the influence of the traumatic historic experience of the early Muslims in their relation with the hostile Arab and Jewish tribes surrounding them. The second is the misconception of the perspective from which the Qur'an speaks. Although the Qur'an and Islam never allow a human being to assume theocratic authority, fanaticism nevertheless emerges when a Muslim allows himself to judge other people by assuming in practice an authority equal to the absolute authority and knowledge of God (Allah) as represented in the Qur'an.[46] For example, Muslims read in the Qur'an:

> The unbelievers say: "listen not to this Qur'an, but talk at random in the midst of its [reading], that ye may gain the upper hand." But we will certainly give the unbelievers a taste of a severe penalty, and we will requite them for the worst of their deeds. Such is the requital of the enemies of God, the fire: therein will be for them the eternal home, a [fit] requital, for that they were wont to reject our signs. [Qur'an 41:27-28]
>
> God hath promised the hypocrites, men and women, and the rejector of Faith, the fire of Hell: therein shall they dwell: Sufficient is it for them: for them is the curse of God and an enduring punishment [Qur'an 9:68].

There are many similar verses, but it is a great mistake for Muslims to assume that their position vis-a-vis non-Muslims is the same as that of God (Allah) in such verses. God speaks in those verses with absolute authority and knowledge. Muslims should not interpret verses referring to God's confrontation with and condemnation of nonbelievers and God's advice on the way Muslims should respond to aggression as the position assigned to all Muslims against all non-Muslims for all time. Such erroneous interpretation would overlook the space-time element in these verses and deal a crushing blow to their role as brokers of the universal mission of Islam. Muslims should read with equal care the other Qur'anic verses which point out their human role as carriers of the Islamic mission. Examples of these verses are:

> It may be that God will grant love [and friendship] between you and those whome ye [now] hold as enemies. . . God forbids you not, with regard to those who fight you not for [your] Faith nor drive you out of your homes, for dealing kindly and justly with them: For God loveth those who are just. [Qur'an 60:7-8]
>
> Mention [heed] one of *'Ād's* brethren: behold he warned his

> people... Worship ye none other than God: truly I fear for you the Penalty of a Mighty Day. [Qur'an 46:21]
>
> Then said the man who believed: "O my people, Truly I fear for you something like the day [of disaster] of the Confederates [in sin],... and O my people, I fear for you a Day when there will be mutual calling (and wailing)..." [Qur'an 40:30-32]
>
> It may be thou frettest thy soul with grief, that they do not become believers. [Qur'an 26:3]
>
> Say: "O ye men, Now truth hath reached you from your Lord, Those who receive guidance, do so for the good or their own souls; those who stray, do so to their own loss: and I am not [set] over you to arrange your affairs." [Qur'an 10:108]

All Muslims should strive to avoid all actions that block channels of communication with other peoples. Historical incidents and renewed conflict should not cause them to respond in a hostile manner to any non-hostile non-Muslim peoples or individuals. Their response to the hostile non-Muslims as circumstances require should be rational and restrained. Allah says:

> Fight in the cause of God those who fight you, but do not transgress limits; for God loveth not transgressers... But if they cease, God is Oft-forgiving, Most Merciful... But if they cease let there be no hostility except to those who practice oppression. [Qur'an 2:190-93]
>
> The recompense for an injury is an injury equal thereto [in degree]: but if a person forgive and make reconciliation, his reward is due from God: for [God] loveth not those who do wrong... The blame is only against those who oppress men with wrong-doing and insolently transgress beyond bounds through the land, defying right and justice: for such there will be a Penalty grievous. But indeed if any show patience and forgive, that would truly be an exercise of courageous will and resolution in the conduct of affairs. [Qur'an 42:40-43]

These examples from the Qur'an show the real danger of fanaticism in relations within Muslim society and with non-Muslims as minorities or foreign entities. If the different positions in these examples are allowed to be interchanged randomly, fanaticism will be the logical conclusion.

To avoid this, Muslims have to differentiate between the role of God and the role of man. The Qur'an is meant to speak in absolute terms and directly to the conscience of man. Muslims are assigned the role of *khalīfah* (vicegerent and custodian) with utmost concern for their fellow men. Muslim authority has a duty to facilitate this Muslim mission of vicegerency, and not to destroy it.[47]

Thus, conceptual clarity in approaching the Qur'an, the *Sunnah*, and the early history of Islam is very important. The desirability of sincere concern and mutual help among people of different races, colors, languages, territories, and ideologies should not be overlooked by any Muslim. Fostered by the Qur'an, traditional Muslim tolerance should again open all possible channels of communication among men. These channels transcend man-made boundaries and grasp at all available opportunities for a better and more just and equitable life for man in this world.

IV. THE ISLAMIC FRAMEWORK

The third step, in addition to respecting the coherence of the Qur'an and maintaining a decent humility among men toward Allah, is to design an Islamic ideological base or framework for a systematic empirical approach to the field of international relations.

When we look at classical Muslim political thought and the administration of the Muslim polity during the classical period, we find that policymakers profited from and were basically guided by the rational Islamic political policies of the Prophet (PBUH). This was possible and reasonable when the foundations of the world's political systems known to the Muslim were fundamentally the same, and when the diplomatic and military techniques and methods were also the same. But when the systems and the techniqeus changed, the benefits from the early Islamic historical precedents and policies in the field of international relations could no longer be realized. A new venture into free investigation is needed, one designed to serve the Muslim policymaker in the face of contemporary needs and techniques. The Muslim policymaker should be aided by a well-established, comprehensive, systematic, empirical Islamic social science. What the Muslim policymaker needs from the early Islamic sources and actual historical policies is an ideological paradigm as a guideline enabling him to continue a cultural and historic heritage, to respond to the conscience of the Muslim people, and to mobilize their energies. The ideological

Islamic framework is required not only to provide Islamic guidelines but to assign basic priorities. The framework should be general enough to remove all unnecessary space-time elements. The Muslim policymaker will thus be able to deal more successfully with concrete realities and options.

At this juncture, it is necessary to abstract some of the basic principles and values central to Islamic thought.[48] With such basics in mind, one can understand and appreciate many decisions and policies of contemporary Muslim decision makers.

A. BASIC PRINCIPLES

1. Tawḥīd

The most basic principal of Islam is *Tawḥīd*, because it gives purpose to the Islamic framework. *Tawḥīd* means the existence, oneness, and uniqueness of Allah (God) the Creator; the unity and equality of man; and man as the vicegerent and custodian (*khalīfah*) of Allah on earth, who should rule in conformity with Allah's will.

The basic concept and the ideological foundation of Islam stems from the concept of *tawḥīd*. *Tawḥīd* is the visualization of human life as a direct relationship between the transcendent Creator and His creation, in which life is seen as a test of excellence and worth. This puts the final responsibility and initiative on the human individual in a society. It leaves no room for man-made divisions based on distinctions of color, language, or wealth in determining the quality of human relationships or the worthiness of an individual. *Tawḥīd* lays the foundation for a human society built on the responsibility of each human being as God's *khalīfah* where superiority and eminence is reserved exclusively for the Unique One, Allah the Creator. Differences in human life and society pertain to function and performance and not to quality. The concept of *tawḥīd* gives society as well as individuals freedom of destiny and self-determination. It is also the basis for Muslim holy tolerance toward non-Muslims.[49]

2. Justice ('Adl)

Fairness and justice are enjoined on Muslims in all dealings, even with their enemies. Allah (SWT) says:

O ye who believe, Be steadfast witnesses for Allah in equity, and let not hatred of any people seduce you that ye deal not justly. Deal justly, that is nearer to your duty. Observe your duty to Allah. Lo! Allah is informed of what ye do. [Qur'an 5:8][50]

Since the concept of justice is a basic principle in Islam, Islam extends Muslim responsibility and commitment to fairness and justice in all Islamic external relationships. What constitutes justice in any specific matter, how to arrive at that judgment, and how Muslims today are to influence the world's international system or reconcile themselves with any part of that system's content and procedures are matters to be decided from within the system and by mutual agreement of the parties concerned.

3. Peace, Mutual Support, and Cooperation

These are the minimum requirements for Muslim unity in the field of international relations. Allah (SWT) says:

The believers are naught else than brothers. Therefore make peace between your brethren and observe your duty to Allah, that haply ye may obtain mercy. [Qur'an 49:10]

Help ye one another unto righteousness and pious duty. Help not one another unto sin and transgression, but keep your duty to Allah. Lo! Allah is severe in punishment. [Qur'an 5:3]

The Prophet (PBUH) summarized these concepts in a *ḥadīth* (tradition) reported by al-Bukhārī and Muslim when he said: "A Muslim is a Muslim's brother. He does not wrong or abandon him. If anyone cares for his brother's need, God will care for his need."[51] The Prophet (PBUH) further summarized the essential ingredient of the relationship between Muslims who share the same faith and outlook in another *hadith* reported by Bukhārī: "A Muslim is he from whose hands and tongue other Muslims are safe."[52]

These verses of the Qur'an and hadiths of the Sunnah and many more provide the basis for relations among Muslims as individuals, groups, and states. They clearly emphasize the minimum requirement of just, brotherly, and peaceful relations among Muslims, the absence of aggression and violence, and the spirit of mutual help and cooperation. Islam also directs Muslims to use all possible peaceful means to preserve peace and establish justice among Muslim peoples. The Qur'an demands that Muslims should, wherever possible, organize themselves and employ a type of collective security, including the use of force against Muslim elements that are disruptive to peace among Muslims. Allah (SWT) says:

And if two parties of believers fall to fighting, then make peace between them. And if one party of them doeth wrong to the other, fight ye that which doeth wrong till it return unto the ordinance of Allah; then, if it return, make peace between them justly, and act equitably. Lo! Allah loveth the equitable. [Qur'an 49:9]

Whatever particulars go beyond these minimum requirements must be considered upon their individual merit without misunderstanding or misinterpretation of such traditions as have been mentioned above in relation to the conditions of the Muslim state and society at the time of the Prophet (PBUH) and the actions taken by his immediate successors.

The absence of armed conflict and aggression and the spirit of symbiosis among Muslims, although it requires political cooperation and organization, does not dictate any specific political structure. Islam encourages Muslims to undertake every possible effort to carry out all constructive and progressive kinds of political, cultural, social, and economic endeavors as much as possible to achieve the most as an Islamic duty and responsibility.

The traditional interpretation of early Islamic sources on the issue of Muslim unity and political organization is a confusing factor in modern Muslim thought and must be clarified. Traditional interpretation of Muslim unity speaks basically of a central political structure tailored after the early Muslim government of the Prophet (PBUH) and his four immediate successors (A.C. 622–660). The traditional position is derived from a few *'aḥādīth* concerning the political organization of the early Muslim government.[53] The traditional interpretation ignored the space-time element involved in these *'aḥādīth*. A brief discussion of some representative *'aḥādīths* will be sufficient to clear the misconception of the traditional interpretation and to open the door for a more basic and intelligible understanding of political unity and power in the Islamic political system. These *'aḥādīth* are the following:

> 'Arfajah said: I heard the Messenger of Allah, peace be upon him, say: 'There is going to be some trouble there (*Hināt wa Hināt*) and whoever wants to split the unity (*'Amr*) while it

is maintained, strike him with the sword, whomever he is.' "[54]

Jābir said: The Prophet, peace be upon him, is said at the Farewell Pilgrimage to have asked the people to listen. Then he said: 'Do not turn after [my death] disbelievers who strike each others' neck (that is rebel and fight each other).'[55]

'Usāmah 'Ibn-Zayd said: The Prophet, peace be upon him, looked out from a Madīnah fortress and then said: 'Do you see what I see?' They said: 'No.' [Then] he said: 'I see killing (*fitan*) and anarchy which goes through your homes like rain (that is, much killing and fighting).'[56]

'Abdullah 'Ibn- 'Amr 'Ibn-al- 'Ās said: While we were [taking care of] some animals, we heard the announcer of the Messenger of Allah, peace be upon him, calling for a meeting at the Mosque (*al-Ṣalāt Jāmi'ah*). We turned in to meet the Prophet [who] said: 'There was no prophet before me who did not find it his duty to point out to his people (*'ummatuhu*) the best thing he knew for them and warn them about the worst he knew for them, and this, the fortune (*'āfiyatuha*) of your generation (*'ummatukum hādhihi*—usually translated community or group or meeting) was decreed at its beginning, and it is going to fall at its end upon a catastrophe and things you do not approve of. . . Whoever wants to be removed from Hell and to enter Heaven, he should treat people the way he would like them to treat him, and whoever gives to an Imam (political leader or khalīfah) his allegiance, approval and loyalty of heart (*thamaratu qalbihi*), he should obey him if he can, and if someone else comes to challenge him, strike the neck of the other (that is, kill him).'[57]

These 'aḥādīth clearly refer to the conditions in Arabia shortly before the death of the Prophet (PBUH). The rebellion of the Bedouin tribes was spreading and many "false prophets," such as Musaylimah and al-Aswad al- 'Insi, had already begun to challenge the Prophet and the central political authority and government of Madinah. These 'aḥādīth refer to the issue of rebellion and the maintenance of the Madinah state political system.

The term *'ummah*, which was used in early Islam for more than one meaning, is a key word in the above 'aḥādīth. The term obviously refers to the generation of the Prophet (PBUH) and his Companions.

The generalization which the traditional interpretation deduces from this usage ignores the space-time element involved in these 'aḥādīth. If the space-time element involved in these aḥādīth. If the space-time element were recognized in these aḥādīth and the meaning of the term *'ummah* corrected (to indicate the generation and the society of early Madīnah), then these aḥādīth create no problem of legitimacy for the necessary political forms and involvements of the different parts of the Muslim world in the modern international political system. In terms of contemporary international law, these aḥādīth deal with the problem of belligerency and the initial right of the state to consider it as an internal matter and to use force to deal with it.[58] Historically speaking, the classical interpretation of these aḥādīth as orders for Muslims to establish and maintain one permanent central political authority for all Muslims helped to preserve and expand the emerging Muslim society. Since then, as we noted, Muslim political thought has lagged behind the political realities and developments taking place in the Muslim world. As we saw in Chapter 2, jurists could not introduce new vision and practical remedies and were forced retrospectively to justify and compromise with the political corruption of military dictators and "illegitimate" new independent sovereigns, until the whole *Khilāfah* system of the Abbasids collapsed.

Since then, they have not genuinely accepted any sort of federal or confederal or multinational political system for the Muslim world, although jurists and writers no longer insist on immediate establishment of one central authority. Any alternative to one central authority is viewed more as a harsh necessity than a desired situation. With this stand, Muslim thought continues to lag behind the trends and currents of the international system and the political realities of the contemporary world, leaving the Muslim peoples in confusion. Muslim understanding of the dynamics of power and politics still needs to develop to the point where Islamic theoreticians can distinguish between functional unity and artificial uniformity and therefore can accept the evolution of sound and realistic combinations as alternatives to a simple central or semi-central political authority as the symbol of Muslim power and authority.

After World War II, Muslim countries in increasing numbers gained political independence and acquired almost all the institutional links for closer association and cooperation. In the Arab World, the League of Arab States was established, which set up a financial institution for economic development (the Arab Development Bank), a council for Arab economic union (the Arab Common Market), joint defense and economic cooperation treaties among the states of the Arab League (Arab Collective Security Pact) and so on.[59] The broader link with the Muslim world was established in the International Organization of the Islamic Conference (OIC), with its permanent secretariat and its many associated cultural, economic, financial and judicial institutions.

These and other agreements, pacts, conventions, and institutions show clearly that there is hardly any need for still more international institutions to help the Muslim Arab and non-Arab people to achieve unity and cooperation, and to decrease the tension and conflict among themselves,[60] thus achieving independence, power, respect, and the constructive participation in international society which they seem to desire.

It is clear that Muslims do not lack either the resources or the institutions necessary for these goals. It seems from our analysis that what is most needed is a change of attitude toward these institutions and ideas. Thus, a new, positive and constructive attitude would allow the flow and accumulation of resources and the growth and development of institutions, ideas, and functions toward the desired goal. The existing political structures of the Muslim world could improve substantially if Muslims approached them with this positive spirit, realistically taking into account as many political and economic issues and problems of social communication and organization as possible.[61]

Islamic thinkers, scholars, and decision makers need to achieve a new orientation, a better understanding of the meaning of politics and power and its dynamics. It is important to study the modern federal and multinational experience of North America, especially of the United States and of the Soviet Union and the emerging united Europe.[62] All these major contemporary federal experiences deal with the problems of multinational states in different ways and provide insights into different approaches and open the way for new Islamic vision. In the case of the United States, the structural approach and the democratic process for the most part leave local problems and issues to local city and state government. In the case of Europe, the pragmatic aspects of economics and common interests are stressed, while the Soviet Union stresses the ideological approach.

4. Al-Jihād (Self Exertion)

For man to carry out his responsibility as the custodian or vicegerent of Allah on earth, he has voluntarily to exert his utmost effort to bring his behavior in line with the guidelines revealed in the Qur'an and *Sunnah* to man by Allah, the Creator and Sustainer of the whole universe. This exertion of the self in all directions, in every effort and act, personal and collective, internal and external, is the essence of *jihād* and *'ibādah* (obedience to Allah in the choice of the right path) in the Islamic sense, which will be rewarded in the hereafter, apart from whatever lawful benefit may result from it in this world. Clearly, *jihād* is supposed to run through all phases of a Muslim's life, as it is his duty in every possible way to do good in the world and prevent harm. This can, of course, include combat on the battlefield, but to equate *jihād* exclusively with war is to be bound only by some aspects of the historical experience of the classical period and to misread the historical experience of the early Muslims.

Al-Bukharī and Muslim reported a conversation between the Prophet (PBUH) and a man who came to him to join his troops in fighting (*jihād*). The Prophet (PBUH) asked the man if his parents were alive, and the man said, "Yes." The Prophet (PBUH) then told him: "Then strive in serving and providing for them (*fafihimā fa jāhid*)."[63] This answer clearly shows that *jihād* is the Muslim's striving to fulfill his every responsibility and to serve the Islamic cause and principles in a manner consistent with the Islamic framework. It is not to be taken to mean warfare alone. *Jihād* in this sense is the active expression of the Islamic commitment, responsibility, and sense of duty, wherever it is required in practical life.

To interpret *jihād* only as an offensive or defensive war is to misunderstand the meaning of the word and the philosophy behind it. It is equally erroneous to assume—as have traditionalists and modernists alike—that *jihād* as holy war was the sole basis for relations between the Muslim and non-Muslim worlds in premodern times. We have already shown in Chapter 2 that *jihād* meant more than one thing to the classical jurists. The Muslim writings of modern times interpret all acts of *jihād* in the field of external relations in Muslim history, and especially in the early period, in terms of defense, while many non-Muslim writers explain the same as offense against other non-Muslim peoples, initiated by Muslims almost entirely for internal reasons. A subjective attitude leaves no final verdict on historical actions that is acceptable to all parties concerned. This is not our concern here, however, and it is enough for us to realize that many things depend on the definitions and assumptions held by each writer. All we are saying here is that the Qur'anic text extends *jihād* far beyond the efforts and sacrifices on the battlefield.[64] But it must be remembered that a realistic analysis of the use of the term *jihād* in the actual course of the foreign policy of any Muslim state should not stop at the ideological aspects of the Islamic framework. The actual course of action taken by any Muslim state, whether called *jihād* or not, always depends on the interaction of internal and external factors as well as the extent of its commitment to the Islamic teachings. These interactions have, in the absence of the leaders' real commitment to a sound Islamic ideology, in some instances led to the proclamation of some most unholy wars, in which it would not be difficult ever for a traditionalist to recognize the fallacy of the claims of *jihād*. Although *jihād* as a basic Islamic principle does not exclude the possibility of armed conflict, students of international relations should pay attention to its variety of meanings and applications in any specific situation. Only then will a better understanding of the motivation and consequences of any specific course of a Muslim foreign policy be possible.

5. Respect and Fulfillment of Commitments

This principle is a natural extension of the principle of *tawḥīd*. The sense of the responsibiity of man and the oneness and equality of human beings requires establishment of the moral obligation of Muslims, individually and collectively, to fulfill their personal, national, and international commitments. The genuine establishment of this principle in Islam is clearly in line with all other basic principles and values of Islam. Numerous Qur'anic verses urging Muslims to fulfill their agreements leave no doubt about the positive moral attitude of Islam in this sphere.[65] It allows no room for double standards. A Muslim decisionmaker or statesman can find no refuge in the Islamic framework of thought or in its principles or values to justify violation of agreements either by intention or by deliberate action.

We refer back to al-Sarakhsī's position that it is permissible for Muslims to make a truce agreement with a stronger enemy for the sake of gaining time and then break the agreement as soon as they are able to fight successfully against that enemy. This stand was taken on the ground that fighting against nonbelievers is a duty, and delaying it is similar to giving more time to a borrower to pay latter.[66] This stand is the exception in Muslim juripsrudence and in my opinion the analogy is a wrong one and the stand is clearly in violation of both the letter and the spirit of every Qur'anic verse related to the subject. Those same verses do not support the static legalistic interpretation relating to the concrete circumstances concerning the Banu-Qurayzah, in conjunction with which Qur'an 8:58 was revealed, as the standard for the interpretation and implementation of the concept of unilaterally withdrawing from or repudiating an agreement.[67]

In the age of nuclear arms and massive destruction, what constitutes "a fear of treachery" as the Qur'an puts it (or "aggression" in political terms)? And by what responsible process should decisionmakers react in such a situation? These are matters to be decided upon according to the prevailing methods and circumstances. The Qur'anic verses (specifically 8:56–58) offer a concept that allows for a realistic, flexible response in a situation of imminent danger. How are decisionmakers to assess the security of the state? What measures should they take? How is the Muslim state to resolve the conflict in different systems of law? The situations are tremendously complicated and change continually.[68] Mechanical and legalistic decisions are not applicable to existing conditions. Decisionmakers must have the freedom to make responsible decisions in such situation.[69] To what extent is a weak party, forced into an unfair agreement such as the former colonies experienced vis-a-vis their colonizers, justified to repudiate treaties and agreements unilaterally? To what extent are the "have-nots" justified in calling for a change of the status quo? It is important to mention here that careful planning of commitments is necessary for Muslim states. Serious political mistakes could lead to a breach of agreements, the destruction of a state's credibility, and a threat to world peace. Policymakers should endeavor to avoid such errors.

The Islamic framework will not tolerate pretense or marginal gains in agreements. In relation to serious considerations defined and worked out with a full sense of responsibility, the Islamic framework and the above verses leave no doubt that a positive attitude is required in international relations. The Islamic frame of mind leaves no doubt that responsible commitment is a basic ingredient for orderly interaction. The Qur'an makes it clear that Muslims are required to observe this injunction scrupulously in their internal and external relations. Thus, members of international systems should not overextend the legal aspects of treaties. They should realize that in bilateral and multilateral agreements, good intentions, friendship, and/or basic mutual interest are necessary conditions for serious implementation of treaties; bad intentions, deceptions, and serious political conflict of interests are bound to end with enmity, breach of agreements, or eventual armed conflict. Once war erupts, most treaties and pledges are repudiated, and thereafter success on the battlefield, as the Prophet put it, basically depends upon mastering the art of maneuver (*al-ḥarbu khidʿah*).[70]

B. BASIC VALUES

Looking closely at the Islamic texts, experience, and history, we find that there are some basic values that color the Muslim attitude and influence the Muslim conscience and strategies for action. The failure of these values to function as effectively as they might is due, as we mentioned earlier, to a misunderstanding of historical experiences, and to the rigid legalistic attitudes of the traditionalists, who tried to set fixed patterns for Muslim action in all aspects of life, including external relations.

The basic values must be freed from space-time elements and kept in focus if Muslim leadership is to regain the efficiency and dynamism that prevailed under the leadership of the Prophet (PBUH), Abu-Bakr, and 'Umar. These values basically promote moderation and self-restraint. They help policymakers to recognize the limits of a particular course of action and not to lose sight of the goals beyond the means. These values, as exemplified by the Prophet (PBUH) in both internal and external affairs, are:

no aggression (*ʿudwān*)

no tyranny (*ṭughyān*)

no corruption (*fasād*)

no excesses (*'isrāf*)

A few Qur'anic verses and *'Aḥādīths* are enough to show the great emphasis of Islam on these values. Allah says:

> And obey not the command of the prodigal [*al-musrifūn*–wasteful or excessive], who spread corruption in the earth, and

re-form not. [Qur'an 26:151-152]

Neither obey thou each feeble oath-monger, detracter, spreader abroad of slanders, hinderer of the good, transgressor, malefactor. [Qur'an 68:10-12]

(O mankind!) . . . He [God] loveth not aggressors. Work not confusion in the earth after the fair ordering [thereof]. [Qur'an 7:55-56]

Go, both of you, unto Pharaoh. Lo! he hath transgressed [the bounds]. And speak unto him a gentle word, that peradventure he may heed or fear. They said: "Our Lord! we fear that he may . . . [abuse] us or that he may play the tyrant." [Qur'an 20:43-45]

The blame is only against those who oppress men with wrong-doing and insolently transgress beyond bounds through the land, defying right and justice: for such there will be a Penalty grievous. But indeed if any show patience and forgive, that would truly be an exercise of courageous will and resolution in the conduct of affairs. [Qur'an 42:41-43]

And let not your hatred of a folk . . .seduce you to transgress; but help ye one another unto righteousness and pious duty. Help not one another unto sin and transgression, but keep your duty to Allah. Lo! Allah is severe in punishment. [Qur'an 5:3]

The Prophet (PBUH) said: Those who are merciful have mercy shown them by the Compassionate One. If you show mercy to those who are in the earth, He who is in heaven will show mercy to you."[71] And, "God will not show mercy to him who does not show mercy to others [*al-nās means humans*].[72]

1. Frameworks of Muslim Attitudes and Policies in External Relations in the Contemporary World

We have already identified some basic attitudes and reviewed some of the external policies of the Prophet (PBUH) in Chapter 2. It is clear that these attitudes were a mixture of friendship and cooperation, and of war and conflict. These attitudes were reflected both in policies and their implementation. The Muslims engaged in policies of cooperation and mutual aid, economic pressure, psychological warfare, guerrilla tactics, and regular warfare.

These policies clearly reflected the influence of the basic Islamic principles and values enunciated by the Prophet (PBUH) in response to the internal and external factors operative at the time. The ultimate goal of these external policies was to serve the Muslim people and their cause under the prevailing circumstances. Policies are action-oriented to carry out the prevailing attitude within the possible alternatives available to the decisionmaker. Early Muslim policies and attitudes, as we observed, were bound to reflect the space-time dimension. Contemporary Muslims should be open to change and innovation in the area of policy.

For example, the attitude of neutrality in relations among nations, if it existed at all in the period was not of major significance because, the basic attitude among major powers during the time was one of hostility. Neutrality was a major ingredient in the European political system of the nineteenth century because of the new and far-reaching means of communication and war. Later changes since World War II in communications and war technology, together with current political alignments, have now reached a point that makes neutrality difficult to practice.

Major disparities between newly created environments and the attitudes persisting from past experience and a serious lack of creative policies threaten to bring about disastrous results. Confusion, misunderstanding of the role of basic principles and values, and a lack of firm adherence to them adversely affect the national conscience of a people and their unity in support of foreign policies. Muslim thought, as we have shown, reflects these serious disparities and the urgent need for self-examination in order to achieve a better understanding of the Islamic framework and of the inner workings of the policy mechanisms involved.

Diagrams 1–3 are intended to delineate the potentially dynamic nature of Muslim states and their attitudes and policies. Diagram 1 illustrates the traditional superimposed understanding of contemporary international relations in terms of the classical jurisprudence of *siyar* and *jihād*, which was explained in Chapter 2. The classical framework is no longer related to current international affairs. As we see it, this traditional approach in the world politics of today is bound to be static and superficial and offers no help for contemporary Muslim policymakers.

Diagram 2 illustrates the modernists' position. Their position and policies on international affairs, while reflecting the influence of foreign powers and a foreign environment, nevertheless lack the capacity to mobilize the people and their potential. This position of the modernists, which represents the prevailing conditions in Muslim political thought, was also discussed in Chapter 2. At the heart of this position is the problem of immature and static Muslim thought. Contemporary Muslim thought has been largely under the influence of the modernist approach, which consists of imitation and piecing together. Positive interaction between ideology and environment and the possible growth of Muslim power and partnership in international affairs are not integral attributes of such an approach. Modernists believe that Muslim foreign policies are deficient not because they lack Islamic motivation and goals but because Muslim policymakers have failed to bring about the economic growth and political power to support their policies and improve the conditions of the Muslim people. Diagram 3 illustrates a proposed Muslim framework in the field of international relation. Islam, in this framework, plays the role of a people's ideology. Islam is presented to the policymakers as a set of abstract principles and values—a framework or set of guidelines—freed from the major weakness of the traditional approach, namely, the space-time element. The proposed framework also eliminates the other major fault of the traditional approach, its lack of systematic empirical analysis, since it accounts for dynamic interaction between the ideology and the environment.

The proposed framework, by taking into account the effective use and acceptance of Islamic ideology in the process of policymaking, also eliminates the major failure of the modernist approach, namely, the lack of capacity to mobilize the Muslim peoples and their potential. It is clear that the proposed framework is aimed at putting an end to the immobilization of Muslim moral and intellectual powers, which occured through incorrect use of historical and alien experiences. The proposed framework provides policymakers with the necessary freedom to plan and execute rational Islamic courses of foreign policy.

Although the principles and the historical precedents referred to in the diagram are clearly moral, they set no rigid formulas for policy action.

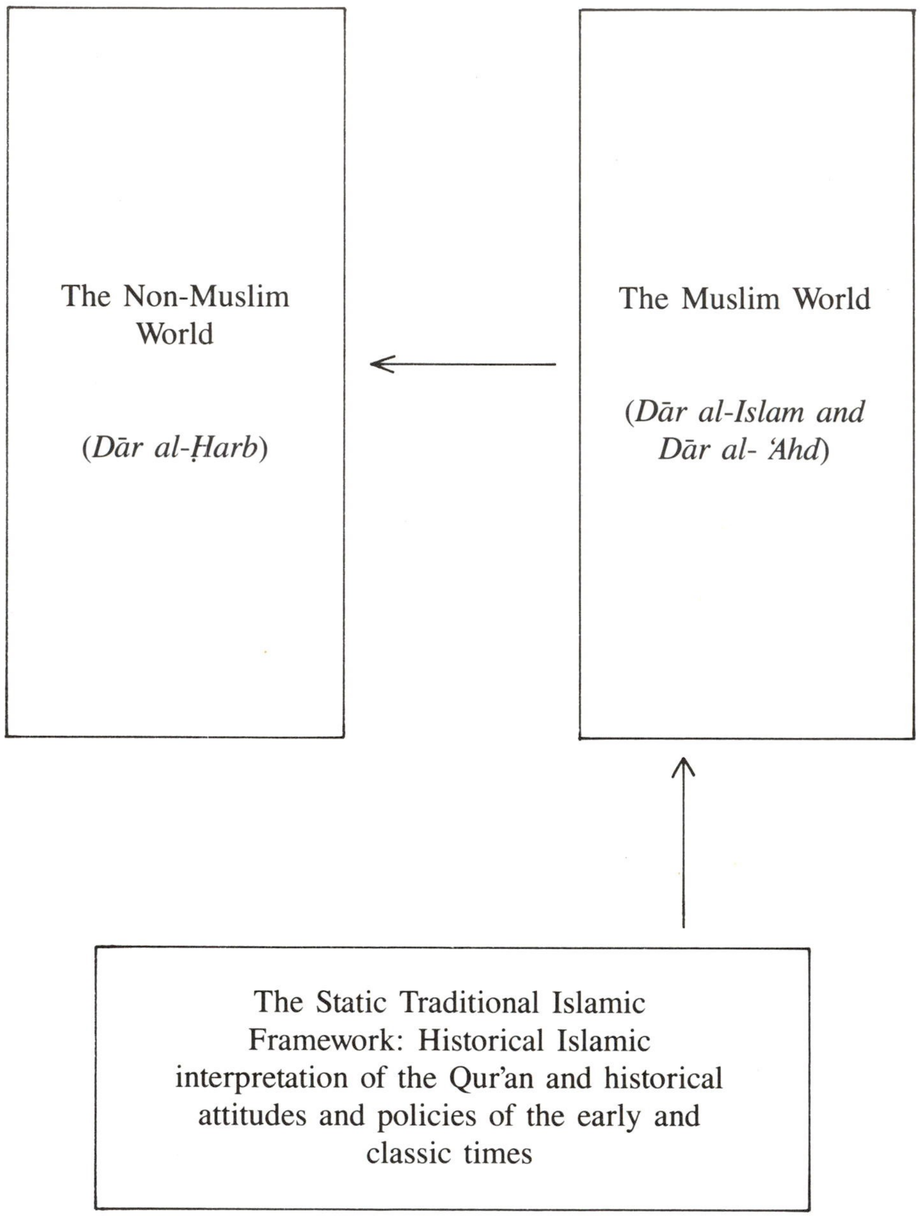

Diagram 1. Traditional Framework

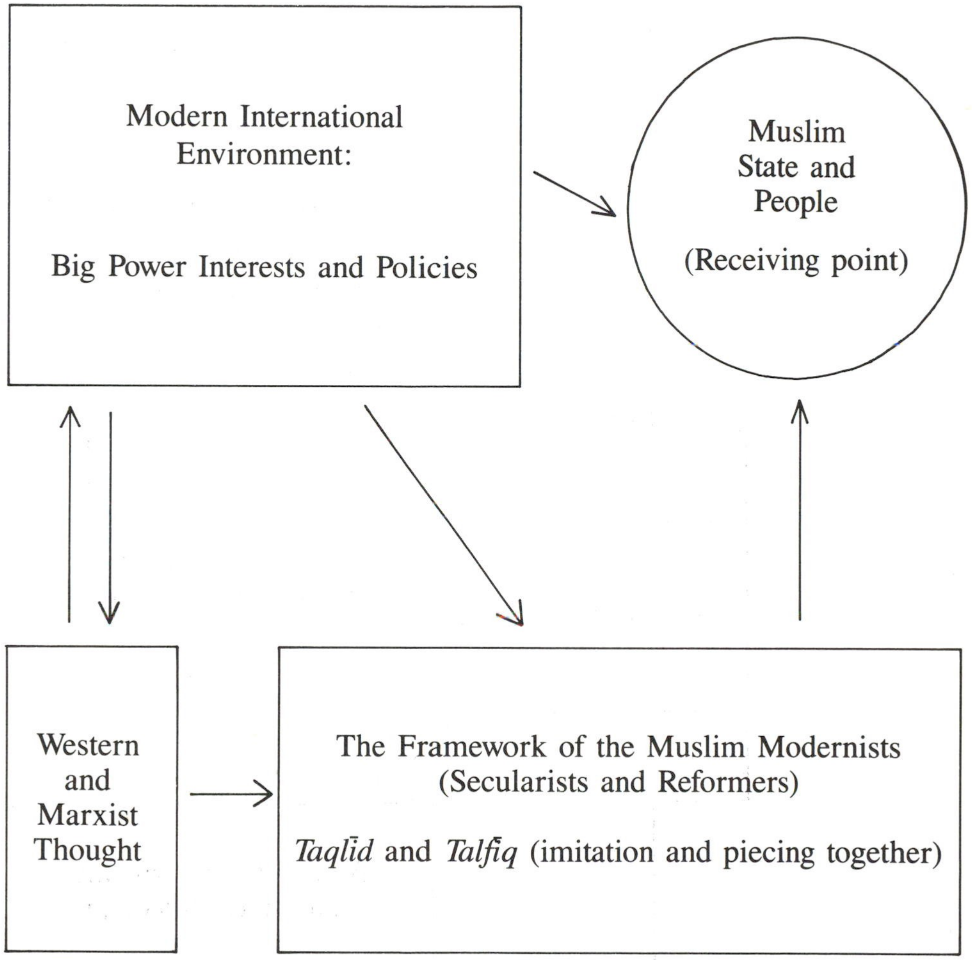

Diagram 2. Modernists and Secularist Framework

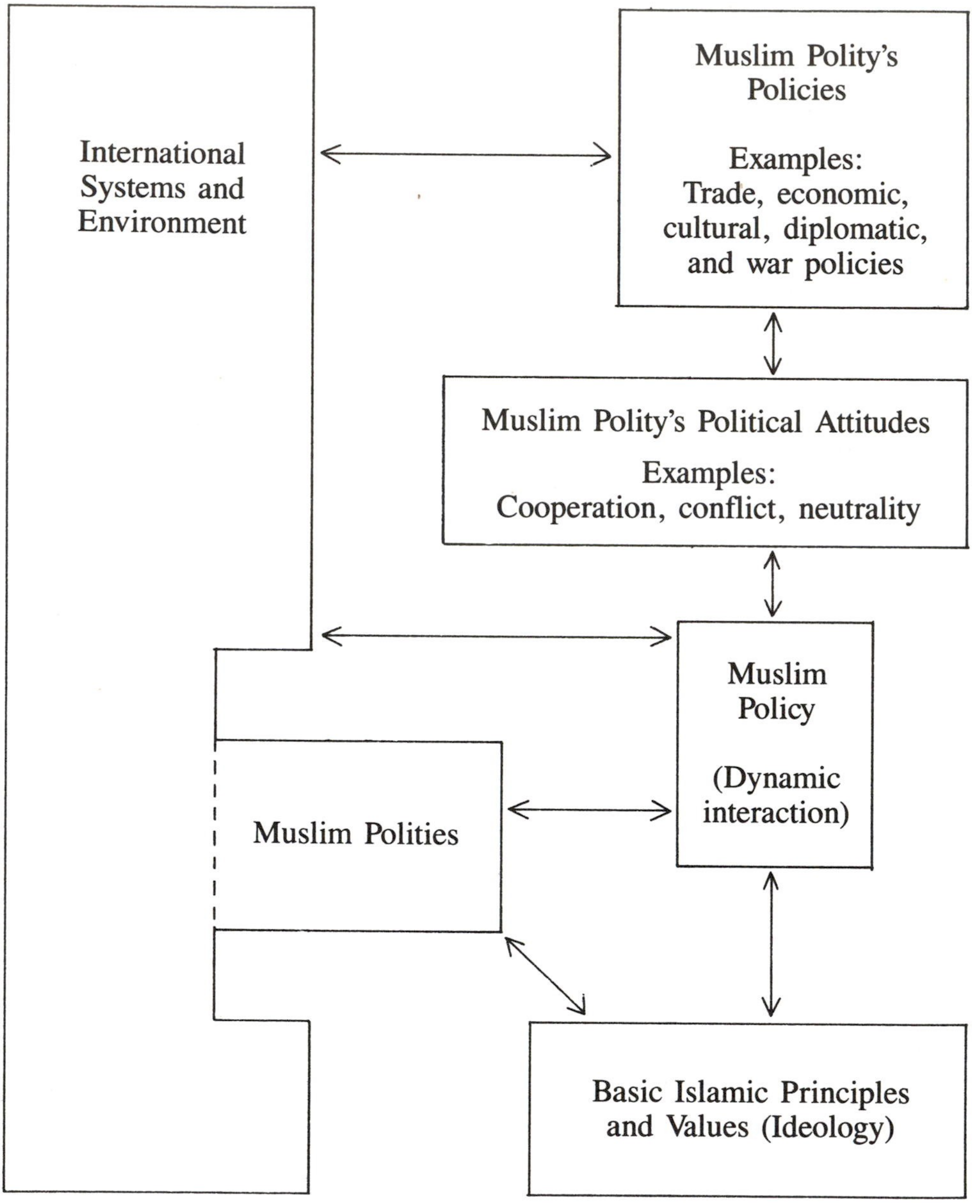

Diagram 3. Modern Dynamic Islamic Framework

Basically what is required of decisionmakers is basic commitment to work within and implement the Islamic framework. Any specific policy devised to meet a specific situation should be undertaken by decisionmakers in the light of five factors: 1) the basic principles and values of Islam; 2) the character of threats to and opportunities for the pursuit of Islamic goals; 3) the strengths and limitations of Muslim societies; 4) the resources of adversaries and allies; and 5) the limitations of the environment.

Hence, this dynamic framework can accommodate every shade of political strategy from that applied in the established international community to the radicalism of policies used in Algeria during the independence struggle against the French army and French colonialist settlers. The nature of policies professed in the Muslim state depends, in the last analysis, on the particular situation at hand. It is simplistic therefore to assume that decisionmakers can afford to obey rigid legal provisions of past ages that supposedly govern the conduct of external affairs in Islam.

2. Major Muslim Policies Examined

The focus of this study now shifts from the early period of Islam to the policies and attitudes of modern Muslim nations. Our purpose in this examination is not to suggest particular changes in any of these policies or for any specific country. Our purpose is to point out the irrelevance of the traditional legalistic approach in assessing the value of any course of foreign policy undertaken by any Muslim state; and, the advantages and opportunities available to Muslim policymakers if they adopt an ideological framework free from space-time limitations and built on a solid dynamic basis of the systematic empirical approach suggested in Chapter. 3.

Three major policies should be analyzed, and their achievements in the service of Muslim states in the field of international relations should be examined. The first policy, already analyzed, is the abandonment of war as the basis of foreign relations with non-Muslims. The second and third are the adoption of diplomatic reciprocity and alliances with non-Muslim states, and the principle of positive neutrality.

At the outset, it is important to mention that our concern is not with the detailed development or technical aspects of these policies. What matters, and what we intend to emphasize here, are the causes of these policies and their goals. Only in the light of the rationales and goals of these policies can we assess the assumed conflict of these policies with Islam and the abandonment of Islamic ideology as a possible cause of their failure.

a. *Strategies of Diplomacy and Alliance*

Starting with the Ottomans, we find that in the history of the victorous early Ottoman *Ghazis* (warriors for the Faith) against the then inferior hostile powers of Europe, diplomacy had a very limited role and value.[73] With the renaissance of Europe and its successful efforts to reach the trade centers of the Far East, however, new attitudes and policies of cooperation in pursuit of mutual interest emerged as did more diplomatic interaction between the Ottomans and the European powers. In what came to be known as the Treaties of Capitulations, the Ottomans provided more facilities for European traders, and European countries sent diplomatic missions to the Ottoman government (the Ottoman sublime porte).[74]

As the contrast between the increasing power and technological capability of Europe and the decaying, corrupt, and stagnant Ottoman cultural, social and political system grew, the Ottoman political authorities began to use and rely on diplomacy to counter the militarily superior European enemies who aimed at dismembering an empire that became increasingly defenseless against their attacks. The Ottomans exchanged diplomatic missions on a permanent basis and entered into treaty and alliance relations with Christian states, though some of these alliances were at the initiative of some European states which wanted to secure better privileges and protect their interests vis-a-vis other European states.[75]

The Ottoman chapter in history closed with World War I and the defeat of the Central Powers. Although Kemalist Turkey continued the Ottoman practice of reciprocal diplomacy, Islam was no longer an approved source for conducting the external relations of the Republic of Turkey. While evaluating the Ottoman policies, some writers took the extreme traditional position for granted and insisted on approaching Islam as a set of traditions and forms, overlooking its fundamental nature as a value system and framework.[76] They strictly measured the Ottoman policies against the Hanafi jurisprudential manuals thereby condemning the Ottoman sultans for deviating from Islam.[77] They raised such questions as whether Islam allows a treaty of more than ten years, or whether a Muslim subject is allowed to be brought to trial in a non-Muslim court. This approach led them to conclude that Muslim deviation from the traditional jurisprudence of one school or another is deviation from Islam.

Islam does not accept the concept of the duality of the secular and the religious. The difference in opinion between a political authority and a jurist or group of jurists does not necessarily mean that the jurist is Islamic and the political authority is not. We have to consider the matter on its merits. While a political authority may tend, under the influence of various political factors, to give less attention to the ideological elements of the system, especially in its rigid juristic form, it is also possible that the jurist lacks an understanding of the political factors at play.

The Islamic orientation of the Ottomans is beyond any doubt. Accusations against the Ottomans are a matter of opinion. Criticism of the Ottoman Sultans is basically a conservative position. The critics, mainly the 'Ulama', considered any deviation from the classical experience as a sort of heresy. Classical thought and certain specific historical precedents were not fully acceptable to Ottoman statesmen, who faced the threat from a rapidly modernizing Europe with its growing power and efficiency. Such accusations of deviation against the Ottoman statesmen are ultimately a denial of their right to exercise judgement to avoid disastrous policies.[78]

The Ottoman Sultans of the eighteenth and nineteenth centuries, whose state was formally admitted as a member of the European state system in the Paris peace agreement of 1856, used the diplomatic approach in order to be able to maneuver under new circumstances and developments.[79] This was necessary for their existence and also for the new program of reforms. These basic requirements elevated the question about the "Islamicity" of the Ottoman approach from such legalistic particulars as the legitimacy of a treaty of more than ten years or the empty textual arguments about the permissibility of a policy of alliance with a non-Muslim state, to the more basic question of interaction and efficiency in pursuing Islamic goals.[80] Why then did the Ottoman political authorities introduce the new diplomatic approach? why did they develop cooperation and co-existence with Christian European powers? and what was the purpose of these new attitudes?

The waning military and economic power of the Empire and the growing strength of the European Powers was the obvious reason. The purpose was to preserve the Empire from dismemberment, by manipulating the balance of power among the Europeans. Reform, in the meantime, was supposed to restore sufficient power to the Empire to withstand any further encroachments.[81] The success or failure of these policies is reflected in the interaction of various sections of a social system in adjusting and responding to real needs, both internal and external.

Obviously, the Ottoman policy-makers failed to achieve their objective of reviving the Ottoman military superiority. They succeeded only in introducing large numbers of technical and constitutional reforms, some of which were superficially implemented or misapplied. They failed to understand the phenomenon of Europe's growth and development, and Ottoman Sunni thought failed to abandon legalism and to introduce a genuine systematic and rational application of the value system to new developments in the socio-political situation. The efforts of more than a century (the nineteenth) basically resulted in secularization and westernization.[82] Islamic thought and consciousness remained static or was further alienated.

When the Empire collapsed and was dismembered at the end of World War I, the gap between the Muslim world and Europe was wider than ever. The fault of the Ottomans was not that they tried to adapt to the changing situation and try to gain time to survive and reform. Their fault was their failure to take a genuine course of Islamic reform and instead their choice of superficial modernist reform. Most of the Muslim world had to wait until the Second World War to gain some degree of independence and freedom before it could move and participate in world affairs. Some Muslim countries followed a course of alliance with the West and recently with the East and the rest adopted what came to be called Positive Neutrality and nonalignment. We now turn to an analytical discussion of these two major contemporary policies to see how much success or failure secular Turkey had in attaining what the Ottomans had aimed at and failed to get.

After the end of World War I and the fall of the Ottoman Empire, the Western powers divided the Ottoman territory under the mandate system. In the period between the two world wars, a number of treaties were made between European powers and Muslim states, full of terms expressing friendship and alliance, but in reality these treaties did not represent policies or agreements between independent states. They were rather the terms dictated by the victorious European powers vis-a-vis the occupied Muslim territories. Examples of these are the treaties between France and Syria of 1936, France and Lebanon of 1936, Egypt and Britain of 1922 and 1936, and Iraq and Britain of 1922 and 1930.[83]

The policy of alliance assumed importance after World War II, when the Western European powers were no longer the major world powers, nor in a position to control the Middle East. This was when the super powers of the world, the United States and the Soviet Union, began to pursue their global interests in the area. Both the new and the old powers started to compete to gain influence and control the area, and this led to the opening of policy alternatives to the Muslim states of the Middle East.[84]

To understand the various attitudes and policies pursued by the Muslim states of the Middle East, we have to keep in mind the different historical and geo-political factors involved which divide them into the frontier zone (or what is called the Northern Tier of Turkey, Iran, Pakistan and Afghanistan) and the Arab World. The threats and dangers to the interests of each area differ; similarly, their attitudes and policies toward the major powers involved in the politics of the area differ. Along the frontier zone are Muslim states facing the Communist Soviet Union. In the past, when these states were a part of the Ottoman Empire and Iran, they had bitter experiences and conflicts with Imperial Russia. Russia projected a threat to these states, and the Western powers, for strategic and geo-political reasons, usually found it in their interest to cooperate with these Muslim states against Russia. The Russian policy of southward expansion toward the warm seas, culminating in the occupation of some of this frontier zone, also constituted a threat to the interests of the Western colonial powers in Asia and Africa.

The countries of the frontier zone or what came to be called the Northern Tier—with the exception of Afghanistan, a small landlocked state of high mountains which shares a long border with the Soviet Union—had their reasons to fear the intentions of the Soviet Union. In the case of Pakistan, its enmity with India and the collaborations between India and the Soviet Union were two more reasons for the pragmatic policy of alliance between these Muslim states and the West, especially the United States.[85] The Northern Tier policy was implemented through the involvement of these states in the alliances of CENTO (Baghdad Pact), SEATO, and NATO. The Arab world, however, was in a different situation, and had different historical and strategic experiences. The Arab world, with its strategic location and possessing major communication lines and vital raw materials, from the eighteenth century experienced an increasing foreign presence and control of its territories. The World War I alliance of the Arabs with the Western powers against the Ottomans and the Central Powers, in an open bid for their independence, ended with the bitter experience of the mandate regimes. In the aftermath of World War II, the dominant Western powers in the area, France and Britain, were weakened and were no longer able to play the same role. The growing oil interests of the United States and its close relations with the emerging Zionist–Jewish state of Israel built on the ruins of Arab Palestine as a result of the British mandate gave an impetus to the movement of liberation and independence from Western domination.

b. *Strategies of Neutrality*

Arab political attitudes toward the West after World War II continued to be largely bitter and hostile. With the growing policy of cold war between the two major powers and the Soviet Union's post-Stalin change of strategy toward the developing areas, particularly the Middle East and its offers of economic and military aid, made possible for a few years, the emergence of new options that came to be known as Positive Neutrality and nonalignment.[86]

Historic and strategic considerations explain why the alliance with the West came to an end for Pakistan, and why it lost some of its strength in relation to Iran and to a lesser extent, Turkey. This happened when the United States provided India, considered the archenemy and a major threat to the existence of Pakistan, with military aid, thus causing serious doubt about the dependability of U.S. commitments to Pakistan.[87] The success of the Egyptian attack on Nuri al-Said's policy of Iraqi alliance with the West (the Baghdad Pact) can also be explained by the historic and strategic factors we analyzed earlier. A policy of alignment with the West against the Soviet Union is contrary to the interests of an area seeking development, liberation, and independence from Western and Zionist control. With the new Soviet approach, the Arab world, especially Egypt, proclaimed the slogan of Positive Neutrality.[88] This slogan has been misinterpreted and misunderstood. In order to understand it, the attitudes and policy underlying this slogan must be explained. Historical developments inevitably turned the Arabs against the West, but at the same time the Arabs were in a position of weakness vis-a-vis the presence of the West in the Area; thus, the Arabs feared the West and had to be cautious in their policies.[89] The Soviet Union, the other superpower and enemy of the West, was a natural ally for the Arabs against the West. Although the Arabs needed Soviet economic and technical aid in their struggle against the West, the ideological differences and the historical experience of their brothers in the frontier zone made the Arabs fear the Soviet Union, which is not basically different from a Western power, and displayed an attitude of caution even while cooperating with the Soviet Union.[90] This explains the bias in the voting pattern of Arab countries, such as Egypt which claims a policy of Positive Neutrality toward the Soviet Union while striking at the communist parties in their own countries.

Although Positive Neutrality represents an attitude of caution on the part of the States that follow it toward the big powers competing in the area, it must be remembered that Positive Neutrality does not represent the entire foreign policy of these states, which simultaneously follow different attitudes and policies toward other Arab and Muslim states. It would be necessary to consider the ideological, national, and historical factors in interaction with the problems in question, the action required, the other party or parties involved, and other policies pursued by the parties involved in order to understand the variety of attitudes and changing policies pursued within the Muslim world.

The change of strategies and policies between the two Super Powers from the Cold War and confrontations to the d'etente' and the subsequent Western abandonment of the Indian Ocean, the South African Region, and Afghanistan to the Soveit Union, the fall of the pro-Western regime of the Shah in Iran, and the devastating Iraqi-Iranian War, indicate strategic change. This could bring harm to the Muslim world in general and the Muslim states of the Middle East in particular, as part of a strategy to provide the Soviet Union with land passage to Warm Water and the Indian Ocean.

Non-alignment and positive neutrality toward the two Super Powers or alliance with either one of them are no longer working policies for the peoples of the Muslim world. Their only option is to find ways and means to achieve workable unity and cooperation among the Muslim countries in politics, economics, and military strategy if they are to avoid more devastating defeats and humiliating control at the hand of the Soviets in the frontier region and at the hands of the West and the Zionist state of Israel in the Arab Middle East.

In the final analysis, the successors of the Ottomans did not do much better than their former masters. Although both alignment and Positive Neutrality aimed at serving the cause of independence, revival, and participation, the situation did not change appreciably. The economic and technological gap and dependence on the big powers have continued to grow and defeats and losses have continued to hit and weaken the Muslim world. Unless there is basic change in the attitude, mentality, and policies of the Muslim peoples and countries, their lot may not be better than the Ottoman Empire and the Arabs of North Africa and Spain who preceded them.

c. *Conclusions*

From the above account of the causes and goals of these two basic foreign policies, we find, according to the suggested Islamic framework (Diagram 3) that there is nothing in the approaches themselves that makes them un-Islamic or anti-Islam. According to the traditional appraoch (Diagram 1), of course, it would be very difficult for these approaches to be accepted as Islamic, since they do not fit the historical Muslim policies in all aspects. Although the modernist/secular approach (Diagram 2) supports these three policies in principle, it assigns little or no value to the revitalization of Islamic thought (*Iṣlāh* and *Tajdīd*) and to the support of Islamic ideology. Thus, the modernist/secular approach, as well as the traditional approach both work negatively against these policies if these policies are to be pursued as expressions of the Islamic approach based on the religious, cultural, and historical affiliation of Muslim people to Islam. The modernist/secular appraoch also allows the Muslim world to continue to be basically a sphere of ideological conflict between the different world powers.

A study of Muslim foreign policies within the limits of the suggested Islamic framework (Diagram 3) points to the need for a basic reform of Muslim political thought. This framework assumes that we can eliminate both the space-time problem of traditional political thought and the lack of originality and consistency of the modernist approach. The suggested Islamic framework, through emphasis on the basic purpose of *tawḥīd* and on the values, principles, and goals of Islam, makes it possible for the policymaker to utilize the moral power of the Muslim ideology inside and outside the Muslim world. The suggested Islamic framework allows, among other things, a more positive Islamic ideological approach to the positions already taken by Muslim nations, heretofore only partially influenced by Islam, against colonialism, imperialism, and racial discrimination, and for justice toward and within the previously colonized areas of the world.

If it is used rationally in the field of international relations, Islamic revival could be used in many constructive ways. For example, according to the suggested framework, Islam could be used to bring about more emphasis on issues such as human dignity and human rights by taking a stand against racial and nationalist discrimination by emphasizing quality and merit, by decentralizing political authority and decisionmaking bodies, and advocating wider coöperation and mutual support in economic, technical, social, cultural, and political matters based on principles of human welfare and progress (*'iṣlaḥ* and *birr*, in a general sense), equity, merit, and social justice.[91]

From the above analysis, it is clear that Muslims do not lack either the resources, the institutions, or the values for them to attain their legitimate goals. What they need is a change of attitude toward the relevant issues, institutions, and ideas. A dynamic, constructive attitude is necessary to make the resources, institutions, and ideas fulfill the desirable goal and achieve the required results.

Change in the approaches and methods of Muslim thought are absolutely necessary for Muslims to create and maintain a successful Islamic social system. These reforms are prerequisities for success in changing the role and condition of the Muslims, both internal and external.

Muslim peoples and Muslim governments should comprehend the real essence of Muslim unity and progress in various times and various fields. They should always be ready and able to establish the right attitudes, the proper alternative solutions, and the necessary organizational structures to serve the unity of Muslim peoples and the real goals, objectives, and interests of Islam.

The Muslim *'ummah* and Muslim peoples should utilize and develop the various international Muslim organizations, especially the Organization of the Islamic Conference and its General Secretariat, and the affiliated cultural, economic and technical organizations to protect and serve Islam and Muslim interests and to strengthen Muslim unity.

The conclusion of this research is that Islam, in its principles, values, and goals pertaining to international relations is still capable of guiding successful and constructive external relationships, provided that Muslims abide by these comprehensive Islamic principles and goals. They should reconstruct their understanding of the early period of Islam and accordingly understand systematically the empirical Islamic study of international relations. In this way, Muslim thinkers and statesmen would be able effectively to evaluate the alternative courses of action available to serve their *'ummah*, man in general, and Islam.

CHAPTER 4

[1] See Chapter 2, footnote [73], p. 92. See also Charles C. Adams, *Islam and Modernism in Egypt* (New York: Russell & Russell, 1933), pp. 248-268; and Erwin I. J. Rosenthal, *Islam in the Modern National State* (Cambridge: At the University Press, 1965), pp. xi-xiii.

[2] See Abu-Muhammad 'Abdul-Malik Ibn Hishām al-Ma'afirī, *Al-Sīrah al-Nabawiyyah* (The Bibliography of the Prophet), eds. M. al-Sagga, I. al-Ibiarī, and A. Shalabī (2nd ed.; Cairo: Sharikat Maktabat wa Maṭba'at Muṣṭafā al-Bābī al-Ḥalabīwa Awladuh bi-Misr 1955), vol. I, pp. 606-715; vol. II, pp. 3-43; and Ibn al- 'Athīr, *Al-Kāmil fī al-Tārīkh*, vol. II, p. 37.

[3] See Ibn Hishām, *Al-Sīrah*, vol. I, pp. 265-395, 642-646.

[4] Ibid., pp. 317-390, 419-429, 591-606.

[5] See M. Hamidullah, *Al-Wathā'iq al-Siyāsiyyah*, pp. 39-47; and Ibn Hishām, *Al-Sīrah*, vol. I, 501-504, 590-606.

[6] See: W. Al-Zuḥaylī, *'Athar al-Ḥarb*, pp. 406-408.

[7] Ibid.

[8] Ibid.

[9] See Muḥammad Aḥmad Ba-Shumayl, *Ghazwat Badr al-Kubrā*, vol. I of *Min Ma'ārik al-Islām al-Fāṣilah* (The Great Battle of Badr, vol. I of the Decisive Battles of Islām), (4th ed.; Beirūt: Maṭba'at Dār al-Kutub, 1969), pp. 227-229; Muḥammad al-Ghazālī, *Fiqh al-Sīrah* (Life of the Prophet) (4th ed.; Cairo: Dār al-Kubub al-Ḥadīthah, 1964), pp. 254-255; and Nadav Safran, *Egypt in Search of Political Community*, p. 213.

[10] See Al-Naysābūrī, *Asbāb a;-Nuzūl*, pp. 132-138; Ibn Hishām, *Al-Sīrah*, vol. I, pp. 666-667; and Al-Ṭabarī, *Jāmi'al-Bayān*, vol. IX, pp. 168-250; vol. X, pp. 1-57.

[11] See Ibn Hishām, *Al-Sīrah*, vol. II, pp. 245-250; Al-Ṭabarī, *Jami'al-Bayān*, vol. X, pp. 25-35; and Qur'ān 8:19, 26, 30, 38, 39, 45, 57, 58, 60, 67, 70, 71, 72, 73, and 81.

[12] See Bernard Lewis, *The Arabs in History*, p. 40

[13] Ibid., pp. 42-45; F. Gabrieli, *Muḥammad*, pp. 64-65, 72-76; Muḥammad Ḥamidullah, *The First Written Constitution in the World: An Important Document of the Time of the Holy Prophet* (2nd rev. ed.; Lahore, Pakistan: Sh. Muḥammad Ashraf, 1968), pp. 48-49, 51-52. It is also useful to see the summary and translation by Moḥammad Tallat al-Ghunaimī, *The Muslim Conception of International Law and the Western Approach* (The Hague: Martinus Nijhoff, 1968), p. 37, for a more accurate evaluation of the Prophet and the political atmoshpere in which the decision against Banu Qurayẓah took place.

[14] See F. Gabrielī, *Muḥammad*, pp. 64-80; Muḥammad Ba-Shumayl, *Ghazwat Banī-Qurayẓah*, vol. IV of *Minm'arik al-Islām al-Fāṣilah* (The Battle of Bani-Qurayẓah, vol. IV of the Decisive Battles of Islām) (Beirūt: dār al-Fatḥ li al-Tibā'ah wa al-Nashr, 1966), pp. 238-270; M. al-Ghazālī, *Fiqh al-Sīrah*, pp. 257-264, 335-346; Maḥmud Shit Khattah, *Al-Rasūl al-Qāid* (The Messenger, the Leader) (2nd rev. ed.; Baghdād: Dār Maktabat al-Ḥayah Maktabat al-Nahḍah, 1960), pp. 161-162; Sayyid Ameer 'Alī, *The Spirit of Islam: A History of the Evolution and Ideals of Islam with a Life of the Prophet* (London: Methuen, 1922), pp. 72-82; H. Watt, *muḥammad*, pp. 166-175; and M. T. al-Ghunaimī, *The Muslim International Law*, pp. 38-39.

[15] See Ibn Hishām, *Al-Sīrah*, vol. II, PP. 51-58, 273-276; M. T. al-Ghunaimī, *The Muslim International Law*, pp. 38-42; and W.M. Watt, *Muḥammad*, pp. 144-176. See also Yūsuf 'Alī, *The Holy Qur'ān: Text, Translation and Commentary* (Brentwood, Maryland: Amana Corporation, 1983), footnote 3701-3704 on pp. 1111-1112.

[16] See Qur'ān 23:8, 17:91, 5:1, 16:91-92, 9:4-14, 2:100, 8:72, 3:76-77, 2:177, 13:20, 25, 6:152, 17:34, 33:15, 8:61. Also see A.a. Manṣūr, *Muqāranāt*, pp. 57-61; Al-Farra', *Al-Aḥkām*, pp. 48-49; Ibn Kathīr, *Tafsir al-Qur'ān*, vol. II, p. 320; M. Abū-Zahrah, *Al- 'Alāqāl al-Dawliyyah*,

pp. 40-41; Mālik Ibn Anas, *Al-Muwaṭṭa*, vol. I, p. 298; M. Ḥamiddullah, *The Muslim Conduct of State, pp. 82 and 208; M. Khaddūri, War and Peace*, pp. 218-220; M.T. al-Ghunaymi, *Muslim International Law*, p. 161, n. 11; Al-Sayyid Muḥammad Rashid Riḍā, *Tafsir a;-Qur'ān al-Ḥakim al-Mushtaharbi Ism Tafsir al-Manār* (Interpretation of the Perfect Qur'ān, known as the Way-Mark Interpretations) (4th ed.; Cairo: Dār al-Manār. 1954), vol. X, pp. 53-60, 169, 178-203, 217-222, 229-234; and vol. XI, p. 281; Al-Shāfi'i, *Al-Umm*, vol. IV, pp. 184-186; and Al-Ṭabari, *Jami'al-Bayān*, vol. X, pp. 26-27. For examples of the implementation of the principle of fulfillment of agreements, see for early period of Islam, M. Ḥamidullah, *Al-Wathāiq*, pp. 58-63, 369, 371-372, 387, and 393-394; for the Ot'toman period and the Capitulation Treaties, J.C. Hurewitz, *Diplomacy in the Near and Middle East*, vol. I, pp. 1-5 and 7-9.

[17] See Ibn Hishām, *Al-Sirah*, vol. II, pp. 389-397.

[18] See Ibn Ibn al- 'Athir, *Al-Kāmil*, vol. II, pp. 239-240.

[19] See Ibn Hishām, *Al-Sirah*, vol. II, pp. 397-407.

[20] Ibid., pp. 482-486.

[21] See Abdul Raḥmān 'Azzām, *The External Message of Muḥammad*, translated from 'Arabic by Caesar E. Rarah (New York: New American Library, 1965), p. 46; Ibn al- 'Athir, Al-Kāmil, vol. II, p. 277; Ibn Hishām, *Al-Sirah*, vol. II, pp. 591-592, 606-607, 641-642; and M. al-Ghazāli Fiqh al-Sirah, pp. 395-396, 435-438, 442.

[22] See Abdul-Karim 'Uthmān, *Al-Niẓām al Siyasifi āl-Islām* (Political system in Islam) (Beirūt: Dār al-Irshād, 1968), pp. 60-67; M. Abū-Zahrah, *Al- 'Alaqāt al-Dawliyyah*, pp. 142-143; Muḥammad 'Abdu, *Al-Islām wa al-Naṣrāniyyah Ma'a al- 'Ilm wa al-Madaniyyah* (Islam and Christianity with Regard to Knowledge and Civilization) (Cairo: Maktabat wa Maṭba'at Muḥammad 'Ali Ṣabiḥ wa Awladuh, 1954), p. 64; M. Al-Bahi, *Al-Fikr al-Islāmi*, pp. 130-137; M. Ghazāli, *Fiqh al-Sirah*, pp. 453-455, 458-464; and M. Sa'idi, *Al-Ḥurriyyah al-Diniyyah*, pp. 25, 30.

[23] See Muhammad al-Ghazāli, *Al-Ta'aṣṣub wa al-Tasāmuh Bayn al-Masiḥiyya wa al-Islām: Ḍaḥd Shubuhāt wa Rad Muftarayāt* (Fanaticism and Tolerance Between Christianity and Islām: and Answering Misunderstandings and False Accusations) (Kuwait: Dār al-Bayān, n.d.), pp. 37-66; and W. C. Smith, *Islām in Modern History*, pp. 266-291.

[24] See Qur'ān 60:8-9, 11:84, 26:135, 46:21; 5:118, 18:87, 26:3, 34:28, 21:107, 3:104, 9:67, 11:116, 16:125, 49:13, 18:87, 26:151-152, 68:10-12, 42:41-43, 16:90-91, 107:1-7, and, 90:12-20. Also see Abi 'Abdullah Muhammad Ibn Ismā'il al-Bukhāri, *Matn al-Bukhāri bi-Ḥashiyat al-Sindi (Bukhāri's Collection of Ḥadith with the Commentary of al-Sindi) (Cairo: Dār Oḥya' al-Kutub al- 'Arabiyyah, 1960), vol. I, p. 228, and vol. II, pp. 159, 161, 171-172; Al-Khaṭib al- Umāri, Mishkah*, Al-Alhani (ed.), vol. II, pp. 605, 608, 613; Al-Fakhr al-Razi, *Al-Tafsir al-Kabir*, vol. XXVI, pp. 54-61; M. Rashid Riḍā, *Tafsir al-Manār*, vol. IV, pp. 25-45, vol. IX, pp. 290-291; Al-Ṭabari, *Jām'i al-Bayān*, vol. XII, pp. 98-105; and Muḥammad 'Izzat Darwazah, *Al-Tafsir al-Ḥadith* (Contemporary Interpretation of the Qur'ān) (Cairo: Maṭba'at 'Isā al-Bābi al-Ḥalabi, 1964), pp. 200-203.

[25] W. al-Zuḥayli, *'Athār al-Ḥarb*, p. 102.

[26] M. Rashid Riḍa, *Tafsir al-Manār*, vol. X, pp. 178-179.

[27] See Abū-Zayd ('Abdul-Raḥmān Ibn Muḥammad) Ibn Khaldūn, *The Muqaddimah* (An Introduction to History), translated from 'Arabic by Franz Rosenthal, ed. N.J. Dawood (Princeton: Princeton University Press, 1967), pp. 118-122; Aḥmad Amin, *Fajr al-Islām: Tabḥath 'An al-Ḥayāt al- 'Aqliyyah fi Ṣadr al-Islām ila Akhir al-Dāwlah al-Amāwiyyah* (The Dawn of Islam: Discourse on Intellectual Life in the Early Period of Islam until the End of the Ummayyad Dynasty) (9th ed.; Cairo: Maktabat al-Nahḍah al-Maṣriyyah, 1964), pp. 30-38; Jawād 'Ali, *Al-Mufaṣṣal fi Tārikh al- 'Arabi Qabl al-Islām* (The Detailed Account of 'Arab History Before Islam) (Beirūt: Dār al'Ilm li-al Malāyin, 1970), vol. IV, p. 334; Muḥammad Kāmil Laylah, *Al-Mujtam'a 'al- 'Arabi wa al-Qawmiyyah al- 'Arabiyyah* (Arab Society and 'Arab Nationalism)

(Cairo: Dār al-Fikr al- 'Arabī, 1966), pp. 85-91, 108-111; and W. Watt, *Islāmic Thought*, pp. 6-7.
[28] See M. Sa'idī, *Al-Ḥuriyyah al-Diniyyah*, pp. 25-33.
[29] 'Afīf 'Abdul-Fattaḥ Ṭabbārah, *Al-Yahūd fī al-Qur'ān: Taḥlic 'Illmī li-Nuṣūṣ al-Qur'ān fī al-Yahūd 'Alā Ḍaw' al-Aḥdāth al-Ḥadirah, Ma'a Qiṣaṣ Anbiyā 'Allah Ibrāhīm wa Yūsuf wa Mūsa 'Alayhim al-Salām* (The Jews and the Qur'ān: Scientific Analysis of the Qur'ānic Text Pertaining to Jews in the Light of the Contemporary Events with the Stories of the Prophets Abraham, Yusuf and Musa, May Peace Be Upon Them) (2nd ed.; Beirūt: Dār al- 'Ibm li-al-Malāyin, 1966), pp. 30-32; and Muḥammad Sayyid Ṭanṭāwī, *Banū Isrā'īl fī al-Qur'ān wa al-Sunnah* (The Descendants of Israel in the Qur'ān and *Sunnah*, pp. 168-263. Also see Ibn al- 'Athīr, *Al-Kāmil*, vol. II, p. 249; and Ibn Hishām, *Al-Sirah*, vol. II, p. 409.
[30] See A. 'Uthmān, *Al-Niẓām al-Siyāsī*, pp. 66-67.
[31] See M. Abū-Zayd, *Al-Nāskh, vol. I, pp. 125-134, vol. II, pp. 553, 563-568, 579-581.*
[32] See M. Abū-Zayd, *Al-Nāskh*, vol. I, pp. 221-285.
[33] Also we have to mention here that we should not commit an old mistake by confusing freezing certain principles (because of the situation calling for another one) for abrogation (Naskh) which means permanent cancellation of the value or principle.
[34] See M. Abū-Zayd, *Al-Nāskh*, vol. I, pp. 205-220. M. Al-Ẓurqanī, *Manāhil al'Irfān*, vol. II, pp. 69-76.
[35] See M. Abū-Zayd, *Al-Nāskh*, vol. I, pp. 236-242, 399-501, vol. II, pp. 503-538; M. Zurqānī, *Manāhil al- 'Irfān*, vol. II, pp. 152-165.
[36] See Ibn Salāmah, *Al-Nāsikh wa al-Mansūkh*, pp. 19, 51; M. Abū-Zayd, *Al-Nāskh*, vol. II, pp. 503, 583; M. Al-Zarkashī, *Al-Burhān*, p. 40; M. Al-Zurqanī, *Manāhil al- 'Irfān*, p. 156; W. Al-Zuḥaylii, *'Athar al-Ḥarb*, pp. 78-89.
[37] See Ibn Kathīr, *Tafsīr al-Qur'ān*, vol. II, pp. 331; Mannā' Qaṭṭān, *Mabāḥith fī 'Ulūm al-Qur'ān* (Studies in the Science of Qur'ān) (Jedda, Saudi 'Arabia: al Dār al Su'ūdiyyah li al-Nashr, n.d.), pp. 49-57.
[38] See Ibn Salāmah, *Al-Nāskh wa al-Mansūkh*, p. 91; M. Abū-Zayd, *Al-Nāskh*, vol. II, pp. 551-553.
[39] See for example the article "Waliyy" in Arabic dictionaries such as *Mukhtār al-Ṣiḥāḥ* (The Correct Selection) of Muhammad ibn Abī Bakr al-Rāzī.
[40] See Al-Fakhr al-Rāzī, *Al-Tafsīr al-Kabīr*, vol. XXVIII, p. 93; Arthur J. Arberry's translation, *The Kor'ān Interpreted* (New York: The Macmillan Company, 1955), p. 227; A. Y. 'Alī's translation, *The Qur'ān*, pp. 1395-1396; M. Pickthall's Translation, *The Glorious Qur'ān*, p. 366.
[41] See Al-Ṭabarī, *Jami'al-Bayan*, vol. II, pp. 82-84.
[42] See Ibn Kathīr, *Tafsīr al-Qur'ān*, vol. IV, pp. 90-93.
[43] See Al-Fakhr al-Rāzī, Al-Tafsīr al-Kabīr, vol. XXVIII, pp. 91-93.
[44] See for example: Ibn Kathīr, *Tafsīr al-Qur'ān*, vol. I, pp. 310-311.
[45] See W. Al-Zuḥaylī, *'Athar al-Ḥarb*, p. 99.
[46] See Hassan al- 'Ishmāwī, *Qalbun Akhar li- 'Ajl al-Za'īm* (Another Heart for the Leader) (Beirūt: Dār al-Fatḥ, 1970), pp. 98-180; M. D. al-Rayyis, *Al-Nadhariyyat al-Siyasiyyah*, pp. 320-341; and M. Khaddūrī, *War and Peace*, pp. 7-18.
[47] The Qur'ān contains many verses that teach Muslims concern and love toward their fellow men and enhance Muslim authority to do its utmost for the service and aid of man. See, for example, Qur'ān 3:159, 14:36, 6:8, 3:103-105, and 2:190.
[48] See Qur'ān 6:101-104, 4:1, 49:13, 67:2, 2:30, 7:32, 21:35, 16:125-126, 3:159, 16:90-91, 3:64, 5:2, 21:94, 9:36, and 2:193. See also, Donald Eugene Smith, *Religion and Political Development* (Boston: Little, Brown & Co., 1970), pp. 20-21.
[49] See also M. Abū-Zahrah, *Al- 'Alagātal Dawliyyah*, pp. 19-47; and Sayyid Qutb, *Al-Salām al- 'Alami wa al-Islām* (The World's Peace and Islām) (Cairo: Dār Iḥyā' al-Kutub al- 'Arabiyyah, 1967), pp. 128-155.

[50] See Qur'ān 16:90, 57:25, 7:29, 4:48, 135, 49:9, and 60:8.
[51] Walī al-Dīn Muḥammad Ibn 'Abdullah al-Khaṭīb al- 'Imārī al-Tabrīzī, *Mishkāt al-Maṣābīh* (Collections of Authentic Traditions of the Prophet the author used the word *maṣābīh*, which means literary lights), ed. Muḥammad Naṣir al-Dīn al-Albānī (Damascus: Al-Maktab al-Islāmī, 1961), vol. I, p. 606.
[52] Muḥammad Muḥsin Khān, *The Translation of the Meaning of Saḥīḥ al-Bukhārī* (Cyranwala, West Pakistan: Sethi Straw Board Mills (Conversion) Limited, n.d.), vol. I, pp. 18-19.
[53] See Aḥmad Amīn, *Yawm al-Islām* (The Day of Islām) (Cairo: Mu'assat al-Khānjī, 1958), pp. 143-152; 'Aziz Aḥmad, *Islāmic Modernism in India and Pakistan: 1857-1964* (London: Oxford University Press, 1967), pp. 139-140; Majīd Fakhrī, *Dirāsāt fī al-Fikr al- 'Arabī* (Studies in Arabic Thought) (Beirūt: Dār al-Nahār, 1970), pp. 250-251; Muḥammad Abduh, *Al-Islām wa Al-Radd 'Alā Muntaqidīh* (Islām and Answers for Its Critics) (Cairo: Al-Maktabah al-Tijār iyyah al-Kubrā, 1928), p. 76; Muḥammad Jalal Kishk, *Mafāhīm Islāmiyyah: Al-Qawmiyyah wa al-Ghazw al-Fikrī* (Islāmic Point of View: Nationalism and Cultural Imperialism) (Kuwait: Maktabat al-Amal, 1967), pp. 187-212; Richard P. Mitchell, *The Society of the Muslim Brotherhood* (London: Oxford University Press, 1969), pp. 264-271; T. Cuyler Young, "Pan-Islamism in the Modern World: Solidarity and Conflict among Muslim Countries," in *Islam and International Relations*, ed. J. H. Proctor, pp. 215-216; and W. C. Smith, *Islam in Modern History*, pp. 37-85.
[54] See Al-Hāfiẓ al-Mundhirī, *Mukhtaṣar Muslim*, vol. II, p. 94.
[55] See Al-Bukhārī, *Al-Jāmi' al-Ṣaḥīḥ*, vol. XI, pp. 42-43; and Al-Hāfiẓ ('Abdul- 'Aẓīm Ibn 'Abdul-Qawiy) al-Mundhirī, *Mukhtaṣar Saḥīḥ Muslim* (Summary of Muslim's [Selection of the] Authentic (Sunnah), ed. Nāṣir al-Dīn al-Albānī (Kuwait: Ministry of Endowments and Islāmic Affairs, 1969), vol. I, p. 19.
[56] Al-Bukhārī, *Al-Jāmi' al-Ṣaḥīḥ*, vol. IX, pp. 40-41.
[57] See Abū-Ya'la al-Farra', "Kitāb al-Imāmah" in *Nuṣuṣ al-Fikr*, ed. Y. Ibish, p. 218; Al-Hāfiẓ al-Mundhirī, *Mukhtaṣar Muslim*, vol. II, p. 87. Notice that in the last *hadīth*, the Prophet was addressing himself to immediate issues and circumstances rather than the future in general.
[58] See Charles G. Fenwick, *International Law* (3rd rev. ed.; New York: Appleton-Century-Grafts, Inc., 1948), pp. 140-148; Hans Kelsen, *Principles of International Law* (2nd ed.; New York: Holt, Rinehart and Winston, Inc., 1966), pp. 414-418; and Muḥammad Hāfiẓ Ghānim, *Mabādi' al-Qānūn al-Dāwlī*, pp. 292-295.
[59] Other such institutions are: The Convention for Facilitating Trade Exchange and the Regulation of Transit Trade Between States of the 'Arab League, the Convention for the Settlement of Payments of Current Transactions and Movements of Capital Between States of the 'Arab League, the Convention on the Privileges and Immunities of the League of 'Arab States, the Federation of 'Arab Lawyers, the 'Arab Journalists' Union, the 'Arab Teachers' Union, the Federation of 'Arab Physicians, the 'Arab League's series of 'Arab social welfare seminars and 'Arab health seminars, etc., the 'Arab Manuscript Institute, the Cultural Museum, the Cooperative Training Center, the Institute of Advanced 'Arab Studies, the Organization of the 'Arab Scientific Federation, the 'Arab Telecommunications Union, the 'Arab Postal Federation, the 'Arab Broadcasting Union, the 'Arab Civil Aviation Council, etc.
[60] See 'Abdul-Qādir al-Jammāl, *Min Mushkilāt al-Sharq al-Awṣat* (Some of the Middle East's Problems) (Cairo: Maktabat al-Anglo al-Maṣriyyah, 1955), pp. 320-477; Norman D. Palmer and Howard C. Perkins, *International Relations: The World Community in Transition* (3rd ed.; Boston: Houghton Mifflin, 1969), pp. 580-583; and Robert W. MacDonald, *The League of 'Arab States: A Study in the Dynamism of Regional Organization* (Princeton, N.J.: Princeton University Press, 1965), p. 241.
[61] See, for example, the following: Daniel Katz, "Nationalism and Strategies of International

Conflict Resolution," in *International Behavior: A Social-Psychological Analysis*, ed. Herbert C. Kelman (New York: Holt, Rinehart & Winston, 1965), pp. 354-391; John H. Herz, "The Territorial State Revisited: Reflections on the Future of the Nation-State," in *International Politics and Foreign Policy: A Reader in Research and Theory*, ed. James N. Rosenau (New York: Free Press, 1969), pp. 76-90; and Karl W. Deusch, *Nationalism and Social Communication: An Inquiry into the Foundation of Nationalsim* (2nd ed.; Cambridge: Massachusetts Institute of Technology, 1966).

[62] Karl W. Deutsch and others, *Political Community and the North Atlantic Area: International Organization in the Light of Historical Experience* (Princeton, N.J.: Princeton University Press, 1968).

[63] See Al-Khaṭīb al- 'Umārī, *Mishkah*, ed. al-Albānī, vol. III, p. 354.

[64] See Qur'ān 22:77-78, 49:14, 29:69, 25:51, 16:110, 3:157, and 2:190-195.

[65] See footnote 24 above.

[66] Al-Shaybānī, *Al-Siyar al-Kabīr*, vol. I, pp. 190-191.

[67] Ibn Kathīr, *Tafsīr al-Qur'ān*, vol. II, p. 320; Al-Ṭabarī, *Jami' al-Bayān*, vol. X, pp. 26-27; also see footnote 24 above.

[68] See A. A. Fatouros, "Participation of the 'New' States in the International Legal Order of the Future," in *The Future of the International Legal Order*, eds. Richard A. Falk and Cyrile E. Black (Princeton, N. J.: Princeton University Press, 1969), vol. I, pp. 350-371; Adda B. Bozeman, *The Future of Law in a Multicultural World* (Princeton University Press 1971), pp. 161-186; B. S. Murty, "Foundation of Universal International Law," in *Asian States and the Development of Universal Internatinal Law*, ed. R. P. Anand (Delhi: Vicas Publications, 1972), pp. 173-178; Josef L. Kunz, *The Changing Law of Nations: Essays on International Law* (Kent: Ohio State University Press, 1968), pp. 3-56; and M. H. Ghānim, *Al-Qānūn al-Dawlī*, pp. 3-16.

[69] See Inis L. Claude, Jr., *Power and International Relations* (New York: Random House, 1962), pp. 197-204.

[70] See Al-Khaṭīb al- 'Umārī, *Mishkāt*, ed. al-Albānī, vol. II, p. 384.

[71] Al-Khaṭīb al- 'Umārī, Mishkat, trans. J. Robson, vol. III, p. 1034.

[72] Ibid., p. 1031; see also the 'Arabic text, ed. al-Albānī, vol. III, p. 605.

[73] See T. Naff, "Reform and Diplomacy," p. 295.

[74] See R. H. Davison, *Turkey*, pp. 46-47.

[75] See Bernard Lewis, *The Middle East and the West* (Harper & Row, 1966), pp. 116-118; R. H. Davison, *Turkey*, pp. 53-90; T. Naff, "The Setting of 'Ottoman Diplomacy," pp. 22, 26; and T. Naff, "The Reform and Diplomacy," p. 310.

[76] See M. Khadduri, "Translator's Introduction" to al-Shaybani, *The Islamic Law of Nations*, pp. 62-67; and M. T. al-Ghunaimi, *The Muslim International Law*, pp. 18-54.

[77] See M. Khadduri, "Translator's Introduction" to al-Shaybānī, *The Islamic Law of Nations*, pp. 63-64.

[78] Note that the 'Ottomans, in defense of their policies, invoked the classical concept of *Maṣlaḥah*, basically in terms of necessity.

[79] See Charles G. Fenwick, *International Law*, p. 18; and Roderic H. Davison, *Reform in the 'Ottoman Empire: 1856-1870* (Princeton, New Jersey: Princeton University Press, 1963), p. 4. Also see: J.C. Hurewitz, *Diplomacy in the Near and Middle East*, pp. 153-156.

[80] See B. Lewis, *The Middle East*, p. 118; and M. Khadduri, "Translator's Introduction" of al-Shaybānī, *The Islamic Law of Nations*, pp. 63-64.

[81] See R. H. Davison, *Turkey*, pp. 68-77.

[82] See T. Naff, "The Setting of 'Ottoman Diplomacy," pp. 62-63; Niyazi Berkes, *The Development of Secularism in Turkey* (Montreal: McGill University Press, 1964), pp. 23-289; R. H. Davison *Turkey*, pp. 62-63 and 53-143; B. Lewis, *The Emergence of Modern Turkey*, pp. 124-128,

230-238; and Don Peretz, *The Middle East Today* (New York: Holt, Rinehart and Winston, Inc., 1965), pp. 53-80 and 445-449.

[83] See, for example, the 'Arabic text of the treaties of alliance and friendship between Great Britain and Iraq of 1922 and 1930 in al-Sayyid 'Abdul-Razzāq al-Husaynī, *Tarīkh al- 'Irāq al-Siyasī al-Ḥadīth* (The Modern Political History of Iraq), (2nd rev. ed.; Sayda, Lebanon: Matba'at al 'Irfān, 1958), II, pp. 30-38, 41-42, 45-81, 204-234; Husayn Fawzi al-Najjār, *Al-Siyāsāh wa al-Istrātījīyyah fī al-Sharq al-Awṣat* (Politics and Strategy in the Middle East) (Cairo: Maktabat al-Nahḍah al-Maṣriyyah, 1953), pp. 501-504, 510-12, 586-610, 470-471, 476, and for the Treaty of Friendship and Alliance between Egypt and Great Britain, see pp. 592-609 of the same work; and Nicola A. Ziyadeh, *Syria and Lebanon* (Beirut: Lebanon Bookshop, 1968), pp. 53-55.

[84] See J. Hurewitz, "Origins of the Rivalry" in *Soviet American Rivalry*, ed. by J. Hurewitz, pp. 1-7.

[85] We should note that in the Baghdad Pact, which after the withdrawal of Iraq changed its name to the Central Treaty Organization (CENTO), Britain was used as the Western connection and the United States was formally only an associate member. Thus, the United States was "in the Pact but not of it, a participant for practical purpose but without the legal commitments." See N. D. Palmer and H. C. Perkins, *International Relations*, pp. 583-584.

[86] See Alvin Z. Rubinstein, (ed.), *The Foreign Policy of the Soviet Union* (2nd ed; New York: Random House, 1966), pp. 379-392, 396-397.

[87] In this book, analysis of contemporary Muslim states' political strategies stops at 1973. I hope to pursue analysis of later major policies in later editions for the benefit of better understanding of Islam and Islamic guidelines in Muslim policies toward internal conflicts, foreign intrusions and their relation to superpower strategies including (Star Wars) the strategic defense initiative. See G. W. Choudhury, *Pakistan's Relations with India* (Meerut, India: Meenakshi Prakashan, 1971), pp. 1-8; Muhammed Aḥsan. *Pakistan and the Great Powers* (Karāchi: Council of Pakistan Studies, 1970), pp. 32-62; Moḥammad Ayūb Khān, *Pakistan Perspective* (Washington, D.C.: The Pakistānī Embassy, n.d.), pp. 17-34; and Muztaba Razui, *The Frontiers of Pakistan* (Karachi: National Publishing House, 1971), pp. 3-11 and 143-168.

[88] Fayez A. Sayegh, "Islam and Neutralism," and P. J. Vaikiotis, "Islam and the Foreign Policy of Egypt," in *Islam and International Relations*, ed. J. H. Proctor, pp. 60-93 and 120-157.

[89] We use the word West in this section on contemporary major foreign policies to mean only Western Europe and the United States.

[90] See Bayard Dodge, "The Significance of Religion in 'Arab Nationalism," in *Islam and International Relations*, ed. J. H. Procter, pp. 112-113.

[91] See Arnold Toynbee, *Civilization on Trial* and *The World and the West* (Cleveland: World Publishing Co., 1958), pp. 182-187; D. Smith, *Religion and Development*, pp. 21-22; and M. Abū-Zahrah, *Al- 'Alāqāt al-Dawliyyah*, pp. 19-46. Also take note of the Qur'ānic verses quoted in this chapter concerning the basic principles and values of Islam.

Appendix

Chapter 1

1. See A. Hoūrānī, *Arabic Thought*, pp. 150, 153, 235, and 272; Jerome N.D. Anderson and Norman J. Coulson, *Islamic Law in Contemporary Cultural Change* (unpublished essay writtin in connection with research work for the "Enzyklopadia des Kulturwandels im 20. Jahrhundert." The author of this thesis owes Professor Coulson special thanks for making this paper available to him. See also Majid Khadduri, "From Religious to National Law," *Modernization of the Arab World*, ed. by Jack H. Thompson and Robert D. Reischauer (New York: Nostrand, 1966), p. 41.

   From this point on, the abbreviations A.C. and A.H. will be omitted. However, the dates will be written down in the same order.

2. See A. al- 'Aqqād, *Mayuqal'an al-Islām*, pp. 129–34; 'Abdul Ḥamīd Mutawallī, *Mabādi' Niẓām al-Ḥukm fī al-Islām: Ma'a al-Muqāranah bi-al-Mabādi' al-Dastūriyyah al-Ḥadīthah* (wa bihi baban Tamhidiyyan 'an Maṣadir al-Aḥkām al-Das-tūriyyah fī al-Sharī'ah al-Islāmiyyah wa Manahij (aw Madāris) al-Tafsīr fi al-Fiqh al-Islāmī) (Principles of Political Systems in Islām: in Comparison with Modern Constitutional Principles (with two introductory chapters about "Sources of Constitutional rules in the Islamic Sharī'ah" and Methods [or Schools] of Interpretation in Islāmic jurisprudence. (Alexandria, Egypt: Dār al-Ma'ārif, 1966), pp. vii-xviii, 7-35, 270-273 and 381-89; 'Abdul Wahhāb Khallāf, *'Ilm 'Uṣūl al Fiqh* (The Science of 'Uṣūl al-Fiqh), (8th ed. Kuwait: al-Dār al-Kuwaitiyyah, 1968), pp. 11-15; 'Abdul Wahhāb Khallāf, *Maṣādir al-Tashrī' al-Islāmī fimā lā Naṣṣa fīh* (The Sources for Islāmic Legislation in Matters for Which There is No Direct Text), 3rd ed., (Kuwait: Dār al-Qalam, 1972) pp. 7-17; J.N.D. Anderson, *Islāmic Law in the Modern World*, (New York: New York University Press, 1959), pp. 2-16; Muḥammad Abū-Zahrah, *'Uṣūl al Fiqh*, (Cairo: Dār al Fikr al 'Arabi, 1957), pp. 3-6 and 379-401; Muṣtafā Aḥmed al Zarqā', *Al-Fiqh al-Islāmī fī Thawbihi al-Jadīd al Madkhal al-Fiqhī* (Reintroduction of the Islāmic Fiqh, vol. 1, In-

troduction to [Islāmic] Jurisprudence), (7th rev. ed., Beirūt: Dār al-Fikr, n.d.) pp. 3-5 and 30-32; and N.J. Coulson, *Islāmic Law*, pp. 6-20, 75-102 and 223-25.

3. The writings on the science of *Fiqh* explain the role and the process of *'ijtihād* and deductions of juristic interpretations and opinions (*al-'Ārā' wa al-Madhāhib al-fiqhiyyah*) from the basic sources (al-Qur'ān and *Sunnah*) in leading to diverse positions. Later on in the course of Muslim history this diversity and duality became more felt in the decisions taken by the sultans. They sanctioned and authorized one opinion or another or acted on their own. Thus there usually existed a gap between what the manuals of *Fiqh* said and what was done by the Muslim laymen and the authorities. Consequently works of *Fiqh* in the modern western sense should be regarded as sources of law. This is very clear in the political sphere as well as in the field of *Siyar* works (relation among nations).
   See: 'Abdul-Wahhāb Khallāf, *Khulāṣat Tārīkh al-Tashrī' al-Islāmī* (The Essence of the History of Islāmic Law), (9th ed., Kuwait: Dār al-Qalam, 1971), pp. 23-49 and 65-82; Muḥammad Abū-Zahrah, *Al-'Imām Zayd: Ḥayātuh wa'aṣruh- 'Ārā'uhu wa fiqhuh* (Imām Zayd: His Life, His Age, His Opinions and His Fiqh) (Cairo: Dāral-Fikr al- 'Arabī, 1959), pp. 11-17, 173-179, and 463-481; Muḥammad Yūsuf Mūsā, *Al-Fiqh al-Islāmī: Madkhal li-Dirāsatihi; Niẓām al-Mu' āmalāt fihi* (Islamic Jurisprudence: An Introduction for its Study and its Approach to Legal Interactions), 3rd ed., (Cairo: Dār al-Kutub al-Ḥad īthah, 1958), pp. 11-83; N.J. Coulson, *Islāmic Law*, pp. 86-88 and 147-48; Sa'īd Ramaḍān, *Three Major Problems Confronting the World of Islām* (Takoma Park, Crescent Publications, n.d.), pp. 1-6; Shihāb al-Dīn Abū-al- 'Abbās Aḥmad Ibn Idrīs al-Qarafī (d. 684/1285), *Al-Iḥkām fī Tamyīz al Fatāwā 'an al-Aḥkām wa Taṣarrufāt al-Qāḍī wa al- 'Imām* (The Perfect Work—Distinguishing Legal Opinions from [Judicial and Executive] Decisions and Functions of the Judge and the Imam), ed. by 'Abdul-Fattāḥ Abū-Ghuddah, (Halah, Syria: Maktab al-Maṭbū'āt al-Islāmiyyah, 1967), pp. 75-85; Wahbah al-Ziḥaylī, *'Āthār al-Ḥarb fī al-Fiqh al-Islāmī: Dirāsah Muqāranah* (The Effects of War in the Islamic Jurisprudence: A Comparative Study), 2nd ed. (Damascus: Al-Maktab al-Hadīthah, 1965), pp. 130, 135.

Chapter 2

4. See: Albert H. Hourānī, "Minorities," in *The Contemporary Middle East: Tradition and Innovation*," Benjamin Rivlin and Joseph S. Szyliowicz (New York: Random House, 1965), pp. 205-217; Amīr Hassān Siddīqī, *Non-Muslim Rule* (Karachi: Jamiyatul Falāḥ Publication) pp. 55-63; M. al-Bahī, *Al-Fikr al-Islāmī*, p. 487; Roderic H. Davison, *Turkey* (England Cliffs, N.J.: Prentice Hall, 1968), pp. 78-108; Sidney Nettleton Fisher, *The Middle East: A History*, 2nd ed. (New York: Alfred A. Knopf, 1969), pp. 295-320; and Thomas Naff, "Reform and the Conduct of Ottoman Diplomacy in the Reign of Selim III: 1789–1807," *Journal of the American Oriental Society* 83:6 (1963), pp. 301-302; also see for documents on capitulations and minorities. J. C. Hurwitz, *Diplomacy in the Middle East: A Documentary Record: 1535*–1914, (New York: 1956), Vol. 1, 20, 24-32, 113-116, 149-53, 164-165, and Vol. 2, 2-3 and 127-128. For the Syrian Lebanese Case, see the three-volume work of Philip and Fred al-Khāzin, *Majmu'at al Muharrarāt al-Siyāsīyah wa al-Mufawaḍāt al-Dawliyyah 'an Sūriyyā wa Lubnān: 1840*–1910 (Collection of International Political Documents and Negotiations about Syria and Lebanon: 1840–1910), (Beirūt: Matba'at al-Ṣabr, 1910).
5. See N.J. Coulson, *A History of Islāmic Law*, pp. 75-85 and 202-203; M. Khadduri, "From Religious to National Law," in *Modernization of the Arab World*, ed. J.H. Thompson and E.R.D. Reischauer (New York: van Nostrand, 1966), pp. 40-41; N.Y. Mūsā, *Al-Fiqh al-Islāmī*, pp. 27-61; and S. Ramaḍan, *Islāmic Law*, 27-30.
6. See A. Hourānī, *Arabic Thought*, pp. 157-160; Muḥammad Husayn, *Al-Islām wa al-Ḥaḍārah al-Gharbiyyah* (Islam and Western Civilization) (Beirūt: Dār al-Irshād, 1969), pp. 91-104; and W.C. Smith, *Islām*, pp. 55-73.
7. It is to be noted that *ḍarūrah* (necessity), being part of the principle of *maṣlaḥah* (public interest) of the Classical Methodology, and *taqlīd* worked together in the process of borrowing political ideas and institutions from the West. See for *ḍarūrah* and *maṣlaḥah*, Wahbah al-Ẓuhaylī, *Naẓariyyat al-Ḍarūrah al-Shar'iyyah Muqāranah ma'a al-Qānūn al-Waḍ'ī (Theory of Necessity in Islamic Law in Comparison with Man-Made Law) (Damascus: Maktabat al-Fārābī, 1969)*, pp. 49-53, 64-69, and 140-272.

Chapter 3

8. H.A. Sharābī "Islām and Modernization in The Arab World" in *Modernization of the Arab World*, J.H. Thompson and R.O. Reischauer ed., p. 32; H.A.R. Gibb, *Modern Trends in Islām*, p. 66; Mālik ibn Nabī, *Wijhat al- 'Ālam al-Islāmī* (The Direction of The Muslim World) 'Abdul-Ṣabūr Shāhīn trans., Mushkilāt al-Ḥaḍārah, 2nd ed. (Beirūt: Dār al-Fikr, 1970), p. 77. Also A. Hourānī, *Arabic Thought*, pp. 372-73, for a brief introduction about Mālik ibn Nabi; Malcolm H. Kerr, *Islāmic Reform: The Political and Legal Theories of Muḥammad 'Abduh and Rashīd Riḍa*, (Berkeley: Univ. of Calif. Press, 1966) pp. 221-22; A. A. Maḥmud, *Al-Da'wah al-Islāmiyyah*, pp. 317-342; M. F. Abū-Ḥadīd, "Risālat al-Salām wa al Taḥrīr" (The Mission of Peace and Liberation), in *Al-Muḥāḍrāt al- 'Āmmah* second ed., The Public Administration for Islamic Culture of Al-Azhar, pp. 367-391; and Maḥmūd Shaltūt, *Al-Islām wa al- 'Alāqāt al-Dawliyyah fī al-Silm wa al-Ḥarb* (Cairo: Maktab Shaykh al-Jāmi' al-Azhar li al-Shu'ūn al-'Āmmah, 1951), pp. 26-69.
9. See 'Allāl al-Fāṣī, *Maqāsid al-Sharī'ah al-Islāmiyyah wa Makārimaha* (Purposes of the Islamic Sharī'ah and its Noble Advantages) (Casablanca, Morocco: Maktabat al-Wiḥdah al- 'Arabiyyah, 1963), 82-194, and Muḥammad Ma'rūf al-Dawālībī, *Al-Madkhal ila 'ilm 'uṣūl al-fiqh* (Introduction to the Science of Sources and Methods of Islamic Jurisprudence), 5th rev ed. (Beirut: Dār al-'Ilm Lil-Malāyīn, 1965), pp. 256-348.

Glossary

Following are definitions for some of the Arabic terms frequently used in the text.

'Adl: justice.
'Ahd: pledge, treaty.
'Ahl al-Kitāb: the tolerated respected and protected people, the People of the Book (primarily Christians and Jews).
Allāh: God, the Creator and Sustainer of the universe.
'Amān: safe conduct or pledge of security.
'Amīr al-Mu'minīn: the Commander of the Faithful, the Caliph.
'Asbāb al-Tanzīl: direct reasons for the revelation of the Qur'ān.
'Aṣl: singular of *'uṣūl*.
'Athār: traditional, *aḥadīth*.
Dār al- 'Ahd (alternatively, Dar al-Ṣulḥ): non-Muslim territories involved in treaty agreements with a Muslim state (term coined by al-Shāfi'ī).
Dār al-Ḥarb: non-Muslim territories hostile to Muslims (opposite of Dār al-Islam).
Dār al-Ṣulh: see Dār al- 'Ahd.
Dār al-Islām: territories and societies in which Muslims are free and secure.
al-Dhimmah: permanent constitutional agreement between Muslim political authorities and non-Muslim subjects whereby subjects receive protection and peaceful relations in exchange for acceptance of Muslim rule and payment of *jizyah*.
Dhimmī: non-Muslim subject of a Muslim state, pl. Dhimmiyyūn.
Fatwā: legal and/or religious judgment, pl. Fatāwā.
Fiqh: the rules and injunctions deduced from the *Sharī'ah* (Qur'ān and *Sunnah*); sum of Muslim legal decisions and opinions; Muslim jurisprudence; the principal vehicle of reflection for classical and traditional Muslim intellectuals.
Ḥadīth: saying; a tradition of the prophet; the (PBUH), (pl. Aḥādīth), see Sunnah.

al-Ḥarbī: an enemy's subjects.
Ḥilf: alliance.
Hudnah: truce.
'Ijmā': consensus.
'Ijtihād: use of human reason (*'aql*) in elaboration and interpretation of the *Shari'ah*; original juristic opinions.
'Imām: Caliph; Muslim leading congregational prayer; a pious Islamic intellectual authority.
'Imāmah: Caliphate.
al-'Istiḥsān: juristic preference.
Jihād: struggle; a Muslim's striving to fulfill his Islamic responsibility, both in outward actions and in inward correction of his own mistakes; working or fighting in the cause of Allah.
Jizyah: tax paid by non-Muslim subjects in a Muslim state, in return for state services; often called poll-tax.
Khilāfah: the caliphate; vicegerency and custodianship on earth.
Khalīfat Rasūl al-Allah: successor of Allah's Messenger; caliph.
Kharāj: land tax paid by non-Muslims to the Muslim state.
Khilāfah: the caliphate.
al-Khulafā' al-Rāshidūn: the first four caliphs.
Makkah: Mecca.
al-Maṣlaḥah or al-Māṣaliḥ al-Mursalah: public interest.
Mīthāq: covenant, pact.
Mu'āhadah: treaty.
Mu'āhid: singular of Mu'ahididūn.
Mu'āhidūn: non-Muslim parties to peace agreement with Muslim state.
Mushrikūn: making partners (literary); those who attribute partners or associates to God (religious); therefore, pagans.
Musta'man: enemy subjects granted safe conduct to enter Muslim territory.
Muwādā'ah: truce, peace.
Nabdh: termination of agreement by Muslim side.
Naskh: abrogation; nullification; suspension.
Naṣṣ: text.
Qiyās: analogy.
Qur'ān: the Holy Book of Islam; the Word of Allah.
Quraysh: Arab tribe of Makkah.
Riddah: apostasy.
Ṣaghār: humiliation.

Ṣahīfah al-Madīnah: constitutional agreement between the Prophet and the Jewish tribes of Madīnah.

Sharī'ah: the will of God for human conduct revealed through the Prophet Muḥammad (PBUH); the Qur'ān and *Sunnah*; Islamic law: fiqh.

Sīrah: the biography of the Prophet (PBUH).

Siyar: account of Muslim external achievements; juristic source for Muslim law of nations.

Ṣulḥ: peace treaty, truce.

al-Sunnah: approved ways, the reported sayings of the Prophet (PBUH) and, all actions performed or consented to by the Prophet (PBUH); *al-ḥadīth*.

Sunnīyyūn: followers of the four schools of Muslim jurisprudence based on the Sunnah; true followers of the Prophet (PBUH); majority of Muslim peoples.

Talfīq: piecing-together.

Taqlīd: imitation.

'Ulamā': Muslim scholars, theologians, and learned men; sing. 'Ālim.

'Ummah: community, people, nation, group of people.

al- 'Urf: the mores of a society.

'Uṣūl: source and method of classical Muslim jurisprudence, i.e., Qur'ān, *Sunnah, Qiyās, Ijmā',* and the other rules and measures of *al-Ijtihād*.

'Uṣūl al-Fiqh: see 'uṣūl.

Zakāh: the poor-due; alms tax paid by Muslims.

SOURCE MATERIALS

Classical Muslim jurists perceived Muslims, in spite of their diversity, as one *'ummah.* [1] This perception of *'ummah* continued in spite of the shift of emphasis and focus from political to moral aspects. The Muslim jurists continued to deal with matters of external relations as basically questions of war and peace vis-a-vis non-Muslim oppressors. Although the affairs of non-Muslim minorities and rebels were dealt with under the heading of *jihād* (struggle) or *siyar* (account of Muslims' achievements), these matters were considered to be internal matters of *Dār-al-Islām* (the Muslim polity).

To understand the classic Muslim thought on international relations, however, we have to discuss the juristic questions of *ahl-al-baghy* (rebels), *khīlafah* or *'imāmah* (caliphate), *Dhimmiyyūn* (the non-Muslim subjects of the Muslim state), and *Mu'āhidūn* (non-Muslim parties to a peace agreement with the Muslim state), and *Musta'manūn* (enemy's subjects granted safe conduct by Muslims to enter Muslim territory). These have to be coupled with the question of *jihād* by *Dār-al-Islām* against *Dār al-Ḥarb* (the non-Muslim states or territories at war with the Muslim state), in order to cover the following three aspects of international relations: relations among Muslim states, relations among Muslim and non-Muslim states, and non-Muslim minorities within Muslim states.

The source material used in this work, besides secondary works on the subject, are the basic works of the *Sunnī fiqh* (jurisprudence of the majority of Muslim peoples), which were originally written in Arabic. These include:

1. Basic works on *jihād* such as *Mudawwanatu-Mālik,* [2] *Sharaḥ al-Siyar al-Kabīr,* [3] *Al-'Umm,* [4] *Al-Mughnī,* [5] and *'Aḥkām 'Ahl al-Dhimmah* of Iby Qayyim al-Jawziyyah. [6]

2. Basic works of *fiqh* on *khilāfah*, such as *Al-Aḥkām al-Sulṭāniyyah* of 'Abū-Ya'lā al-Farrā' (al-Ḥanbalī) and that of al-Māwardī (al-Shafi'ī, [7] and *Al-Siyāsah al-Shar'iyyah* by 'Ibn Taymiyyah. [8]

3. Basic works of *tafsīr* (commentary on the Qur'ān) by classical authorities such as al-Ṭabarī, al-Rāzī, and Ibn Kathīr. The classical works of *tafsīr*, such as those by 'Ibn Kathīr or al-Ṭabarī, provide substantial information on the actual situations that led to specific revelations of the Qur'ānic verses *'Asbāb al-Tanzīl*) and on the question of abrogation (*al-nāskh*), besides the traditions and opinions of the first two generations of *al-Ṣaḥābah* (the Companions of the Prophet (PBUH)) and *al-Tābi'īn* (the scholars who worked with them).

4. Basic works on *asbāb al-tanzīl* (direct reasons for revelations), such as *Asbāb al-Nuzūl* of al-Wahidī al-Nayasābūrī, [9] and *Kitāb al-I'tibār fi al-Nāsikh wa al-Mansūkh* by 'Ibn Ḥazm al-Hamadhānī.[10]

5. Basic works of *al-ḥadīth* (containing the *Sunnah*, the teachings of the Prophet), especially *al-Siḥāḥ* (the accepted authentic works on tradition by *Sunni* Muslims) of al-Bukharī and that of Muslim.

6. Basic works of *al-sīrah* (Biography of the Prophet (PBUH)), and the early Muslim period such as *Al-Sīrah al-Nabawiyyah*[11] of 'Ibn Hishām.

In handling these classical materials including the great Muslim juristic works, we have to be aware of difficulties in structure and terminology. Although these works deal with the same areas, their structure is not always unified. For example, questions related to the area of external relations may be discussed as part of the issue of applying criminal law to *Dhimmiyyūn*. It can be found either under sections dealing with *Dhimmiyyūn* or hudud (Islamic criminal law) or both.

The terms used are not always standardized either. While the issue of war and peace is discussed under the heading of *siyar*, its basic elements or in most works are dealt with under the title of *'al-jizyah* (poll tax). Similarly, the subject of rebels is commonly handled under the title of *'ahl al-baghy*, but 'Ibn Rushd (Averroes) deals with it in his book *Bidayatu al-Mujtahid*[12] under the title of *al-ḥarbī*.

FOOTNOTES for Source Materials

[1] The word *'ummah* usually translates as nation. The Qur'ān uses the term *'ummah* in more than one sense, such as a group of people, people collectively or in general, community, and nation. See 'Abbās Maḥmud al- 'Aqqād, *Māyugāl 'an al-Islām* (On What Has Been Written About Islam) (2nd ed.; Beirūt: Dār al-Kitāb al' 'Arabī, 1966), pp. 183-186.

[2] The following edition has been used for reference: Malik ibn Anas al-Asbuḥī, *Al-Madawanah al-Kubrā* (The Great Written Work [of Jurisprudence]) (Beirūt: Dār-Sadir, 1905).

[3] See also Muḥammad ibn al-Ḥasan al-Shaybānī, *Sharḥ al-Siyar al-Kabīr* (Commentary on the Book of the Great Siyar), dictated by Muḥammad ibn Aḥmad al-Sarakhsī and ed. by Ṣalāḥ al-Munajjid (Cairo: Ma'had al-Makhṭūṭāt bi-Jāmi'at al-Duwal al 'Arabīyyah, 1958). Notice that the book (*Kitāb*) belongs to al-Shaybānī while the commentary (*Sharḥ*) belongs to al-Sarakhsī.

[4] See Abū- 'Abdullāh Muḥammad ibn Idrīs al-Shāfi'ī, *Al-Umm* (literally, The Mother, meaning a basic work of jurisprudence) (series Kitāb al-Sha'b; Cairo: Dār al-Sha'b, 1903).

[5] See Abū-Muḥammad 'Abdullah ibn Aḥmad ibn Qudāmah (d. 620/1223), *Al-Mughnī* (the Sufficient) (Cairo: Maṭba'at al- 'Aṣimah, n.d.,).

[6] See Al-Shaykh Shamsuddīn Abū'Abdullāh Muḥammad Ibn Abū-Bakr Ibn Qayyim al-Jawziyyah, *Aḥkām ahl-al-Dhimmah* (The Islamic Rules of the Dhimmi peoples), Ṣubḥī al-Ṣāliḥ, ed. (Damascus: Maṭba'at Jāmi'at Dimashq, 1961).

[7] See Abū-al-Ḥasan 'Alī ibn Muḥammad ibn Ḥabīb al-Baṣrī al-Baghdādī al-Māwardī (d. 450/1057), *al-Aḥkām al-Ṣulṭānīyah wa al-Wilāyāt al-Dīniyyah* (The Ordinance of Government and the Religious Offices) (2nd ed.; Cairo: Sharikat Maktabat wa Matba'at Musṭafā al-Bābī al-Ḥalabī wa Awlāduh bi-Miṣr, 1966), and Abū-Ya'la Muḥammad Ibn al-Husayn al-Farra' al-Ḥanbalī (d. 458/1065), *al-Aḥkām al-Sulṭānīyah* (The Ordinance of Government), Muḥammad Ḥāmid al-Faqī, ed. (Cairo: Sharikat Maktabat wa Maṭba'at Musṭafā al-Bābī al-Ḥalabī wa Awlāduh bi-Miṣr, 'Abbās wa Muḥammad Mahmūd al Bābī wa Shurakāhum Khulafa, 1966).

[8] See Taqiyal-Dīn Aḥmad ibn 'Abdul-Ḥalīm Ibn Taymiyyah, *Al-Siyāsah al-Shar'iyyah fī Iṣlaḥ al-Rā'ī wa al-Ra'iyyah* (The Policies of the *Sharī'ah* in Reforming the Affairs of the Ruler and the Ruled), introduction by Professor Muḥammad al-Mubārak, Rawa'i al-Fikr al-Islāmī no. 1 (Beirūt: Dār al-Kutub al- 'Arabiyyah, n.d.).

[9] See Abū-al-Hasan 'Alī ibn Aḥmad al-Wāḥidī al-Nāysābūrī (d. 468/1075), *Asbāb al-Nuzūl* (The [Direct] Reasons for the Revelations [of Qur'ān]) (Cairo: Sharikat wa Maṣtba'at Muṣtafā al-Bābī al-Ḥalabī wa Awladuh, 1959).

[10] See Abū-Bakr Muḥammad ibn Mūsa ibn Ḥazm al-Hamadhānī, *Kitāb al-I'tibār fī al-Nāsikh wa al-Mansūkh min al- 'Athār* (Book of Lessons about the Abrogator and the Abrogated of the Traditions), Rātib al-Ḥakīm, ed. (Hioms, Syria: Matba'at al-Andalus, 1966).

[11] See Abū-Muḥammad 'Abdul-Malik ibn Hishām al Ma'afirī, al-Sīrah al-Nabawiyyah (The Bibliography of the Prophet), Muhammad al Saqqā, Ibrāhīm al-Ibiārī, and Aḥmad Shalabī, eds. (2nd ed.; Cairo: Sharikat Maktbaat wa Maṭba'at Muṣtafā al-Bābī al-Ḥalabī wa Awladuh bi-Miṣr, 1955).

[12] Abū-al-Walīd Muḥammad ibn Aḥmad ibn Muḥammad ibn Rushd al Qurṭubī al-Andalusī (al-Shahīr bi ibn Rushd al-Ḥafīd) (Averroes), *Bidāyat al-Mujtahid wa Nihāyat al-Muqtaṣid* (A Beginning for the Ambitious and an End for the Contented), edition of the late Muhammad Amīn al-Khānjī (Cairo: Maktabat al-Khānjī, n.d.).

BIBLIOGRAPHY

References (Arabic)

Al-Bukhārī, Abī 'Abdullāh Muḥammad 'Ibn 'Ism'āil, *Matn al-Bukhārī bi Ḥāshiyat al-Sindī* (The Bukhari's Collection of Ḥadīth with the Commentary of al-Sindi. (Cairo: Dar Iḥyā'al-Kutub al- 'Arabīyyah, 1960).

Ḥamidullah, Muḥammad, *Majmu' Wathāi'q al-Siyāsīyyah li'al 'Ahd al-Nabawīwa al-Khilāfah al-Rāshidah* (Political Detriments Concerning the Period of the Prophet and the Rightly Guided Caliphs. (Beirūt: Dār al-Irshād li'al-Tibā'ah wa al-Nashr wa al-Tawzī', 1959).

Ibn Manzūr, Al-Imām al- 'Allāmah Abī al-Faḍl Jamāl al-Dīn Muhammad Ibn Muqarrin, *Lisān al- 'Arab* (The Arab Language). (Cairo: Al-Maṭba'ah al-Kubrā, 1882).

Kaḥḥālah, 'Umar Riḍā, *Mu'jam al-Mu'allifin: Tarājim Muṣannifī al-Kutub al- 'Arabiyyah* (Index of Authors: Bibliography of Authors of Arabic Books) (Damascus: Al-Maktabah al- 'Arabiyyah, 1957).

Al-Khāzin, Philip and Fred, *Majmū'at al-Muḥarrarāt al-Siyasiyyah wa al-Mufāwaḍāt al-Dawliyyah 'an Sūriyya wa Lubnān: 1840-1910* (Collection of International Political Documents and Negotiations About Syria and Lebanon: 1840-1910) (Beirūt: Maṭba'at al-Ṣabr, 1910).

Al-Mujaddidī, Al-Muftī al-Sayyid Muḥammad 'Amīm al-Iḥsān, ed., *Qwā'id al-Fiqh wa hiya Taḥtawī'alā Khams Rasā'il* (The Rules [and Definitions of Terms] of Muslim [Ḥanāfī] Jurisprudence) (Dacca: The Secretary Research and Publication Committee, Madrasah-i-Aliah, 1961).

Al-Mundhirī, Al-Ḥāfiz ['Abdul- 'Aẓīm Ibn 'Abdul-Qawiyy], *Mukhtaṣar Saḥīh Muslim* (Summary of Muslim's [Selection of the] Authentic [Sunnah]), edited by Nāṣir al-Dīn al-Albānī (Kuwait: The Ministry of Endowments and Islamic Affairs, 1969).

Nusayr, 'Āydah Ibrāhīm, *Al-Kutub al- 'Arabiyyah allatī Nushirat fī al-Jumhūriyyah al- 'Arabiyyah al-Muttiḥidah (Miṣr) Bayna 'Amay 1926-1940* (The Arabic Books Which Were Published in the United Arab Republic [Egypt] Between 1926-1940) (Cairo: The American University of Cairo, 1969).

Al-Rāzī, Muḥammad Ibn Abī-Bakr, *Mukhtār al-Ṣiḥāḥ* (Selection of Correct Definitions [an Arabic dictionary]) (Cairo: Sharikat wa Maṭba'at Muṣṭafā al-Bābī al-Ḥalabī wa Awlāduh, 1950).

Al-Tabrīzī, Walī al-Din Muḥammad Ibn 'Abdullah al-Khaṭīb al-Imārī, *Mishkāt al-Maṣābīh* (Collections of Authentic Traditions of the Prophet), edited by Muḥammad Nāsir al-Dīn al-Albānī, (Damascus: Al-Maktab al-Islāmī, 1961.)

References (English)

'Alī, 'Abdullah Yūsuf, *The Holy Qur'ān, Text, Translation and Commentary* (Washington, D.C.: The American International Printing Co., 1945).

Gibb, H.A.R., and others, *The Encyclopaedia of Islām* (new ed.; Leiden: E.J. Brill, Luzac and Co., 1960).

Hurewitz, J. C., *Diplomacy in the Near and Middle East: A Documentary Record 1535-1914* (New York: Van Nostrand, 1956).

Khān, Muḥammad Muḥsin, *The Translation of the Meaning of Saḥīḥ al-Bukhārī* (Cyranwala, Pakistan: Sethi Straw Board Mills Conversions, Ltd., n.d.)

Pearson, J.D., compiler, with the assistance of Julia F. Ashton; *Index Islamicus: A Catalogue of Articles on Islāmic Subjects in Periodicals and Other Collective Publications* (Cambridge: W. Heffer and Sons, Ltd., 1972).

Peaslee, Amos J., *Constitutions of Nations*, prepared by Dorothy Peaslee Xydis (The Hague: Martinus Nijhoff, 1965).

Pickthall, Muḥammad Marmaduke, *The Meaning of the Glorious Korān* (New York: New American Library, n.d.)

[Al-Tabrīzī], Waliy al-Dīn Muḥammad Ibn 'Abdullah al-Khaṭīb al-'Imārī, *Mishkāt al-Maṣābīh* [sic], translated with explanatory notes by James Robson (Lahore, Pakistan: Sr. Muḥammad Ashraf, 1963).

Works Consulted (Arabic)

'Abduh, Muḥammad, *Al-Islām wa al-Naṣrāniyyah Ma'a al- 'Ilm wa al-Madaniyyah* (Islām and Christianity with Regard to Knowledge and

Civilization) (Cairo: Maktabat wa Maṭba'at Muḥammad 'Alī Sabih wa Awlāduh, 1954).

'Abduh, Muḥammad; *Al-Islām wa al-Radd 'Alā Muntaqidīh* (Islām and Answers for Its Critics) (Cairo: Al-Maktabah al-Tijārīyyah al-Kubrā, 1928.)

Abū-Zahrah, Muḥammad, *Al- 'Alāqāt al-Dāwlīyyah fī al-Islām* (International Relations in Islām), Al-Maktabah al- 'Arabīyyah (Cairo: Al-Dār al-Qawmīyyah li al-Ṭibā'ah wa al-Nashr, 1964).

Abū-Zahrah, Muḥammad, *Al-Imām Zāyd: Hayātuh wa' asruh- 'Arā'uhu wa Fiqhuh* (Imām Zayd: His Life, His Age, His Opinions and His Fiqh) (Cairo: Dār al-Fikr al- 'Arabī, 1959).

Abū-Zahrah, Muḥammad, *Al-Mujtama'al' Insānī fī Ẓil al-Islām (Human Society under the Rule of Islām) (Beirūt: Dār al-Fikr, n.d).*

Abū-Zahrah, Muḥammad, *Ibn Ḥanbal: Ḥayātuh wa' as ruh- 'Arā'uhu wa Fiqhuh*, (Ibn Ḥanbal: His Life, His Time, His Opinions, and His Fiqh) (Cairo: Dār al-Fikr al- 'Arabī, 1947).

Abū-Zahrah, Muḥammad, *Mālik: Ḥayātuh wa 'asruh 'Arā'uhu wa Fiqhuh* (Mālik: His Life, His Age, His Opinions and His Fiqh) (Cairo: Dār al-Fikr al- 'Arabī, 1963).

Abū-Zahrah, Muḥammad, *'Usūl al-Fiqh* (Methodology of Muslim Jurisprudence) (Cairo: Dār al-Fikr al- 'Arabi, 1957).

Abū-Zāyd, Muṣṭafa, *Al-Nāsikh wa al-Mansūkh: Dirāsah Tashrī'iyyāh Tārīkhīyyāh Naqdiyyāh* (The Abrogator and the Abrogated: A Juristic, Historical and Critical Study) (Cairo: Dār al-Fikr al- 'Arabī, 1963).

'Alī, Jawād, *Al-Mufaṣṣal fī Tārīkh al- 'Arabī Qabl al-Islām* (Detailed Account of Arab History Before Islām) (Beirūt: Dār al- 'Ilm li-al-Malaayīn, 1970).

Amīn, Aḥmad, *Fajr al-Islām: Yabḥath 'An al-Ḥayāh al- 'Aqliyyāh fī Ṣadr al-Islām ilā 'Ākhir al-Dāwlah al- 'Amawīyyah* (The Dawn of Islām: Discussion on Intellectual Life in the Early Period of Islām Until the End of the Umayyad Dynasty) (9th ed., Cairo: Maktabat al-Nahḍah al-Maṣriyyah, 1964).

Amīn, Aḥmad, *Yāwm al-Islām* (The Day of Islām) (Cairo: Mu'assat al-Khānjī, 1958).

Al- 'Aqqād, 'Abbās Maḥmūd, *Ḥaqā'iqi al-Islām wa Abāṭil Khusūmih* (The

Facts of Islām and the Allegations of Its Adversaries) (3rd ed.; Cairo: Dār al-Qalam, 1966).

Al- 'Aqqād, 'Abbās M., *Al-Islām fī al-Qarn al-'Ishrīn: Ḥāḍiruh wa Mustaqbaluh* (Islām in the Twentieth Century: Its Present and Its Future) (2d. ed.; Beirūt: Dār al-Kitāb al- 'Arabī, 1969).

Al- 'Aqqād, 'Abbās Maḥmūd, *Māyuqāl 'an al-Islām* (On What Has Been Written About Islām), (2nd ed.; Beirūt: Dār al-Kitāb al 'Arabī, 1966).

Arslān, Shakīb, *Limādha Ta'akhara al-Muslimūn wa Limādhā Taqaddama Ghāyruhum* (Why Muslims Are Declining and Why Others Are Progressing) (Beirūt: Dār Maktabat al-Ḥayāh, 1965).

Badawī, 'Abdulrahmān, ed., *Al-Trāth al-Yūnānī fī al-Ḥaḍārah al-Islāmīyyah: Dirāsāt li Kibār al-Mustashriqīn* (The Greek Heritage in the Islāmic Civilization: Studies for Most Important Orientalists) (Cairo: Dār al-Nahḍah al- 'Arabiyyāh, 1965).

Al-Bahī, Muḥammad, *Al-Fikr al-Islāmī al-Ḥadīth wa Ṣilatuh bi al-Isti'mār al-Gharbī* (Contemporary Islāmic Thought and Its Relations to Western Imperialism) (4th ed.; Cairo: Maktabat Wahbah, 1964).

Boer, T.J.: *Tārīkh al-Falsafah fī al-Islām* (History of Philosophy in Islām), translated from German by Muḥammad 'Abdul-Hādī Abū-Riḍah (4th ed.; Cairo: Lajnat al-Ta'līf wa al-Tarjamah wa al-Nashr, 1957).

Darwazah, Muḥammad 'Izzat, *Al-Tafsīr al-Hadīth* (Contemporary Interpretation of the Qur'ān) (Cairo: Maṭba'at 'Isā al-Bābī al-Ḥalabī, 1964).

Fakhrī, Majīd, *Dirāsah fī al-Fikr al- 'Arabī* (Studies in Arabic Thought) (Beirūt: Dār al-Nahār, 1970).

Al-Farra', Abū-Ya'la Muḥammad Ibn al-Ḥusayn, *Al-Aḥkām al-Ṣulṭānīyyah* (The Ordinance of Government), ed. Muḥammad Ḥāmid al-Faqī (Cairo: Sharikat Makṭabat wa Maṭba'at Muṣṭafā al-Bābī al-Ḥalabī wa Awlāduh bi-Misr, 'Abbās wa Muḥammad Maḥmūd al-Bābī wa Shurakahum Khulafa, 1966).

Ghānim, Muḥammad Hāfīẓ, *Mabādi'al-Qānūn al-Dawlī al- 'Am* (Principles of International Law) (4th ed.; Cairo: Maṭba'at Nahḍat Miṣr, 1964).

Al-Ghazālī, Muḥammad, *Al-Islām fī Wajh al-Zaḥf al-Aḥmar* (Islām Fighting Communist Expansion) (Kuwait: Maktabat al- 'Amal, n.d).

Al-Ghazālī, Muḥammad, *Al-Ta'assub wa al-Tasāmuḥ Bāyn al-Masīḥīyyah wa al-Islām: Dahḍ Shubuhāt wa Rad Muftarayāt* (Fanaticism and

Tolerance Between Christianity and Islām: Rebutting and Answering Misunderstandings and False Accusations) (Kuwait: Dār al-Bayān, n.d).

Al-Ghazālī, Muḥammad, *Fiqh al-Sīrah* (Life of the Prophet) (4th ed. Cairo: Dār al-Kutub al-Ḥadīthah, 1964).

Al-Ḥamadhānī, Abū-Bakr Muḥammad Ibn Mūsa Ibn Hazm, *Kitāb al-I'tibār fī al-Nāsikh wa al-Mānsukh Min al' Āthār* (Book of Lessons about the Abrogator and the Abrogated of the Traditions), ed. Rātib al-Ḥakīm (Hims, Syria: Maṭba'at al- 'Andalus, 1966).

Hawātmah, Nāyif, *Azmat al-Thāwrah fī al-Janūb al- 'Arabī: Naqdun wa Taḥlīl* (The Crisis of the Revolution in South Yemen: Analysis and Criticism) (Beirūt: Dār al-Ṭalī'ah, 1968).

Hell, J., *Al-Ḥaḍārah al- 'Arabiyyāh* (Arab Civilization), translated from German by I al- 'Adawī, ed. H. Mu'nis, Al-Alf Kitāb no. 88 (Cairo: Maktabat al-Anglu al-Maṣrīyyah, 1956).

Ḥusāyn, Muḥammad, *Al-Islām wa al-Ḥaḍīah al-Gharbīyyah* (Islām and Western Civilization) (Beirūt: Dār al-Irshād, 1969).

Al-Ḥusāynī, Sayyīd 'Abdul-Razzāq, *Tārīkh al- 'Iraq al-Siyāsī al-Ḥadīth* (The Modern Political History of Irāq) (2nd rev. ed.; Sāydā, Lebanon: Maṭba'at al- 'Irfan, 1958).

Ibish, Yūsuf, *Nuṣūṣ al-Fikr al-Siyāsī al-Islāmī: Al-Imāmah 'Ind al-Sunnah* (Readings in Islāmic Political Theory: The Sunnī Doctrine of the Imāmah) (Beirūt: Dār al-Ṭalī'ah, 1966).

Ibn Anas, Mālik, *Al-Mudawanah al-Kubrā* (The Great Written Work [of Jurisprudence], (Beirūt: Dār Sadir, 1905).

Ibn al- 'Athīr, 'Izz al-Dīn Abī al-Ḥassan 'Alī Ibn Abī al-Karam Muḥammad Ibn 'Abdil-Karīm Ibn 'Abdil Wāḥid al-Shaybānī, *Al-Kāmil fī al-Tārīkh* (The Comprehensive [Study] of History) (Beirut: Dar Beirūt li al-Ṭibā'h wa al-Nashr, 1965).

Ibn Hishām, Abū-Muḥammad 'Abdul-Mālik, *Al-Sīrah al-Nabawīyyah* (The Biography of the Prophet), ed. M. al-Saqqa, I. al-Ibiarī and A. Shalabī (2nd ed.; Cairo: Sharikat Maktabat wa Maṭba'at Muṣṭafā al-Bābī al-Ḥalabī wa Awladuh bi-Miṣr, 1955).

Ibn al-Qāyyim, A. Shāykh Shamsuddin Abū- 'Abdullah Muḥammad Ibn Abī-Bakr, *Aḥkām Ahl al-Dhimmah* (The Islamic Rules of the Dhimmis), ed. Subḥī al-Ṣāliḥ (Damascus: Maṭba'at Jāmi'at Dimashq, 1961).

Ibn Qadāmah, Abū-Muḥammad 'Abdullah Ibn Aḥmad, *Al-Mughnī* (The Sufficient) (Cairo: Maṭba'at al- 'Asimah, n.d).

Ibn Rushd al-Ḥāfid (Averroes), Abū al-Wālik Muḥammad Ibn Aḥmad Ibn Muḥammad Ibn Rushd al-Qurṭubī al-Andalusī', *Bidāyat al-Mujtahid wa Nihāwat al-Muqtaṣid* (A Beginning for the Ambitious and an End for the Contented), the edition of the late Muḥammad Amīn al-Khānjī (Cairo: Maktabat al-Khānjī, n.d).

Ibn Salāmah, Abī al-Qāsim Hibatullāh, *Al-Nāskih wa al-Mansūkh* (The Abrogator and the Abrogated) (2nd ed.; Cairo: Al-Ḥalabī wa Awlāduh bi-Misr, Maḥmud Naṣṣār al-Ḥalalu wa Shurakāh, Khulafa' , 1967).

Ibn Tāymiyyah, Taqiyal-Dīn Aḥmad Ibn 'Abdul-Ḥalīm, *Al-Siyāsah al-Shar'iyyāh fī Iṣlāh al-Ra'i wā al-Ra'iyyah* (The Policies of the Sharī'ah in Reforming the Affairs of the Ruler and the Ruled) (Beirūt: Dār al-Kutub al- 'Arabīyyah, n.d).

Al- 'Ishmāwī, Ḥassan, *Qalbun 'Ākhar li- 'Ajl al-Za'īm* (Another Heart for the Leader) (Beirūt: Dār al-Fatḥ, 1970).

Al-Jammal, 'Abdul-Qādir, *Min Mushkilāt al-Sharq al-Awṣaṭ* (Some of the Middle East's Problems) (Cairo: Maktabat al-Anglo al-Maṣriyyāh, 1955).

Al-Kahlānī, Al-Imām Muḥammad Ibn Ismā'īl, *Subul al-Salām: Sharḥ Bulūgh al-Murām min Adillat al-Aḥkām* (The Ways of Peace: A Commentary on the Attainment of the Desired Support [of Qur'ān and Sunnah] of [the Islāmic] Rules) (Cairo: Al-Maktabah al-Tijāriyyāh al-Kubrā, n.d).

Khallaf, 'Abdul Wahāb, *'Ilm 'Usūl al-Fiqh* (The Science of Usūl al-Fiqh) (8th ed.; Kuwait: al-Dār al-Kuwaitiyyah, 1968).

Khallāf, Abdul Wahāb, *Khulāṣat Tārīkh al-Tashrī' al-Islāmī* (The Essence of the History of Islāmic Law) (9th ed.; Kuwait: Dār al-Qalam, 1971).

Khallaf, Abdul Wahāb, *Maṣādir al-Tashrī' al-Islāmī fīma lā Naṣṣa fīh* (Sources for Islamic Legislation for Matters in Which There Is No Direct Text) (3rd ed.; Kuwait: Dār al-Qalam, 1972).

Khaṭṭab, Maḥmūd Shīt, *Al-Rasūl al-Qā'id* (The Messenger, the Leader) (2nd rev. ed.; Baghdād: Dār Maktabat al-Ḥayah was Maktabat al-Nahḍah, 1960).

Kishk, Muḥammad Jalāl, *Mafāhīm Islāmiyyah: Al-Qāwmīyyah wa al-Ghazw al-Fikrī* (Islāmic Point of View: Nationalism and Cultural Imperialism) (Kuwait: Maktabat al- 'Amal, 1967).

Laylah, Muḥammad Kāmil, Al-Mujtama' al- 'Arabī wa al-Qāwmiyyāh al- 'Arabīyya'h (Arab Society and Arab Nationalism) (Cairo: Dār al-Fikr al- 'Arabī, 1966).

Maḥmasānī, Subhī, *Al- 'Awda' al-Tashri'iyyāh fī al-Duwal al- 'Arabiyyāh; Māḍiha wa Ḥāḍiraha* (Legal System in the Arab States: Past and Present) (3rd rev. ed.; Beirūt: Dār al-'Ilm li al-Malayīn, 1965).

Manṣūr, 'Alī, *Muqāranah Bāyn al-Shāri'ah al-Islāmiyyāh wa al-Qwānīnn al-Waḍ'iyyāh* (Comparative Study Between the Islāmic Shāri'ah and Secular Laws) (Beirūt: Dār al-Fatḥ, 1970).

Al-Māwardī, Abū al-Ḥassan 'Alī Ibn Muḥammad Ibn Ḥabīb al-Baṣrī al-Baghdādī, *Al-Ahkām al-Ṣulṭānīyah wa al-Wilāyāt al-Dīnīyyah* (The Ordinance of Government and the Religious Offices) (2nd ed.; Cairo: Sharikat Maktabat wa Maṭba'at Muṣṭafā al-Bābī al-Ḥālābī wa Awlāduh bi-Miṣr, 1966).

Al-Mawdūdī, Abū al-A'lā, *Naẓarīyyāt al-Islām wa Hadyuh* (The Islamic Theory and Guidance), translated from Urdu by Jalīl Ḥasan al-Iṣlaḥi (Beirūt: Dār al-Fikr, 1967).

Al-Māwdūdī, Abū al-A'la, Al-Banna, Ḥassan, and Quṭb, Sāyyīd, *Al-Jihād fī Sabīl Allah* (Jihad for the Cause of Allāh) (Beirūt: Al-Ittiḥād al- 'Alamī li al-Jam'īyyāt Ṭullābīyyah, 1970).

Al-Māwdūdī, Abū al-A'la, *Al-Islām fī Muwājahat al-Taḥaddiyāt al-Mu'āṣirāh* (Islām in Confrontation with Contemporary Challenges), translated by Khalīl Aḥmad al-Ḥamidī (Kuwait: Dī al-Qalam, 1971).

Al-Mubārak, Muḥammad, *Al-Fikr al-Islāmī al-Ḥadīth fī Muwajahat al-Afkār al-Gharbiyyāh* (Contemporary Islāmic Thought in Confrontation with Western Ideas) (Beirūt: Dār al-Fikr, 1968).

Al-Mundhirī, Al-Hāfiẓ ['Abdul- 'Aẓīm Ibn 'Abdul-Qawiy] *Mukhtaṣar Ṣaḥīḥ Muslim* (Summary of Muslim's [Selection of the] Authentic [Sunnah]), ed. Nāṣir al-Dīn al-Albānī. (Kuwait: The Ministry of Endowments and Islāmic Affairs, 1969).

Mūsā, Muḥammad Yūsuf, *Al-Fiqh al-Islāmī: Madkhal li-Dirāsatih: Nidhām al-Mu'āmalati fihi* (Islāmic Jurisprudence: An Introduction to Its Study and Its Approach to Legal Interactions) (3rd ed.; Cairo: Dār al-Kutub al-Ḥadīthah, 1958).

Mutwallī, 'Abdul-ḥamīd, *Mabadi' Niẓām al-Ḥukm fī al-Islām: Ma'a al-*

Muqāranah bi al-Mabādi' al-Dastūrīyyah al-Ḥadīthah (Principles of Political System in Islām: In Comparison with Modern Constitutional Principles) (Alexandria, Egypt: Dār al-Ma'ārif, 1966).

Al-Najjār, Hūsāyn, *Al-Sīyāsah wa al-Istrātījīyyah fi al-Sharq al-Awṣaṭ* (Politics and Strategy in the Middle East) (Cairo: Maktabat al-Nahḍah al-Maṣrīyyah, 1953).

Al-Nāysābūrī, Abī al-Ḥasan 'Alī Ibn Aḥmad al-Waḥidī, *Asbāb al-Nuzūl* (Reasons for the Revelation of Qur'ān) (Cairo: Sharikat wa Maṭba'at Muṣṭafa al-Bābī al-Ḥalabī wa Awlāduh, 1959).

Qal'ajī, Jihād, *Al-Islām Aqwā* (Islām Is Stronger) (Beirūt: Dār al-Kitāb al- 'Arabī, n.d).

Al-Qarafī, Shihāb al-Dīn Abū al- 'Abbās Aḥmad Ibn Idrīs, *Al-Iḥkām fi Tamyīz al-Fatawā 'an al-Aḥkām wa Taṣarrufāt al-Qāḍī wa al-Imām* (The Perfect Work in Distinguishing Legal Opinions from [Judicial and Executive] Decisions and Functions of the Judge and the Imām), ed. 'Abdul-Fattaḥ Abū-Ghuddah (Ḥalab, Syria: Maktab al-Maṭba'at al-Islāmiyyā, 1967).

Qutb, Sayyīd: *Al-Salām al- 'Alamī wa al-Islām* (The World's Peace and Islām) (Cairo: Dār Iḥyā al-Kutub al- 'Arabīyyah, 1967).

Al-Rāyyis, Muḥammad Ḍiya'al-Dīn, *Al-Naẓariyyāt al-Siyāsīyyah al-Islāmīyyah* (Islamic Political Theories) (4th ed.; Cairo: Dār al-Ma'arīf, 1967).

Al-Rāzī, Al-Imām al-Fakhr, *Al-Tafsīr al-Kabīr* (The Big Commentary on Qur'ān) (Cairo: 'Abdul-Rahmān Muḥammad, 1938).

Riḍā, Al-Sayyīd Muḥammad Rashīd, *Tafsīr al-Qur'ān al-Ḥakīm al-Mushtahar bi-Ism Tafsīr al-Manār* (Commentary of the Perfect Qur'ān, well-known as the Way-Mark Commentary) (4th ed.; Cairo: Dār al-Manār, 1954).

Sābiq, Al-Sayyīd, *Fiqh al-Sunnah* (Understanding of the Sunnah) (Kuwait: Dār al-Bayān, 1968).

Al-Sa'idī, 'Abdul Mut'āl, *Al-Ḥurrīyyah al-Dīnīyyah fi al-Islām* (Religious Freedom in Islām) (2nd ed.; Cairo: Dār al-Fikr al- 'Arabī, n.d).

Al-Shāfi'i, Abū- 'Abdullah Muḥammad Ibn Idrīs, *Al-Umm* (The Mother) [i.e., a basic work of jurisprudence] (Cairo: Dār al-Sha'b, 1903).

Shaltūt, Maḥmud, *Al-Islām wa al- 'Alāqāt al-Dawlīyyah fi al-Silm wa al-Ḥarb* (Islām and International Relations in Peace and War) (Cairo: Maktabat Shāykh al-Jami'al-Azhar li al-Shu'ūn al- 'Āmmah, 1951).

Al-Shāybānī, Muḥammad Ibn al-Ḥasan, *Sharḥ al-Siyar al-Kabīr* (Commentary on the Book of the Great Siyar), dictation of Muḥammad Ibn Aḥmad al-Sarakhisi, ed. Salaḥ al-Munajjid (Cairo: Ma'had al-Makhṭūṭāt bi-Jami'at al-Duwal al- 'Arabiyyah, 1958).

Shumayl, Muḥammad, *Ghazwat Banī-Qurayzah,* vol. IV of *Min Ma'ārik al-Islām al-Fāṣilah* (The Battle of Bani-Qurayzah, vol. IV of The Decisive Battles of Islām) (Beirūt: Dār al-Fatḥ li al-Tibā'ah wa al-Nashr, 1966).

Shumayl, Muḥammad Aḥmad, *Gazwat Badr al-Kubrā,* vol. I of *Min Ma'ārik al-Islām al-Fāṣilah* (The Great Battle of Badr, vol. I of The Decisive Battles of Islam) (4th ed.; Beirūt: Maṭba'at Dār al-Kutub, 1968).

Al-Ṭabarī, Abū-Ja'far Muḥammad Ibn Jarīr, *Jāmi' al-Bayān 'an Ta'wīl 'Ayī al-Qur'ān* (The Master of Clarity in Interpretation of Qur'ān) (2nd ed.; Cairo: Sharikat Maktabat wa Maṭba'at Muṣṭafā al-Bābī al-Ḥalabī, 1945).

Ṭabbarah, 'Afīf 'Abdul-Fattāḥ, *Al-Yahūd fi al-Qur'ān: Taḥlīl 'Ilmī li-Nuṣūṣ al-Qur'ān fi al-Yahūd 'Ala Dāw' al-Aḥdāth al-Ḥāḍirah, Ma'a Qaṣaṣ Anbīya' Allah Ibrahīm wa Yūsuf wa Mūsā 'Alāyhim al-Salām* (The Jews and the Qur'ān: Scientific Analysis of the Qur'ānic Text Pertaining to the Jews in the Light of the Contemporary Events with the Stories of the Prophets Abrāham, Yūsuf and Mūsā, May Peace Be upon Them) (2nd ed.; Beirūt: Dar al-'Ilm li al-Malāyīn, 1966).

Al-Tabrīzī, Walī al-Dīn Muḥammad Ibn 'Abdullah al-Khatīb al-Imarī, *Mishkāt al-Maṣābiḥ* (Collections of Authentic Traditions of the Prophet), ed. Muḥammad Na'ṣir al-Dīn al-Albānī (Damascus: Al-Maktab al-Islāmī, 1961).

'Uthmān, 'Abdul-Karīm, *Al-Naẓām al-Siyāsī fi al-Islām* (Political System in Islām) (Beirūt: Dār al-Irshād, 1968).

'Uthmān, Muḥammad Fathī, *Dawlat al-Fikrah allatī Aqāmaha Raṣūl al-Islām 'Aqib al-Hijrah: Tajrubah Mubakkirah fi al-Dāwlah al-Iydyūlujīyyah fi al-Tārīkh* (The Ideological State Which the Messenger of Islām Established After the Immigration: An Early Attempt at an Ideological State in History) (Kuwaīt: Al-Dār al-Kuwaytiyyah, 1968).

'Uthmān, Muḥammad Fatḥī, *Al-Fikr al-Islāmī wa al-Taṭawwur* (Islāmic Thought and Change) (2nd rev. ed.; Kuwait: Al-Dār al-Kuwaytiyyah, 1969).

Zarakshī, Al-Imām Badr al-Dīn Muḥammad Ibn 'Abdullah, *Al-Burhān fī 'Ulūm al-Qur'ān* (The Proof in the Sciences of Qur'ān), ed. Muḥammad Abū al-Faḍl Ibrāhīm (Cairo: Dār Iḥyā' al-Kutub al- 'Arabīyyah, 'Isā al-Bābī al-Ḥalabī wa Shurakāh, 1957).

Al-Zarqā, Muṣṭafā Aḥmad, *Al Fiqh al-Islāmī fī Thāwbihi al-Jadīd,* vol. I of *Al-Madkhal al-Fiqhī* (Reintroduction of the Islāmic Fiqh, vol. I of Introduction to [Islāmic] Jurisprudence) (7th rev. ed., Beirūt: Dār al-Fikr, n.d).

Al-Zarqānī, Muḥammad 'Abdul- 'Azīm *Manāhilal- 'Irfān fī 'Ulūm al-Qur'ān* (Sources of Knowledge of the Sciences of Qur'ān) (Cairo: Dār Iḥyā al-Kutub al- 'Arabīyyah, 'Īsā al-Bābī al-Ḥalābī wa Shūrakāh, n.d).

Ziyadeh, Nuqulla (ed.), *Dirāsāt Islāmiyyāh* (Islāmic Studies) (Beirūt: Dār al-Andalus, 1960).

Al-Zuḥāyhī, Wahbah, *'Āthār al-Ḥarb fī al-Fiqh al-Islāmī: Dirāsah Muqāranah* (The Effects of War in Islāmic Jurisprudence: A Comparative Study) (2nd ed., Damascus: Al-Maktabah al-Ḥadīthah, 1965).

Al-Zuhāylī, Wahbah, *Nazarīyyāh al-Ḍurūrat al-Shar'iyyāh Muqāranah Ma'a al-Qanūn al-Waḍ'ī* (Theory of Necessity in Islāmic Law in Comparison with Man-Made Law) (Damascus: Maktabat al-Farābī, 1969).

Works Consulted (English)

'Abdul-Ḥakīm, Khalīfa, *Islām and Communism (3rd ed.; Lahore, Pakistan: Institute of Islāmic Culture, 1962).*

Adams, Charles C., Islām and Modernism in Egypt (New York: Russell & Russell, 1933).

Aḥmad, 'Azīz; *Islāmic Modernism in India and Pakistan: 1857-1964* (London: Oxford University Press, 1967).

Aḥmad, Khūrshīd, *Fanaticism, Intolerance and Islām* (3rd ed.; Karachi: Islāmic Publications, Ltd., 1967).

'Alī, Sayēd Ameer, *The Spirit of Islām: A History of the Evolution and Ideals of Islām with a Life of the Prophet* (London: Methuen, 1922).

Anand, R.P. (ed.) *Asian States and the Development of Universal International Law* (Delhi: Vicas Publications, 1972).

Anderson, Jerome, N.D., and Coulson, Norman J., *Islāmic Law in Contemporary Cultural Change* (unpublished essay written in connection with the *Enzyklopadie des Kulturwandels im 20. Jahrhundert).*

Anderson, J.N.P., *Islāmic Law in the Modern World* (New York: New York University Press, 1959).

Arnold, Sir Thomas W., *The Caliphate,* with a concluding chapter by Sulbia G. Haim (New York: Barnes, Noble, 1965).

'Azmī, Moḥammad Muṣṭafā, *Studies in Early Ḥadīth Literature with a Critical Edition of Some Early Texts* (Beirūt: Al-Maktab al-Islāmī, 1968).

'Azzām, 'Abdul-Raḥmān, *The Eternal Message of Muḥammad,* translated from 'Arabic by Caesar E. Faraḥ (New York: New American Library, 1965).

Berkes, Niyāzī, *The Development of Secularism in Turkey* (Montreal: McGill University Press, 1964).

Bozeman, Adda B., *The Picture of Law in a Multicultural World* (Princeton: Princeton University Press, 1971).

Brockelman, Carl: *History of the Islāmic Peoples,* translated by Joel Carmichael and Moshe Perlman (New York: Enpriarn Books Edition, Alien Property Custodian, 1960).

Brohi, A.K., *Islām in the Modern World,* compiled and edited under the auspices of the Islāmic Research Academy of Karachi by Khurshīd Aḥmad (Karachi: Chiragh-E-Rah Publications, 1968).

Chaudhri, Muḥammed Aḥsan, *Pakistan and the Great Powers* (Karachi: Council for Pakistan Studies, 1970).

Choudhury, G.W., *Pakistan's Relations with India* (Meerut, India: Meenakshi Prakashan, 1971).

Claude, Inis L., Jr., *Power and International Relations* (New York: Random House, 1962).

Coulson, N.J., *A History of Islāmic Law* (Edinburgh: Edinburgh University Press, 1964).

Daniel, Norman, *Islām and the West* (Edinburgh: Edinburgh University Press, 1960).

Davison, Roderick H., *The Modern Nations in Historical Perspective: Turkey* (Englewood Cliffs, N.J., Prentice-Hall, 1968).

Deutsch, Karl W., *Nationalism and Social Communication: An Inquiry into the Foundation of Nationalism* (2nd ed.; Cambridge: Massachusetts Institute of Technology, 1966).

Deutsch, Karl W., and others, *Political Community and the North Atlantic Area: International Organization in the Light of Historical Experience* (Princeton: Princeton University Press, 1968).

Dougherty, James E., and Pfaltzgraff, Jr., Robert L., *Contending Theories of International Relations* (Philadelphia: J.B. Lippincott, 1971).

Falk, Richard A., and Black, Cyrile E., eds., *The Future of the International Legal Order* (Princeton, N.J.: Princeton University Press, 1969).

al Fārūqī, Ismā'īl Rājī: "Toward a New Methodology for Qur'ānic Exegesis," *Islāmic Studies,* I (March 1962).

Fenwick, Charles G., *International Law* (3rd rev. ed.; New York: Appleton-Century Crofts, 1948).

Fisher, Sidney Nettleton, *The Middle East: A History* (2nd ed.; New York: Alfred A. Knopf, 1969).

Gabrielli, Francesco, *Muḥammad and the Conquests of Islām,* translated from Italian by Virginia Luling and Rosamund Linell (New York: World University Library, McGraw-Hill Co., 1968).

Ghunaīmī, Moḥammad Ṭala'at, *The Muslim Conception of International Law and the Western Approach* (The Hague: Martinus Nijhoff, 1968).

Gibb, H.A.R., *Modern Trends in Islām* (Chicago: University of Chicago Press, 1947).

Gibb, H.A.R. *Muḥammadanism: A Historic Survey* (2nd ed.; New York: Oxford University Press, 1962).

Gibb, H.A.R., *Studies on the Civilization of Islām,* edited by Stanford J. Shaw and William R. Polk (Boston: Beacon Press, 1962).

Halpern, Manfred H., *The Politics of Social Change in the Middle East and North Africa* (Princeton, N.J.: Princeton University Press, 1963).

Ḥamidullah, Muḥammad, *The Muslim Conduct of State* (5th rev. ed.; Lahore, Pakistan: Sh. Muḥammad Ashraf, 1963).

Ḥamidullah, Muḥammad, *The First Written Constitution in the World: An Important Document of the Time of the Holy Prophet* (2nd rev. ed.; Lahore (Pakistan: Sh. Muḥammad Ashraf, 1968).

Ḥourānī, Albert, *"Minorities" in the Contemporary Middle East: Tradition and Innovation,* eds. Benjamin Riulin and Josephs Szyliowics (New York: Random House, 1965).

Ḥourānī, Albert, *Arab Thought in the Liberal Age: 1798-1939* (London: Oxford University Press, 1970).

Ibn Khaldūn, Abū-Zayd ['Abdul-Raḥmān Ibn Muḥammad], *The Mu-*

qaddimah (An Introduction to History), translated from Arabic by Franz Rosenthal, ed. N.J. Dawood, Bollingen series (Princeton, N.J.: Princeton University Press, 1967).

Kelman, Herbert C. (ed.), *Behavior: A Social-Psychological Analysis* (New York: Holt, Rinehart, Winston, 1965).

Kelsen, Hans, *Principles of International Law* (2nd ed.; New York: Holt, Rinehart, Winston, 1966).

Kerr, Malcom H., *Islāmic Reform: The Political and Legal Theories* of Muḥammad ʿAbduh *and* Rashīd Riḍā (Berkeley: University of California Press, 1966).

Khadduri, Majīd, *War and Peace in the Law of Islām* (Baltimore, John Hopkins Press, 1952).

Khān, Moḥammad, Ayub, *Pakistan Perspective* (Washington, D.C.: Pakistani Embassy, n.d).

Khan, Muḥammad Muḥsin, *The Translation of the Meaning of Saḥīḥ al-Bukhārī* (Cyranwala, Pakistan: Sethi Straw Board Mills Conversion Ltd., n.d).

Kunz, Josef L., *The Changing Law of Nations: Essays on International Law* (Kent: Ohio State University Press, 1968).

Lewis, Bernard, *The Arabs in History* (New York: Harper & Row, 1960).

Lewis, Bernard, *The Middle East and the West* (New York: Harper & Row, 1966).

Lewis, Bernard, *The Emergence of Modern Turkey* (2nd ed.; London: Oxford University Press, 1968).

Lewis, Bernard, *Race and Colour in Islām* (New York: Harper & Row, 1970).

MacDonald, Robert W., *The League of Arab States: A Study in the Dynamism of Regional Organization* Princeton (N.J.: Princeton University Press, 1965).

Mitchell, Richard P., *The Society of the Muslim Brotherhood* (London: Oxford University Press, 1969).

Naff, Thomas, *The Setting and Rationale of Ottoman Diplomacy in the Reign of Selim III* (1789-1807), unpublished paper.

Naff, Thomas, "Reform and the Conduct of Ottoman Diplomacy in the Reign of Selim III, 1789-1807, " *Journal of the American Oriental Society*

83:6 (1963).

Nāṣr, Sayyed Ḥosseīn, *Islāmic Studies: Essays on Law and Society, the Science and Philosophy of Sūfism* (Beirūt: Librarie du Libanon, 1967).

Palmer, Norman D., and Perkins, Howard C., *International Relations: The World Community in Transition* (3rd ed.; Boston: Houghton Mifflin Co., 1969).

Peretz, Don, *The Middle East Today* (New York: Holt, Rinehart & Winston, 1965).

Proctor, J.H. (ed.), *Islām and International Relations* (New York: Frederick A. Praeger, 1965).

Qadirī, Anwar Aḥmad, *Islāmic Jurisprudence in the Modern World: A Reflection Upon Comparative Study of the Law* (Bombay: N.M. Tripathi Pvt., Ltd., 1963).

Raf'i-Ud-Din, M., *Ideology of the Future* (3rd ed.; Lahore, Pakistan: Sh. Muḥammad Ashraf, 1970).

Raḥmān, Fazlur, *Islāmic Methodology in History* (Karachi: Central Institute of Islāmic Research; 1965).

Ramaḍān, Saīd, *Three Major Problems Confronting the World of Islām* (Takoma Park, Md.: Crescent Publications, n.d).

Ramaạn, Said, *Islāmic Law: Its Scope and Equity (London: P.R. MacMillan, Ltd., 1961).*

Razui, Muztaba, The Frontiers of Pakistan (Karachi: National Publishing House, 1971).

Rosenau, James N, *International Politics and Foreign Policy: A Reader in Research and Theory* (New York: Free Press, 1969).

Rosenthal, Erwin, I. J., *Islām in the Modern National State* (Cambridge: University Press, 1965).

Rosenthal, Erwin I. J., *Political Thought in Medieval Islam* (Cambridge, University Press, 1958).

Rubinstein, Alvin Z. (ed.),*The Foreign Policy of the Soviet Union* (2nd ed.; New York: Random House, 1966).

Safran, Nadav, *Egypt in Search of Political Community* (Cambridge, Mass.: Harvard University Press, 1961).

Schacht, Joseph, *The Origins of Muḥammadan Jurisprudence* (Oxford: Oxford University Press, 1950).

al-Shaybānī, Muhammad, *The Islāmic Law of Nations,* translated from Arabic by Majīd Khadduri (Baltimore: Johns Hopkins University Press, 1966).

Siddiqī, Amīr Ḥassan, *Non-Muslim under Muslim Rule and Muslim under Non-Muslims Rule* (Karachi: Jamiyatul Falāḥ Publications, n.d).

Sills, David L. (ed.), *International Encyclopedia of the Social Sciences* (New York: MacMillan Free Press, 1968).

Smith, Donald Eugene, *Religion and Political Development* (Boston: Little, Brown & Co., 1970).

Smith, Wilfrid Cantwell, *Islām in Modern History* (Princeton, N.J.: Princeton University Press, 1957).

Thompson, Jack H., and Reischauer, R.D. (eds.) *Modernization of the Arab World* (New York: Van Nostrand, Inc., 1966).

Toynbee, Arnold, *Civilization on Trial* and *The World and the West* (Cleveland: World Publishing Co., 1958).

Turhan, Mumtāz, *Where Are We in Westernization?* translated by David Garwood (Istanbul: Research Centre, Roberts College of Istanbul, 1965).

Watt, W. Montgomery, *Muḥammad: Prophet and Statesman* (London: Oxford University Press, 1961).

Watt, W. Montgomery, *What Is Islām?* (New York: Frederick A. Praeger, 1968).

Ziyadeh, Nicola A., *Syria and Lebanon* (Beirūt: Lebanon Bookshop, 1968).

INDEX